English with an Accent

Professor Lippi-Green has authored the perfect (and much needed) book for students to help them consider the ideologies that undergird many of our myths about language and how language enables, even encourages, people to limit social access to minorities of all types. She gives the reader a brilliant analysis of such topics as language as it relates to social control, authority, social identity, change, and individual rights. The book is superbly written in a careful yet creative style. I recommend it most highly to scholars and practitioners who deal with language, education, and social concerns.

Roger W. Shuy, Distinguished Research Professor of Linguistics,
Georgetown University

In *English with an Accent* Rosina Lippi-Green does for language what others have done for race and gender. She shows that the "dialectists" among us have done the same sorts of damage to individual advancement and self-esteem that racists and sexists have done.

Dennis R. Preston, *Michigan State University*

In *English with an Accent*, Rosina Lippi-Green scrutinizes American attitudes towards language. Using examples drawn from a variety of contexts: the classroom, the court, the media, and corporate culture, she exposes the way in which discrimination based on accent functions to support and perpetuate unequal social structures and unequal power relations.

English with an Accent:

- focuses on language variation linked to geography and social identity;
- looks at how the media and the entertainment industry work to promote linguistic stereotyping;
- examines how employers discriminate on the basis of accent;
- reveals how the judicial system protects the status quo and reinforces language subordination.

This fascinating and highly readable book forces us to acknowledge the ways in which language is used to discriminate.

Rosina Lippi-Green is Associate Professor of Linguistics at Western Washington University.

English with an Accent

Language, ideology, and discrimination
in the United States

Rosina Lippi-Green

LONDON AND NEW YORK

First published 1997
by Routledge
11 New Fetter Lane, London EC4P 4EE

Simultaneously published in the USA and Canada
by Routledge, Inc.
29 West 35th Street, New York, NY 10001

Reprinted 1998 (twice), 2000, 2001, 2003 (twice)

Routledge is an imprint of the Taylor & Francis Group

Typeset in Times Ten by Florencetype, Stoodleigh, Devon
Printed and bound in Great Britain by Biddles Ltd, Guildford and King's Lynn

British Library Cataloguing in Publication Data
A catalogue record for this book is available from the British Library

Library of Congress Cataloguing in Publication Data
Lippi-Green, Rosina
     English with an accent: language, ideology, and discrimination in the
     United States/Rosina Lippi-Green.
       1. English language – Social aspects – United States.   2. English language
     – Political aspects – United States.   3. English language – Variation – United
     States.   4. Speech and social status – United States.   5. Language and
     culture – United States.   6. Language policy – United States.
     7. Discrimination – United States.
     I. Title.
     PE2808.8.L57 1997
     306.4´4´0973–dc20   96-33234

ISBN 0–415–11476–4 (hbk)
       0–415–11477–2 (pbk)

In memory of my father, Arturo Lippi
1911–1985
who had an accent that I couldn't hear

The work of an intellectual is not to mould the political will of others; it is, through the analyses that he does in his own field, to re-examine evidence and assumptions, to shake up habitual ways of working and thinking, to dissipate conventional familiarities, to re-evaluate rules and institutions and ... to participate in the formation of a political will (where he has a role as a citizen to play).

Michel Foucault, "The concern for truth" (1989)

Contents

Figures

Tables

Preface

By almost anybody's modern US standards, I have no accent. Because of the English I speak, the hurtful and exclusionary practices you will read about in this book have never been directed at me.

In fact, objectively, I do have an accent. My English tells anybody who wants to listen to me who I am: I am a white woman of middle age who has lived most of her life in the heart of the country, in the midwest. By fortunate circumstance, I had a longer and more exclusive education than most people have, which has also influenced my accent – because it took me away from the midwest, primarily, but also because it put me in social circumstances which were foreign to me, against which I struggled and will always struggle, even as I adjust.

This is a written work, and so it is by virtue not of my accent but of my education that I am granted a voice. For that reason some would say that my authority derives exclusively from privilege. It is true that I cannot claim the authority of personal experience in the matters I am going to describe and discuss, but I can and do claim the authority of careful observation and study, and of interest and participation.

I am taking a chance. My thoughts may be dismissed, my observations put aside. In a time when authorial voices are questioned very closely, I have no credentials which allow me to speak – nor do I wish to speak – for African Americans or Asian Americans. But because I am not a Latina or Lakota Sioux, because I am not from Mobile, the Bronx, Bombay, Singapore, or Nairobi, readers may question my data before ever considering my analysis and conclusions. In that case, I invite them to investigate for themselves before dismissing what I have to say. The purpose of this study is not to answer the questions raised in a definitive way, but to open up a discussion and examination which has been suppressed for too long.

This book is divided into three parts. In the first chapter, I attempt to provide a brief introduction to linguistic facts: empirically won knowledge about the structure and function of language. These facts are crucial to the development of the central arguments of this book. Some of the material presented (for example: that language change is normal, functional, and inevitable) will evoke emotional responses, because beliefs about the way language should be used are passed down and protected in much the same way that religious beliefs are passed along and cherished. Nevertheless, they are facts, and anyone who is willing to read and consider with an open mind will find enough evidence here, and in other volumes, to establish that clearly.

Once facts are established, I cannot claim that this work is solely a neutral exercise in the presentation of behaviors around language and the analysis of those behaviors. Chapters 2 and 3 explore some of the commonly held myths about language: where they came from, and how they function to specific social ends. Thus questions are raised which have consequence in the real world; I have personal beliefs about how those questions should be resolved. My opinions are informed by careful thought and by research, but they are opinions. To be clear, my analytical framework (presented in Chapter 4) takes as a departure point these positions:

- There is something deeply inequitable and unacceptable about the practice of excluding the few from the privileges of the many on the basis not of what they have to say, but of how they say it.
- The demand that the disempowered assimilate linguistically and culturally to please the empowered is – purely in linguistic terms – an impossibility. For that reason, such demands are misleading, unreasonable, and demeaning.

In Chapter 4 I present a working model of what I call the language subordination process, as well as an analysis of the concept of communication barriers. The purpose of these tools is in part to provide readers with a means to undertake their own critical analysis of language subordination outside the examples provided here.

Parts II and III approach the issue of language and discrimination from complementary angles. In Part II, I explore the way institutions have worked together to interweave a set of ideological practices which effectively limit access to discourse on the grounds of language linked to race, ethnicity, economics, and homeland. In Part III I then step back to look at how specific groups and individuals are affected by the lifelong exposure to institutionalized language ideology. In a case-study approach, I consider how some come to embrace common-sense arguments and perpetuate them, and how others manage to resist.

There is a challenge here for the reader. Can you be objective about language? Can you examine what you think you know about your own language? And more difficult, are you willing to explore why you may be so very protective of common-sense arguments about language which have no demonstrable basis in fact?

This book is about reluctance to acknowledge language for the social construct that it is, and the repercussions of such resistance.

Acknowledgements

It's been a long haul. It is only because I am fortunate in my colleagues, students, family, and friends that this study sees the light of day.

First and foremost I owe a debt to my students, in particular those who signed up for my course on Language and Discrimination without knowing what exactly they were getting into, but who stayed anyway. The classroom discussions of many topics in this book – often loud, sometimes disturbing, but seldom boring – have directed my research and influenced the development of my thought. I am also particularly endebted to those graduate students who worked with me on the Disney analysis pilot project: Carlee Arnette, Jennie Dailey-O'Cain, Rita Simpson, and Matt Varley. Their enthusiasm and energy gave me a sorely needed jump start, and my discussions with them on the difficult points of coding and analysis were invaluable.

In the course of collecting material for this book, I have interviewed people all over the country. While many of them wish to remain anonymous, I am nonetheless very thankful for their candid discussion of sometimes difficult topics. I am also endebted to the librarians at the Margaret Herrick Library Center for Motion Picture Study at the Academy of Motion Picture Arts and Sciences in Los Angeles, and to the staff of the Vanderbilt Television News Archives in Nashville.

I have had excellent research assistance, particularly from Pamela Friedman, Lisa Quiroga, Sonia Unchu Park, and Daniel Brenner. Rita Simpson was a careful and constructive editor of the final draft with many useful and substantive comments; Alicia Beckford read and provided crucial commentary on Chapter 9 while Deborah Minter did the same for Chapter 6.

My colleagues Patrice Beddor, Joe Salmons, Debby Keller-Cohen, Lesley Milroy, and James Milroy have been a constant source of encouragement, providing careful readings and constructive criticism. Jim read the last draft of almost all the chapters and provided very close comments, for which I am especially thankful. In addition, there were other thoughtful readers who provided a lot of material which was especially valuable, precisely because they are not linguists. These include David Karraker, who will Ever Continue to Resist; Emmy Liston, who brought her fine feel for language to the first chapters; and Jack Whyte, who questioned me closely about turns of phrase which needed more careful attention. The usual disclaimers apply, of course; this is my work and I am ultimately responsible for any infelicities.

Finally I am thankful to my husband, Bill, for his usual patience in the face of my last-minute jitters, and to my daughter Elisabeth for reminding me that her past participles are nobody's business but her own.

Permissions

The author and publishers would like to thank the following for permission to reproduce copyright material:

New York University Press for the extract from "The order of discourse" by Michel Foucault, in *Language and Politics*, edited by Michael Shapiro, 1984;

Verso for the extract from *Ideology: An Introduction* by Terry Eagleton, 1991;

A. P. Watt Ltd on behalf of The National Trust for Places of Historic Interest or Natural Beauty for the extract from "The stranger," in *Rudyard Kipling's Verse: Definitive Edition*;

The Society of Authors on behalf of the Bernard Shaw Estate for the extract from *Man & Superman* by Bernard Shaw;

Providence Journal-Bulletin for the extract from "The voice of success silences dialect: program helps shed telltale tones" by Bob Kerr, in the *Providence Journal-Bulletin*, April, 1994;

Miami Herald for the Dave Barry quotation in Chapter 10, taken from his column in *Bad Habits*. Dave Barry is a columnist for the *Miami Herald*;

The Prince of Wales's Press Office for the extract from His Royal Highness's speech at the presentation of the Thomas Cranmer Schools Prize on 19th December 1995.

The extract from *The Story of English* by McCrum and MacNeil is reprinted by permission of the Peters Fraser & Dunlop Group Ltd. Excerpt from *The Color Purple*, copyright © 1982 by Alice Walker, reprinted by permission of Harcourt Brace & Company.

While the publishers have made every effort to contact copyright holders of material used in this volume, they would be happy to hear from any they were unable to contact.

Part I

Linguistics, language, and ideology

Introduction

Language ideology: science fiction?

> The American ideal, after all, is that everyone should be as much alike as possible.
>
> James Baldwin, "The Harlem Ghetto" (1948)

This book is about language, but let's begin with a bit of science fiction. Imagine the following:

On January 1 of the next new year, each person residing in the United States wakes up to find themselves physically transformed: regardless of race or ethnicity, all adult males 18 and older will be exactly 6' tall and weigh 175 pounds; adult females, 5'9", at 140 pounds. All persons will show exactly the same physical measurements (length of tibia, diameter of wrist) and body fat ratios, with a differential arising from gender-specific roles in the propagation of the species. All persons newborn through age 17 will approach the adult model on a scale graduated exactly to age. Metabolism has adjusted so that the ratios of height to weight are maintained regardless of diet or development of musculature.

Let's take this strange idea a step further and imagine what this revolution would mean to us in our day-to-day lives. Some of the repercussions might be seen as positive:

- The end of the diet industry and tremendous behavior shifts in matters of mate selection and sexuality. Every woman will wear what is now a size 10, but as sizes are no longer relevant or meaningful, the social connotations of clothing sizes (*petite* or *queen*, *extra tall*, *extra long*, *extra broad*, *extra narrow*) will quickly be lost.
- Sudden resolution of health problems related to weight control. Heart disease, hypertension, anorexia – a whole range of difficult health problems greatly simplified or resolved overnight.
- Dramatic changes in the way we think about food. As metabolism is now fine-tuned to deal with excessive or insufficient calories, carbohydrate and fat intake, much of the culture and psychology about eating would evolve in new directions.

- Revolution in the design and manufacture of easy chairs, rollerskates, toothbrushes, gloves, skis, kitchen counters, bathtubs, lawn-mower handles, car seats, bedsheets, violins, submarines, auditoriums, coffins, and everything else which now makes allowance for variation in physical size. This would mean a tremendous economic advantage for businesses which could streamline production in ways never imagined.
- Sports, professional and otherwise, would change greatly. But because muscle tone, agility, speed, and strength would remain matters of life style, nutrition, and training, sports as we know them would not disappear, but shift in focus and nature.

These are just a few areas which would be changed. The list can easily be expanded as we anticipate the major social and cultural impact on our lives.

When I discuss this fictional United States with my classes, the students are eager to list things that would be easier, cheaper, more streamlined and efficient if this physical world were suddenly to become a reality. Slowly, different considerations begin to emerge, which students are sometimes reluctant to express. They have to do with issues which are more subtle, which touch on identity and self-awareness, aesthetic and value systems. *It sounds like this would be a good thing overall, for us as a country*, says one student. *But my father and my grandfather and my great grandfather were all 6'5" or bigger.* With less of an apologetic tone, a Japanese American woman tells the class *I can't imagine being that tall.* Another student asks, *Who decided on these particular figures? Why 140 pounds for women – wouldn't 125 be more aesthetically pleasing?*

Before I let the class discuss these questions in any depth, there is one more step in the science-fiction fantasy which we must consider.

Imagine now that this unanticipated and unwilled transformation does not take place. Instead, a junior congresswoman rises before the House of Representatives and she presents a precise, well-written proposal for a law which dictates the physical world imagined above, in which a woman who is 6'2" or a man who weighs 225 pounds are either violating federal law willfully, or must be labeled handicapped.

In support of her proposal, the congresswoman outlines the many social ills which will be instantaneously fixed, and the economic advantages for the manufacturing and business communities. She provides projections which promise that billions of dollars will be saved if this law is put into effect, money which can be put into education and job training. Her presentation includes complex essays and calculations by a panel of experts who have, on the basis of considerable study, determined what ideal heights and weights must be – what makes a superior, efficient, aesthetically pleasing human being. *Let us all be one height and weight,* she says. *For we are all one nation.*

This is a funny idea; students laugh. What is wrong with it is so obvious as to be trivial, they tell me. First, we cannot all be the same height and weight and physical type: variation and diversity are inescapable biological facts. Thus, this law would be unenforceable. Second, even if this were not an impossibility, it would be wrong – an invasion of personal liberties – to *require* people to change their physical beings to approximate some model set up by others, in the name of perceived economic or social advance, even their own. Third, and finally: the premise that we will be a better nation, a more unified nation, if we all *look* the same, is suspect.

Now what does this hypothetical world, this hypothetical congresswoman and her proposal have to do with language, and more to the point, with language and discrimination? People will immediately claim that language cannot stand in for height and weight in this story. The argument will go that language is an ethereal, mutable thing, something we learn, something within our control. Height and weight are biological facts of the physical world, determined by genetics and nutrition in the first line, and by will only secondarily. Language – which languages we speak, and how we speak them – is a matter of *choice*, people will argue, whereas height is not.

In the course of this book I will argue that language has more in common with height and weight than is readily apparent, and that the same reservations which are so self-evident when we talk about manipulation of our physical bodies can and must be applied to discourse about language, and the manipulation and evaluation of language. Language, a possession all human collectives have in common, is more than a tool for communication of facts between two or more persons. It is the most salient way we have of establishing and advertising our social identities. It may not be as tangible as height and weight, but the way we use language is more complex and meaningful than any single fact about our bodies.

The degree of control we have over language is limited. We can choose to be polite or obtuse, to use forms of address which will flatter or insult, to use gender-neutral language or language that is inflammatory; we can consciously use vocabulary which is simple, or purposefully mislead with language. But there are many dimensions of language which are not subject to conscious or direct control. Nevertheless, as speakers we are obsessed with the idea of control: we talk a great deal about language as if it were an indispensable but often wayward and unpredictable servant, in need of our constant attention and vigilance if the job is to get done.

Crucial questions have been raised here which will occupy the rest of this study:

- What is the relationship between language and social identity? How do we use language to construct "self" and "other"?
- What is or is not mutable about language, specifically about phonology (accent)?
- Do individuals have language rights which render the question of mutability irrelevant? That is, is it desirable or even possible to balance the

individual's language rights with the needs of the community? Is this an appropriate matter for majority rule, or is it an area where the tyranny of the majority is a real threat, and individual liberties must be evoked?

- Who claims authority to make these decisions, how do they manage to do this, and why do people let them?

All of these questions are important to this study, but the last question is perhaps the most complex and difficult one. There is a common conception that there is a *good* English, and following from that, *bad* English. Further, there is a good deal of consensus on who speaks good English, and who has authority to decide what is good. While anyone would anticipate heated debate on the height/weight legislation (who has the authority to decide what an ideal person looks like, and on what aesthetic, biological, or other grounds?), it is interesting to note that there is little debate at all about who sets the standards for spoken and written language, standards which have been the focus of legislation, standards which affect our everyday lives.

Before we can set out on an exploration of these issues, however, some common ground must be identified, built of established facts about language structure and function. This will be undertaken in the first three chapters.

1 The linguistic facts of life

Language is very difficult to put into words.
                                    Voltaire

This study is about the English language as it is spoken and written in the United States.[1] Nevertheless, the linguistic principles which provide groundwork for the discussion are not limited to English. Instead, they are generalizations about all human language, and they need to be understood before we proceed. There are some obstacles to laying out these ideas, however, and some ironies which bear consideration.

Linguists do not form a homogenous club. Like any other group of scholars divided by a common subject matter, there are great rivalries, ancient quarrels, picky arguments, and plain differences of opinion. It could hardly be otherwise in a discipline diverse enough to include topics such as neurological structures and linguistic capacity, grammaticalized strategies for encoding social information in systems of address, and creolization. Thus it should be no surprise that those who study the rules which generate the ordering of words into sentences (syntacticians and cognitive grammarians, for example) are often openly disdainful of each other's approach, on theoretical grounds, and of the study of the social life of language, more generally. Linguists concerned with the relationship between structured variation in language and social identity (sociolinguists, variationists, some anthropological linguists) chide both syntacticians and cognitive grammarians for what they see as unreasonable abstractions and lack of reproducible results; phoneticians go about their business of understanding and theorizing the way humans produce and perceive sound – the architects and engineers of linguistics – and wonder what all the noise is about; historical linguists concern themselves with the written data of lost language communities and write complex formulas for the reconstruction of sounds that might have been heard around the early Roman explorations of central Europe, or in more extreme cases, when the first people wandered from Asia to the North American land mass.

However, there is a great deal that linguists do agree about, in simply factual terms. For example, the statement *All living languages change* is one that no linguist would counter, unless they were to ask for a definition of "living" and to debate the parameters and implications of that term, just for the fun of it. And, of course, not all linguists find the fact that all living languages change to be equally interesting or worthy of study. Nonetheless, that statement is part of the core of knowledge about language, hard won, with which all linguists begin.

It is also true that the very subject of this book – how people think about language, how and why they try to control it, to what social ends, and with what linguistic and social repercussions – has often been put aside as uninteresting by linguists themselves. Traditionally, linguists draw a strict line in the sand between what they hope is their own objective description of language phenomena and subjective, usually prescriptivist limits on language by misinformed or underinformed lay persons (language "mavens" or "shamans").[2] More recently, however, some linguists have put aside this strict division in recognition of the fact that how people think about language *is* in fact relevant to the study of language as a social construct, and that claims of objectivity on the part of linguists are sometimes suspiciously self-protective. Deborah Cameron points out, for example, that the descriptive/prescriptive line used by linguists to validate their own pursuit of knowledge about language and devalue or dismiss other types of discourses about language can be challenged:

> the overt anti-prescriptive stance of linguists is in some respects not unlike the prescriptivism they criticize. The point is that both prescriptivism and anti-prescriptivism invoke certain norms and circulate particular notions about how language ought to work. Of course, the norms are different (and in the case of linguistics, they are often covert). But both sets feed into the more general arguments that influence everyday ideas about language. On that level, "description" and "prescription" turn out to be aspects of a single (and normative) activity: a struggle to control language by defining its nature.
>
> (1995: 8)

Cameron's observations are accurate on many levels: the struggle between linguists and non-linguists are often about authority. The issues she raises are relevant ones for sociolinguists and other linguists interested in the relationship between power and language to think about, but she is not the first to raise them.[3] An extreme representation might be that prescriptivists claim the right to tell people how to talk, and that linguists claim the right to tell prescriptivists what not to say.

There is a qualitative difference between the two approaches, however. The linguist and the non-linguist claim *different kinds and sources of authority* to validate their individual approaches to language. Linguists are often impatient when they are cornered at cocktail parties and asked to debate language issues which to them brook no debate, just as geologists and biologists would be hard-pressed to debate (with any degree of seriousness or interest) arguments against evolutionary theory based on the writings of the Bible. Linguists claim some authority in the description of language based on observation, experimentation, and deduction, so that the claim *All living languages change* is not a matter of faith or opinion or aesthetics, but observable fact (which is not to say that all claims by linguists are equally supportable by fact).

The rest of this chapter is an attempt to pull together some statements about language which enjoy widespread support of the majority (but probably not all) linguists and which are demonstrably true, in as much as anything can be demonstrated as consistently true for any social behavior: that is, the nature of linguistic argumentation is probabilistic and not predictive.

This small collection of "facts" is where most linguists would come together. The irony is that where linguists settle down to an uneasy truce, non-linguists take up the battle cry. The least disputed issues around language structure and function, the ones linguists argue about least, are those which are most often challenged by non-linguists, and with the greatest vehemence and emotion.

This phenomenon has been observed widely. In *The Language Instinct: How the mind creates language*, Steven Pinker notes to his readers:

> Most educated people already have opinions about language. They know that it is man's most important cultural invention, the quintessential example of his capacity to use symbols, and a biologically unprecedented event irrevocably separating him from other animals. They know that language pervades thought, with different languages causing their speakers to construe reality in different ways. They know that children learn to talk from role models and caregivers. They know that grammatical sophistication used to be nurtured in the schools, but sagging educational standards and the debasements of popular culture have led to a frightening decline in the ability of the average person to construct a . . . grammatical sentence. They also know that English is a zany, logic-defying tongue. . . . In the pages that follow, I will try to convince you that every one of these common opinions is wrong!
>
> (1994: 17–18)

My purpose in this book is somewhat less comprehensive than Pinker's: I will concern myself primarily with the part of common beliefs about language which concern attitudes towards language variation, and the personal and institutionalized behaviors resulting from these beliefs. Moreover, I will outline only those *linguistic facts of life* which are essential to the arguments which follow in the remainder of this book.

The linguistic facts of life which are of central concern to the issues in this book are the following:

- All spoken language changes over time.
- All spoken languages are equal in linguistic terms.
- Grammaticality and communicative *effectiveness* are distinct and independent issues.
- Written language and spoken language are historically, structurally, and functionally fundamentally different creatures.
- Variation is intrinsic to all spoken language at every level.

ALL SPOKEN LANGUAGE CHANGES OVER TIME

All language changes over time, in terms of lexicon, sound structures, tone, rhythm, the way sentences are put together, the social markings of variants, and the meanings assigned to words. Only unused, dead languages are static.[4] This is true in Great Britain as it is on the North American continent, as it is for every other spoken language in the world.

Even the most conservative of language observers cannot argue that Chaucer, Shakespeare, Milton, Austen, Woolf, Wharton, and Morrison (to take us from the fourteenth to the twentieth century), some of the men and women who wrote what is commonly regarded as the great literature of the English-speaking world, wrote the same English. From there it follows that they did not *speak* the same English. It is not conceivable that anyone would care to argue that because Toni Morrison does not write or talk like Shakespeare did that her English is bad, less efficient, less capable of carrying out the functions for which it is needed. Table 1.1 provides examples which demonstrate how written language changes over time.

Language changes whether we like it or not. Attempts to stop spoken language from changing are not unknown in the history of the world, but they are universally without success, unless they are instituted by means of genocide.[5] Sometimes languages die a less sudden death, for example when the community of speakers who use them disperse, succumb to plague, or otherwise are forcibly assimilated into dominating cultures (as in the case of most of the languages indigenous to this continent); languages are born, for example through the processes of pidginization and subsequent creolization.

Language standardization, which is in some ways an attempt to stop language change, or at least to fossilize language by means of controlling variation, will be considered in more depth in the next chapters. That discussion will be part of a more in-depth consideration of the ideological structures which make such a process seem good and necessary.

Table 1.1 The English language changing over time

1480	As it is knowen how many maner of peple ben in the jlonde ther ben also so many langages and tonges ... (William Caxton, *Of the languages of maners & Vsage of the people of Y' Londe)*
1596	I doe not well know, but by ghesse, what you doe meane by these termes ... therefore I pray you explaine them. (Edmund Spenser, *A View of the State of Ireland*)
1640	Custome is the most certaine Mistresse of Language, as the publicke stampe makes the current money. (Ben Jonson, *Timber or Discoveries*)
1740	The Opportunities we have lost for propagating *our Language* on the Continent, are more to be lamented, since perhaps the same, or so great, may never again be offer'd ... how easily might we have made the Frenchmen eat their own Words, and obliged them to speak plain *English*. (M. Briton, "An apology for the English language," *London Magazine.* Quoted also in Bailey 1991: 99)
1818	Man have had every advantage of us in telling their own story. Education has been theirs in so much higher a degree; the pen has been in their hands. I will not allow books to prove any thing. (Jane Austen, *Persuasion*)
1990	His voice was clear and ringing, not Scots, full of what Roland might inaccurately have called toffee-nosed sounds, or plummy sounds, sounds he had spent his childhood learning to imitate derisorily, hooting, curtailed, drawling, chipping sounds that pricked his non-existent hackles with class hostility. (A. S. Byatt, *Possession*)

ALL SPOKEN LANGUAGES ARE EQUAL IN LINGUISTIC TERMS

All spoken languages are equally capable of expressing a full range of ideas and experiences, and of developing to meet new needs as they arise. This claim by linguists is usually countered by non-linguists with examples of languages which reportedly have no terms for snow, or for which a vocabulary to discuss nuclear fusion does not exist. *Try talking about the Geneva Convention's guidelines on chemical weapons in Arawakan*, this argument goes, *and see if English or French or Chinese are not more capable of carrying the discussion.* The fact is, however, that English has not always had the vocabulary necessary to talk about chemical weapons, or aeronautical engineering, or genetic mapping – just as speakers of Germanic languages in central Europe once had no terms with which to discuss Christian theology. Language is an incredibly flexible and responsive social tool; we make or borrow what we don't have. In this flexibility and ability to change and adapt when necessity or will arises, all languages are equal. If through a sudden and unexpected shift in the world's economy the Arawakan speakers of Peru suddenly were sole possessors of some resource everyone else needed, then Arawakan would develop a variety of new vocabularies and grammatical strategies to deal with new challenges.

Languages are similar and different from one another in many ways beyond matters of vocabulary, however. Nevertheless, it is not a useful exercise to compare Swahili to Tagalog in order to find out which one is the "better" or "more efficient" language: these are not cars. We cannot compare manufacturing costs, gas mileage, performance on rough terrain. Each language is suited to its community of speakers; each language changes in pace as that community and the demands of the speakers evolve. This applies not just to languages which are unrelated to one another, but also to varieties of a single language. Cockney and the dialect of Chicago, or African American Vernacular English and the dialect of Smith's Island in Chesapeake Bay, while very different varieties of English in many ways, are all equally efficient as languages, although they do not enjoy the same degree of wider social acceptance.

If efficiency and clarity in communication are an ultimate goal in language use (an idea which will be considered below), then a non-linguist might argue that English is neither efficient nor clear in terms of its pronouns, as a speaker cannot make clear, in purely grammatical terms, if she is addressing her comments to one speaker or more ("Would you like to have dinner with me?"); further, this statement is completely without any indication of the social relationship between the speaker and the person she wants to have dinner with. Other languages are not so lax: most of the Germanic and Romance languages, as well as the Slavic and many Asian languages, distinguish between singular and plural personal pronouns, and many languages also have a complex system of honorifics which requires that speakers situate themselves in social space in relationship to the person addressed.

Another example of a lack of grammatical complexity in English has to do with the issue of verb mood. If asked why George is not in class, his classmates may answer "He's working." If George's classmates are trying to be helpful to him, they may say this in a way which passes on no additional information about the truth value of the statement. In some spoken varieties of German, however, they have no choice but to take a stance on their report. In Alemannic (the spoken varieties of German used in eastern Switzerland, western Austria and some parts of south-western Germany) there are three possibilities:

Ar ischt am schaffa	indicative
Ar sii am schaffa	present subjunctive
Ar wär am schaffa	past subjunctive

In the first case, use of the indicative mood indicates that the speaker believes the report he or she is passing on to be factually true. Using the present subjunctive, however, indicates that the report is being passed on neutrally. A good, idiomatic translation of this would be "I am told he is working; I do not know if this is true or not true." The third option, however, says very clearly that the speaker is passing on the report but does not believe it. Thus, Alemannic speakers, when asked to report something said by another speaker, must take a stance on the truth value of what they are reporting.

It is a credit to the power of language prescriptivists that many native speakers of English will look at this example and say, well yes, now that you mention it – in this particular instance, English is less effective or systematic than Alemannic.

But let's consider some facts. First, a language which does not have an overt strategy for dealing with a grammatical or semantic distinction will have other ways of doing just that. We cannot claim that English speakers are incapable of making themselves clear on just who it is they are inviting to dinner, or what they believe about the reports they pass on. Social and regional varieties of English have developed a multitude of strategies for dealing with the singular/plural distinction. For example, in Belfast and some parts of the US *you* and *youse*; in the midwest and some parts of the far west *you* and *you guys*; in much of the southern US *you* and *you'uns* or *ya'll*; in parts of Pennsylvania *you* and *yousns*. Intonation and lexical choice will make it clear whether or not the speaker believes George is actually working, or just cutting class. An additional strategy employed by all speakers of English would involve a range of lexical choices which might not engender negative social reactions, but which show strategic maneuvering: "Would you folks/people/chaps/fellows/kids like to . . ."

It is true that these examples all come from regionally restricted "dialects" of English, not "standard" English (with the possible exception of some of the lexical strategies in the last example). Could we then claim that supra-regional or standardized English – bound by adherence to a sometimes inflexible grammar – is not as efficient as the social and regional dialects? This is a tempting argument, but it cannot survive close examination.

All language, even standardized and idealized language, will cope with ambiguity of all kinds. If socially motivated rules forbid reliance on certain grammatical strategies or lexical terms, then discourse, intonation, and body-language strategies can be called into play:

"Would you [single eye contact] like to have a meal with me?"
"Would you [multiple eye contact] like to have a meal with me?"

It is a strange and interesting thing that we should think about language as if it were a machine invented to serve the purpose of communication, and thus open to criticism on the same grounds in which we talk about our lawn mowers and food processors. In the next sections we will see that these misconceptions have less to do with inherent qualities of language than they do with a preoccupation with functional aspects of language use, which in turn originates in part with struggles over authority in the determination of language and social identity.

GRAMMATICALITY AND COMMUNICATIVE EFFECTIVENESS ARE DISTINCT AND INDEPENDENT ISSUES

There are two interrelated concepts which must be distinguished: first, what constitutes the rules of a grammar, and the violation of those rules; and second, the lack of relationship between some kinds of grammaticality and the inherent value, content, and purpose of the message contained in the utterance. The first issue, grammaticality, has been discussed widely, but will be outlined here briefly. Evaluation of language *content* is brought up in this context less often, but because the two issues are so often confused in public discourse, this subject will be explored.

Grammaticality

Linguists use the term *grammatical* to refer to any utterance which could occur in a given language. In terms of linguistic grammaticality, the following are perfectly functional utterances in English:[6]

Ain't no way he's gonna.
Danny gone – he be working down to the factory.
Whatsa matter you?
He said he may can have these by the first of the month (Feagin 1979: 335).
Between you and I, he's wrong.
Coffee I can always drink, so pour me.
Meat's so expensive anymore that we eat a lot of macaroni.
Down the shore everything's all right.
Those boots sure are fly (Morgan and DeBerry 1995: 12).
If you're going out, I'm coming with.
Mrs. Vincent took a heart attack.
So she goes, like, no, it's way late for that.
The data shows that the hypothesis can't be supported.
Put it in your pocket.

To non-linguists, the "mistakes" in these sentences would be more or less obvious, with the possible exception of the last two examples. In those cases, academics especially would argue that the noun *data* must be used as a plural, with a plural verb; particularly hard-line prescriptivists would be sure to point out that things are put *into* a pocket.

Linguists and non-linguists both see *grammar* as a set of rules which must be obeyed, but they differ on the nature and origination of those rules. When linguists talk about grammar, they are conceptualizing the internalized, rule-driven structure of a language which facilitates the generation of all possible sentences for that particular language, and at the same time, rules out sentences like *lizard the leaped*, for English.[7] (There are no varieties of English which allow a definite article to be placed after the noun to which it belongs, although Swedish, another Germanic language, does this as a matter of course.) For non-linguists, grammar rules are usually socially constructed, having more in common with norms that forbid men to wear skirts in public or people to eat mashed potatoes with their fingers in restaurants. Pinker (1995) uses the example of a taxicab to illustrate this distinction, and as it is a useful illustration I have adapted it here:

The Taxicab Maxim
A taxicab must obey the laws of physics, but it can flout the laws of the state of Michigan (or Florida, or London, etc.).

Thus it is never necessary to remind a child about language-internal, rule-governed grammaticality (*Susie! Stop putting your articles after your nouns!), but it may seem very necessary, in social terms, to stop that same child from announcing "I gotta pee" during religious services, or for saying "I ain't got none" if she is asked about her brothers and sisters by a stranger; although these two instances invite correction for different reasons, none of those reasons have to do with *linguistic* grammaticality. Both "I gotta pee" and "I ain't got none" are completely viable, for English. Social conventions around language, however, are less tolerant. In terms of language, as for social behaviors like dress and eating behaviors, there are complex histories and rationalizations underlying each point of authority, and mechanisms for enforcing them which are quite effective. Thus it is useful to make a distinction between *linguistic* grammaticality and *socially constructed* grammaticality.[8]

Danny gone – he be working down to the factory is linguistically grammatical because it follows from the rule-governed structure of African American Vernacular English (AAVE), known also as Black English or Black English Vernacular (BEV). AAVE has complex morphosyntactic rules which contrast with those for other varieties of US English in many ways. So for example we see in this sentence a grammatical distinction in the conjugation of the verb "to be" in *Danny gone* and *he be working*. In the first case, AAVE allows deletion of the copula where other varieties of US English allow contraction ("Danny's gone").[9] In the case of *he be working*, AAVE provides a grammatical strategy to distinguish between durative and non-durative action: *Danny working down to the factory* means that he is there right now; *Danny be working down to the factory* means he goes there daily, that this is an on-going, repetitive action.[10]

A non-linguist would very likely call *Danny gone – he be working down to the factory* ungrammatical because it violates subject–verb agreement rules which are functional in *other* varieties of English. The question then becomes: is there only one valid variety of English, with one set of morphological rules, and can all spoken language varieties be held to that single set of rules?

That is a question for the later chapters in this book. For the moment, it is enough to note that linguists reserve the term *ungrammatical* for those constructions or usages which do not occur in the language at all, and cannot be generated from its grammar.

Content

I have put forth as facts that any language is capable of adapting to any linguistic need, and that every native speaker produces utterances which are by their very nature grammatical. What I have not and cannot claim, is that message *content* can be judged in the same way. This is where the potential of the language and the grammar as abstractions come into conflict with language as it is used by individuals. Linguists differentiate between *language system* and *language use*, which may be loosely interpreted as the acknowledgement that each utterance, while grammatical, *may or may not* fulfill the purpose for which it was conceived and formulated, for a wide variety of reasons. Consider the following hypothetical responses (B1–B5) to a simple question (A):

A: "Can I have your phone number?"
B1: "I'll have a beer."
B2: "Uh, well, I'm not sure – what *is* my phone number, it's – ah – I don't –"
B3: "What's a phone, and why does it have a number?"
B4: "When hell freezes over."
B5: "It's 555-3333."

To determine linguistic grammaticality, a very simple question suffices: *Can this utterance be generated by the grammar of the language?* Each of the responses above is a grammatical construction for my own variety of English, and for many others. But an evaluation of content and *socially-construed* well-formedness or efficiency moves to issues of intent, composition, and delivery. In each case, we could ask a number of questions to evaluate the responses given.

Is the message clear?
Is it easily broken down into its constituents?
Does one point follow logically from the previous point?
Is it couched in concise language and free of excess and overly complex
    construction?

Is it persuasive?
Is its delivery pleasing?

The five possible responses provided for the question *Can I have your phone number?* could be judged on the basis of clarity, logic, conciseness, persuasiveness, and delivery, but not until we have more information, because the communicative intent of both the question posed and the answer received are multidimensional. It is possible to imagine many underlying purposes to the question *Can I have your phone number?* depending on the context in which it is asked, and the relationship of speaker to listener. In one possible situation (in which one person is trying to establish a romantic or sexual relationship), the answer "Uh, well, I'm not sure – what is my phone number, it's – ah– I don't –" may not be concise (in the sense of "succinct"), but the underlying message is, after all, a complex one: *I have evaluated you as a potential mate and found that you are not acceptable, but I have no wish to insult you directly or embarrass you, and in fact I am afraid of the social consequences of doing so*. Within its social context, the reply is very clear, and it is also concise in that it gets its message across with fewer lexical items than the alternate proposed. Alternatively "When hell freezes over" is a longer answer than "No" but it is also much more descriptive. A simple negation leaves room for interpretation of motive; "When hell freezes over" leaves very little doubt about the evaluation of the question.

In the medieval and early modern periods, liberal arts consisted in part of the study of grammar, logic, and rhetoric (the *trivium*), where rhetoric is taken to mean language used effectively and persuasively. This concern with "effective" language persists, although the term remains, as always, a subjective one.[11] If effectiveness in language is the sum of more specific qualifiers (clarity, logic, conciseness, persuasiveness, and delivery), then calculation of effectiveness is complicated by the fact that these are subjective rather than objective measures. Whether or not these are *reasonable* demands of language as a vehicle of communication is also debatable.[12] Is language more effective when sentences are short, or long? When it is spoken fast, or slow? When the vocabulary used is primarily Germanic (*help!*), or Romance (*assistance!*)?

I will argue at various points in this study that the evaluation of language effectiveness – while sometimes quite relevant – is often a covert way of judging not the delivery of the message, but the social identity of the messenger. It is a basic truth about language that *the variety of the language spoken cannot predict the effectiveness of the message*.

It is not hard to get people to acknowledge that an individual who speaks a variety of English which is highly evaluated in social terms is not necessarily a *good* speaker, or that a socially "right" variety of English does not automatically bring with it the ability to write well. The National Council of Teachers of English put out a publication called *Quarterly*

Review of Doublespeak which is dedicated to documenting how spoken
and written language are used to obscure poor reasoning and to deliber-
ately mislead. The persons who are quoted in these pages are speakers
of what would be called an educated, mainstream US English, for example
the following transcript of Supreme Court Justice Harry Blackmun:

> Today's majority ... decides that the forced repatriation of the Haitian
> refugees is perfectly legal, because the word "return" does not mean
> return, because the opposite of "within the United States" is not outside
> the United States, and because the official charged with controlling
> immigration has no role in enforcing an order to control immigration.
>
> (Justice Harry Blackmun, *The Progressive*, August 1993: 10,
> as cited in *Quarterly Review of Doublespeak*, October 1993: 2–3)

Political debate provides daily examples of highly educated and
powerful people who speak what is generally considered "the best"
English, who are still incapable of expressing simple ideas clearly, at least
in a public forum. When former Vice President Dan Quayle stated with
great confidence: "I believe we are on an irreversible trend toward more
freedom and democracy – but that could change" (Slansky and Radlauer
1992: 41) many people shook their heads at his doublespeak, but no one
called his English ungrammatical. When the media drew attention to
Quayle's language use it was not because of the *kind* of English he speaks,
but more usually because of his lack of logic, poor information, mala-
propisms, or on one highly publicized occasion, his inability to spell.[13]

Of course, there are many speakers of what would generally be called
Standard US English who also are capable of expressing their thoughts
clearly and concisely, both in speech and writing. But can effective
messages be given in AAVE? In Appalachian English, or Chicano
English? What happens when the message comes in a variety of English
which is not highly evaluated in social terms?

In the course of this book, I will argue that the statement *the variety
of the language spoken cannot predict the effectiveness of the message*, while
true, is only a partial truth. The variety of the language spoken cannot
predict the effectiveness of the message, but it can predict some of the
social evaluation the listener brings to the message, and his or her willingness to listen.

WRITTEN LANGUAGE AND SPOKEN LANGUAGE ARE HISTORICALLY, STRUCTURALLY, AND FUNCTIONALLY FUNDAMENTALLY DIFFERENT CREATURES

This point is easy enough to bolster with factual evidence, but it is perhaps
the single most difficult point for non-linguists to fully understand and
accept. In our minds the spoken and written languages are so intertwined
that we seem sometimes incapable of distinguishing between them.

Prince Charles often demonstrates this tendency in public speeches, as we see in the following example given when he was judging a reading competition:

> If English is spoken in heaven ... God undoubtedly employs Cranmer as his speechwriter. The angels of the lesser ministries probably use the language of the New English Bible and the Alternative Service Book for internal memos.
>
> (Tytler 1989: 1)

I suppose we must be fair and point out that the Prince of Wales does not automatically assume that English is spoken in heaven. Nevertheless, his further assumptions are quite interesting. It is useful to point out first that those language authorities cited here as perfect all draw their power from religious institutions. Thomas Cranmer was the Archbishop of Canterbury (the head of the Anglican Church) under Henry VIII, and he is cited by the Prince of Wales as an authority because he simplified and translated the Latin prayer books into one English volume, the Book of Common Prayer, which eventually became the only book used, by means of England's Act of Uniformity (1662). It is also interesting that the written documents which are cited here as appropriate models for the spoken language are British ones (in other places, Prince Charles has been very critical of what has been done to English by its speakers on the North American continent). But most important to the discussion immediately at hand is the way this picture of language perfection assumes that the various mediums of language are one and the same. Here we see mention of spoken language, speeches (which can be given as planned but extemporaneous speech, or the reading out loud of written language), and written language.

This proclamation by the future king of England also builds on a tradition of drawing on divine authority in language which goes back to Socrates, who in writing about the self-sufficiency and perfection of classical Greek makes the argument that it is the language "in which the Gods must clearly be supposed to call things by their right and natural names" (Plato 1970: 138). More recently, in an event which has been quoted so widely as to have passed into linguistic legend, a congressman in Texas (or, in some accounts, Oklahoma) is said to have expressed the decisive argument against bilingual education (and unwittingly, for more and better history and geography instruction) by drawing on the ultimate authority: "If English was good enough for Jesus Christ," he intoned, "then it's good enough for the schoolchildren of Texas."

The issue of rightful authority in determining standards for language obscures one primary issue: written and spoken language lend themselves differently to standardization. Why should this be? Halliday points out that "writing and speaking are not just alternative ways of doing the same things; rather, they are ways of doing different things" (1989: xv). Before we examine what it is that they do differently, an overview of the major differences between the two language channels will be useful, as seen in Box 1.1:

Box 1.2   A comparison of written and spoken language

Spoken language . . .	*Written language . . .*
is an innate human capacity which is acquired by all human children who are not isolated from other language users during the critical acquisition period	is not universal, and must be consciously and rigorously taught; it is a skill which will be acquired with differing degrees of success
draws heavily on paralinguistic features to convey information in more than one way: tone of voice, body language	cannot rely on these resources and must use punctuation, additional lexical items or constructions when written letters alone do not suffice
is primarily a social activity, carried out between two or more persons	is carried out as a solitary pursuit, with an audience removed in time and space
allows confusion and ambiguity to be resolved directly by repair and confirmation procedures	does not allow confusion and ambiguity to be immediately resolved
is used in a social and temporal context, and thus brings with it a great deal of background information; draws on context to complement meaning and fill in ellipses	is contextless and thus more prone to ambiguity; intolerant of ellipses
can be planned or spontaneous	is by nature planned
is ephemeral	is permanent
is inherently and unavoidably variable on every level, language internally (structurally) and externally (socially); exploits variation to pass on information in addition to that of the surface message	actively suppresses and discourages variation of all kinds

While written and spoken language seem on the surface to be very similar, a comparison of one with the other soon demonstrates how different they are. Why should this be the case?

Writing systems are a strategy developed in response to demands arising from social, technological, and economic change. The purpose of writing systems is to convey decontextualized information over time and space. We write love letters, laundry lists, historical monographs, novels, family trees, car-care manuals, menus, "out to lunch" signs, biochemistry text-books. We write these things down because our memories are not capable of storing such masses of information for ourselves or those who come after us, or because we consider the message one worthy of preserving past the limitations of memory.

The demands made on written language are considerable: we want it to span time and space, and we want it to do that in a social vacuum, without the aid of paralinguistic features and often without shared context of any kind. Thus, the argument goes, written language needs to be free of excessive variation: it must be consistent in every way, from spelling to sentence structure.[14] The process of learning how to write involves learning a new set of rules which in effect translate the spoken language into a written language form. The acquisition of this skill is a complex one that demonstrates the differences between the two mediums, as seen below in the writings of one school-aged Michigan child, Robert, as he moves from second to fourth grade.[15]

> We prettended we we[re] explorers and Jesse's house was the world and went all the way around the world. We had a little bit of popcorn and we played some other stuff. About the funniest thing was when we made products and we made up a story about are [our] products and told while we were presenting our products after about two hours and I went home.
>
> (second grade)

> Bicicles come in all sizes and colors. It is easy to ride with training wheels, because they [are] hard to tip. Riding without training wheels is easy to[o], once you get the hang of it.
>
> (early third grade)

> At last, when night fell Richard came to the top of the mountain. There he saw that it was not a mountain after all, it was a volcano! For in the center of it there was an ab[y]ss, and when Richard stared down into it, he saw nothing but an ebony void.
>
> All of a sudden an immense cloud of smoke blasted out, streaking toward the heavens. . . .
>
> (late third grade)

In the first example, composed when he was in the second grade, Robert writes of a visit to a friend in the same relaxed and easy manner he might have told these same details to his family over dinner. There are no para-graph breaks at logical points, and there is little punctuation, although he shows an unusually early awareness of the function of apostrophes to mark possessive *s*. The final sentence is actually in four distinct thoughts, joined by the conjunction *and*, as is common in spoken language. There is only one subordinate clause.

The second example was written barely six months later when Robert was in third grade, and it demonstrates that he has learned how to divide language into the chunks which are expected of a written description. He uses commas to set off dependent clauses.

In the final example, written late in the third-grade school year, Robert has mastered many narrative techniques unique to the written language: *at last, when night fell,* and *there he saw* are the type of construction rarely heard in spontaneous oral discourse. Robert has learned to use exclamation points when in an oral narrative he might raise an arm or his voice to signal a high point in the story. He begins a new paragraph to signal a pause or change of direction in the narration.

The transition from spoken to written language is the acquisition of a skill; it is, in broad terms, learning to plan an otherwise spontaneous activity with extreme attention to detail. Generally, all language can be divided into two rough categories, planned and unplanned, but writing predominates on the planned side, and the spoken language is usually unplanned. For the most part planned speech occurs in particularly formal or stylized contexts, for example, a traditional marriage proposal or a presentation before a bank's board of directors. In this case, spoken language often shows traces of syntactical constructions or lexical items normally reserved for the written language.

While writing is planned language, most speech is unplanned, and fulfills a wide range of possible functions. Many (or, some linguists would claim, all) of these are communicative in nature.[16] There are distinct functions, which in the Jakobsonian model include

1 The pragmatic functions, in which commands or requests are made, things are sold, or warnings are issued. *Newspaper! Get your newspaper! Put it here!* or *Your hair is on fire!* are all examples of speech functioning in a pragmatic way.
2 Emotional components, which serve to express an internal state on the part of the speaker or instill an emotional state on the part of the decoder, as in *I could just spit!*
3 Cognitive aspects, in which the use of speech is to convey information associated with thought, theory, data, or other facts. This subsumes the explanation of procedures and the expression of opinion, such as *I like it like that,* or *Giraffes have longer necks than turtles.*
4 Speech as a tool to establish, maintain, and reaffirm social roles within an organized society. Salutations (*Hey! Look who the cat dragged in! How are you today? Girlfriend! Good afternoon, gentlemen*) which seem to be pragmatic or cognitive are often in fact primarily social.

While the pragmatic, emotional, cognitive and social functions of speech can and do co-occur in single utterances, sociolinguists seem to agree that no matter how strictly pragmatic or cognitive, the majority of utterances have some element of the social in them. The social life of language often exists in subtle shifts and choices below the level of consciousness, in the way our vowels and consonants are pronounced and in the intonational patterns we use. *Newspaper! Get your newspaper!* is not the same utterance in Portland, New Orleans, Iowa City, San Diego, or Missoula, because it is not the same person calling out this very pragmatic message.

So what is the confusion between spoken and written language? It seems straightforward enough: we write things that tax our ability to remember, or to project our thoughts through space. We speak everything else. But aren't they the same thing, just as water is water whether it flows, or freezes so that we can walk on it? Isn't it just a matter of presentation? Can't speech and writing be treated as different manifestations of the same mental phenomenon? Wouldn't spoken language be more efficient if we treated it like written language?

We might think of the difference between spoken and written language as the difference between walking and machines built for the purpose of transporting human beings. Unless a child suffers a terrible turn of fate, he or she will learn to walk without focused instruction. People move themselves over space to pursue food and shelter, to associate with each other, to explore their world. Over time, the human race developed a series of technologies to improve the ability to move themselves: they tamed horses, camels, oxen; they built carts, carriages, boats, trains, bicycles, cars, airplanes. All of these things are faster than walking, and, if speed is the primary criterion by which we judge efficiency of movement, they are superior to the skill all humans have in common. But it would not occur to us to set up standards for walking on the basis of the speed of any of these vehicles: it is a physical impossibility to walk 60 miles an hour for any amount of time. We cannot walk like we ride.

Why then do we not think anything of Prince Charles telling us that in heaven, people will speak like they write, as if this were the ultimate good, the ideal?

In their seminal work on authority in language, James and Lesley Milroy point to the underlying issue which may explain – in part – why we are so willing to see the spoken language subordinated to the written.

> As writing skills are difficult, our educational systems have concentrated on inculcating a relatively high degree of literacy, with little attention paid to the nature of spoken language as an everyday social activity. Training in the use of "English" ... is usually assumed to be training in the use of *written* English. ... Spoken language is taken for granted. As a result of this constant emphasis on written language, there is an understandable tendency for people to believe that writing

is somehow more complicated and difficult (and more important) than speech.

(1991: 65–66)

The preoccupation of the schools with the written language to the exclusion of the spoken is quite easy to document. The National Council of Teachers of English, for example, publishes guidelines for the curriculum in English on a regular basis; of the twelve points addressed, only three include mention of spoken language skills, and then in a very vague and indirect way (a topic which will be taken up in more detail in Chapter 6). From the spoken to the written language is a large step; it is another significant step from the written language to the possession of literacy.[17] However, the possession of a skill, and facility to use that skill to *construct a product*, are cultural resources not equally available to all persons, and are heavily endowed with social currencies. Generally, the public does not consider oral cultures as equal to literate ones, and there has been scholarly work in linguistics and education which would seem to provide evidence for the inherent validity of this position. Some scholars have argued, with differing degrees of subtlety, that certain kinds or modes of thought cannot develop in oral cultures, and that for this reason literate cultures are superior. This type of argument has come under attack on both methodological and theoretical grounds. Most relevant here is Bernstein's theory of restricted and elaborated codes, which attempted (and failed) to establish that children who spoke "elaborated" languages at home (those more syntactically complex) were more capable of logical thought (among other cognitive advantages) and that children who heard only "restricted" codes in the home were at a disadvantage. While Bernstein never made explicit the connection between languages of oral cultures and "restricted" codes, or languages of literate cultures and "elaborated" codes, this reading of his work is not an unusual one. Gordon (1981) provides an excellent review of Bernstein's work and the literature.[18]

It is demonstrably true that in a literate culture, illiteracy is a social brand like few others. Cameron calls what goes on around the written language "a circle of intimidation":

> mastering a complex and difficult craft gives you an inbuilt incentive to defend its practices. If I have invested time and effort learning how to write according to a particular set of prescriptions, I will take some convincing that those prescriptions are not necessary and desirable; to admit that the rules are both arbitrary and pointless is to devalue my own accomplishment in mastering them.

(1995: 14)

Gee (1990) goes a step farther when he outlines the complex associations and expectations of literacy:

literacy is claimed to lead to logical, analytic, critical and rational thinking, general and abstract uses of language, a skeptical and questioning attitude, a distinction between myth and history, the recognition of the importance of time and space, complex and modern governments . . . political democracy and greater social equity, economic development, wealth and productivity, political stability, urbanization, and contraception (a lower birth rate). It is also supposed to lead to people who are innovative, achievement oriented, productive, cosmopolitan, media and politically aware . . . with more liberal and humane social attitudes, less likely to commit a crime, and more likely to take education, and the rights and duties of citizenship, seriously. The common popular and scholarly conception that literacy has such powerful effects as these constitutes what Harvey Graff has called the "literacy myth."

(32)

What is of interest in this study is the force of a *literacy myth* (Graff 1987a, b) which has brought about the subordination of the spoken language to norms – in themselves sometimes arbitrary, and with differing degrees of effectiveness – which were developed for the written language. This process is part of what Foucault has called the *disciplining of discourse*, or the way we decide who has the right to talk, and to be listened to (1984, and elsewhere), the major topic of interest in the second and third parts of this book.

VARIATION IS INTRINSIC TO ALL SPOKEN LANGUAGE AT EVERY LEVEL

Spoken language varies for every speaker in terms of speech sounds, sound patterns, word and sentence structure, intonation, and meaning, from utterance to utterance. This is not a frivolous or useless feature of language.[19] Quite the contrary: "Heterogeneity is an integral part of the linguistic economy of the community, necessary to satisfy the linguistic demands of everyday life" (Labov 1982a: 17). There are three sources of variation in language: first, language-internal pressures, arising in part from the mechanics of production and perception; second, language-external influences on language, as a social behavior subject to normative and other formative social pressures; and third, variation arising from language as a creative vehicle of free expression. These forces can and do function in tandem, and any good study of language change in progress will consider at least the first two together.

There is great similarity in the way we produce and perceive the sounds of language, because the human neurological and vocal apparatus used in speech is architecturally and structurally universal. As a child acquiring language, every person has potentially available to them the full range of

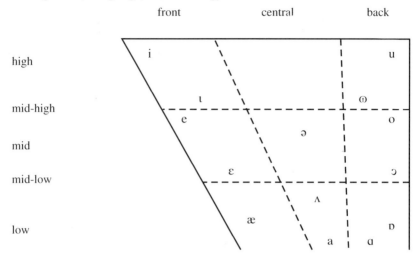

Figure 1.1 International Phonetic Symbols for the vowels of English, showing relative vowel qualities
Source: Ladefoged 1982: 34

possible sounds. The sounds which will eventually survive and become part of the child's language are arranged into language-specific *systems*, each sound standing in relation to the other sounds. In linguistic terms, the study of production and perception of speech sounds is the science of phonetics; concern with how sounds are organized into systems is called phonology. It is in the production and perception of speech sounds as systematic entities functioning in relationship to each other that there is perhaps the greatest potential for variation in language, and following from that, variation leading to change.

We begin with brief descriptions of some points of phonological or morpho-phonological variation currently active in all or parts of the US, as well as descriptions of two grammatical points and one stylistic point. If variation in language were "free" (a term often used in those branches of linguistics uninterested in the social life of language, where variation is seen as a kind of "noise in the channel"), then it would follow logically that the social structures of the communities in which the language functions could not predict any of the variation.

Phonological variation

The cot–caught merger

When two distinct, meaning-bearing sounds – vowels in this case – begin to merge, homonyms may result. For much of the midwestern US, for example, the words *Mary*, *merry* and *marry* are pronounced exactly the same. Currently, there is a great deal of activity in US English for the vowels in the words *cot* and *caught*, or *hock* and *hawk*, whereby the vowel of *caught* and *hawk* is being replaced by the vowel in *cot* and *hock*. For some readers of this book, this may be a meaningless statement because the merger will already be complete, and the whole process came and went without ever drawing attention to itself. For them, it must be pointed out that *cot* and *caught* are not the same word for everybody: some pronounce the first word with the sound [ɑ] and the second with [ɔ]. (See Figure 1.1 for a schematic representation of these and other sounds.) This change is moving through the language lexical item by lexical item (which is only one way in which phonological change is realized). In my own speech, best termed "Midwest Northern Cities," it has already come to pass for the words *hot* and *solitary*; it is variable for the words *water* and *hog*, but not yet active for the words *fought, awkward, dawn,* or *horrible* (although I have heard [ɑ] used in those words by others, including my seven-year-old daughter). This is part of the large-scale vocalic system shift discussed at length in Labov (1991).

*The **short–forty** and the **park the car** variables*

For some varieties of US English the combination of [or] with a following consonant triggers variation between two possible realizations of the vowel, [o] or [ɒ] (a low, back, slightly rounded vowel) in words such as *short, forty, orchestra,* and *corporation* with subsequent addition of an "off-glide" in monosyllables (Laferriere 1986). In a related set of phenomena, the sound (r) is often deleted after vowels, and sometimes inserted where none is expected.[20] An example of this particular variation known to many is John Kennedy's Boston variety of English; aware of the way his own accent was perceived by the public, he once noted that Bostonians "saved all the r's *paaking aa caas in Haaavaad yaad* [parking our cars in Harvard yard] in order to put them on the end of *idear* and *Cuber* [idea and Cuba]."

*The **walkin'** and **talkin'** variable*

English uses "ing" suffixes of verbs in a number of ways: as gerunds (*Skiing is hard work*), or in the progressive verbal construction (*He's playing games again*). The suffix written with three letters has a number of possible realizations in speech: the one which is considered "proper" [ɪŋ] does not actually have a "hard *g* sound", or stop, at its end. The second most common realization is [in], often represented in writing as *walkin'* and *talkin'* as if a *g* had been deleted, when in fact one sound, [n], has been substituted for another, [ŋ]. There *is* in fact a third possible realization of this suffix as [ɪŋg], but it is limited in geographic and perhaps social ways.[21]

This variation is not active where *-ing* is part of the root of the word rather than a suffix: we do not find the variable pair ring [riŋ] and rin' [rin].

The *coupon* variable

For a subset of lexical items with the sound [u] in a stressed syllable, there is at least a possibility of adding a "glide" or a *y* sound before that vowel, so that *duke* has two possible realizations: [duk] and [djuk] ("dyook"). This variation works below the level of consciousness, for the most part, with the exception of one lexical item: people do seem to be aware of the choice between *coupon* and *c-y-oupon*.

Grammatical variation

While variation in grammatical structure is quite salient, it is less often studied than phonological variation. Variations in verbal morphology are probably some of the most productive grammatical points of change in progress, and also the most complex.

Multiple negation

Generally in mainstream, non-stigmatized varieties of US and other Englishes, a single negative element is all that is allowed when we negate a sentence, although there are usually a number of possible strategies in negation available. In fact negation is a very complex business in any variety of English, and it is further complicated by prescriptivist, socially motivated grammatical rules which insist, for example, that two negatives make a positive, a piece of logic borrowed – rather oddly – from mathematics. The fact that two negatives do not make a positive in a variety of other languages does not seem to shake the public's firm commitment to this rule of thumb; nevertheless, mainstream varieties of spoken English do sometimes allow multiple negation of the sort found in *Nobody much likes Harry, I don't think.* Further, if one person rages "No, no, no no no no!" it is not likely that his or her audience would then determine that the six "no's" (a number divisible by two) render this a positive statement.

In other, stigmatized varieties of English, a single underlying negation may be realized at multiple points in an utterance: *We ain't never had no trouble about none of us pulling' out no knife* (Wolfram 1969: 153).

In non-stigmatized US English the possible variants for this sentence include:

We never had any trouble about pulling out a knife.
We didn't have any trouble about pulling out a knife.

None of us ever had any trouble about pulling out a knife.
Not one of us ever had any trouble about pulling out a knife.

Whether the variety of English in question allows multiple negation or not, there is a great deal of variation available in the process.

Invariant forms of "to be"

Another point of variation in verb usage is commonly called "subject–verb" agreement. For example, a standardized US English requires that the past tense of the verb "to be" distinguish between plural and singular; first, second, and third persons: I was, you (singular) were, he/she/it was, we were, you (plural) were, they were. There are, however, both social and regional dialects which tend toward what has been called "invariant *was*," or the use of the singular form regardless of the subject, as in *We was in an ideal place for it* or *Was you a majorette?* (Feagin 1979: 204). This particular point of variation shows up more widely in conjunction with the impersonal subject *there*, as in *There was twenty dollars in my purse when I last looked.* This is true as well for the present tense, where the verb form is often contracted: *There's donuts left if you're hungry* or *There's stars out tonight.*

Lexical variation

This is the kind of linguistic variation which people are most often aware of, and which causes heated discussion at cocktail parties. In southeastern Michigan, there are often good-natured classroom arguments on the use of *pop* (the variant most likely found farther west) versus *soda* (the variant found to the east); people seem to find discussions of the distribution of the roughly equal terms *tennis shoe, gym shoe, sneaker* quite interesting. Sociolinguists find this kind of variation less compelling, unless there is correlation to other points of variation which are more socially or geographically complex.

There are lexical items which function as discourse markers, however, and which are so complex in structural, social, and stylistic terms that linguists spend a lot of time worrying over them. Terms like *you know*, *well*, and *but* show us "how speakers and hearers jointly integrate forms, meanings, and actions to make overall sense out of what is said" (Schiffrin 1987: 49). A particularly interesting but not widely studied discourse marker is the use of *like*, as in the sentence *Most of them like maybe like drink and stuff* (California Style Collective 1993: 8). At first glance it would seem that this must be nothing more than a random and strictly age-graded phenomenon and devoid of any meaning, but first glances are often deceptive.

STRUCTURED VARIATION: THE HIDDEN LIFE OF LANGUAGE

The examples of variation in language provided above might seem, at first glance, to be obvious and uninteresting in any real way. People say things different ways at different times, but the meaning of the utterance remains the same whether we are told that *Republicans don't like liberals* or *Ain't no Republican likes no liberal.*

But language isn't simple, and variation isn't without consequences. Human beings choose among thousands of points of variation available to them not because the human mind is sloppy, or language is imprecise: just the opposite. We *exploit* linguistic variation available to us in order to send a complex series of messages about ourselves and the way we position ourselves in the world we live in. We perceive variation in the speech of others and we use it to structure our knowledge about that person. Listening to strangers calling into talk-radio programs, it is more than grammar and vowel sounds that we evaluate, more than the content of their comments that we walk away with. "What's a Dago know about the price of oil?" my father asked once while listening to an anonymous caller to a talk-radio program rant about the gasoline crunch in the late 1970s. My father, a native speaker of Italian, recognized the caller as socially and ethnically similar to himself and made a series of evaluations. We all have experiences like this: it is part of speaking a language. The inability to use or recognize the social markings of linguistic variants is one of the most significant problems of second-language learners, and one that is rarely dealt with in the classroom, where the myth of standard language has a stronghold.

The parameters of linguistic variation are multidimensional. In large-scale terms, these are social, stylistic, geographic, or temporal, and in any one case of active variation, more than one of these factors is probably at play, and works in complex ways with language-internal influences on variation.

Social parameters of linguistic variation can be approached a number of ways. There is a great deal of discussion among sociolinguists about the underlying conceptions of the language community and the methodologies for approaching and quantifying the community's language. What is relevant here is not a history of the theory and methodology of sociolinguistic inquiry (that has been done elsewhere, and with great care; see for example Chambers 1995), but what generalizations are possible about the relationship between linguistic variation and social identity based on some thirty-five years of inquiry. We know, for example, that gender, age, and geographical loyalties are often coded by means of language variation. When we choose among variants available to us, we take those that will effectively mark us as belonging to specific social groupings. We do this sometimes even when we are trying not to (in the next chapters we will return to this very relevant subject of mutability of language).

Sociolinguistics becomes complicated as soon as we recognize that social identities only begin with questions of geography, gender, and age. In many years of studying the way structured variation in language reflects the social structures of the community, it has become clear that language can serve to mark a number of kinds of identity. The way individuals situate themselves in relationship to others, the way they group themselves, the powers they claim for themselves and the powers they stipulate to others are all embedded in language. National origin, socioeconomic class, communication networks based on the workplace and occupation, degree of integration into kinship structures: all these things and many more can be marked by means of variation in very clear ways. To add to this complexity, topic and setting put their own demands on variation.

Figures 1.2 through 1.9 provide data from a variety of sociolinguistic studies conducted in the US, with a range of relevant variables. What should be striking here is that for each case of variation (which we must recall is a small portion of the total range of variation happening in any of the speech communities at a given time) another constellation of possible social, stylistic, and geographic factors are at play.

Laferriere's 1979 study of the *short–forty* variable active in Boston found that the use of the innovative or newer value, [ɒ], for a less regionally-marked [o], was not random, but correlated strongly with one of three ethnic identities and formality of the speech event:

> All groups use the dialect variant [ɒ] most frequently in casual speech, as expected, and least in formal speech; but the three groups contrast in the degree to which they use the variant. Jewish speakers have the lowest percentages of [ɒ] in all styles; Italians have the highest; and Irish speakers have values parallel to and between the other two.
>
> (605)

We see in Figure 1.2 that stylistic formality is consistently relevant to a person's participation in this variation, regardless of ethnicity. Again and again, sociolinguistic studies have shown that amount of attention paid to speech is a crucial factor in the propagation of any change in progress.

Is there some more general relevance of this particular variable to ethnicity? To the vowel sound [o] before [r]? Absolutely not. When a sociolinguist goes into a community to study variation in the language, there is no way to predict what elements will be changing, in what directions, or based on what social differences between speakers. But because we have seen time and time again that certain kinds of social contrasts are likely to be embodied in linguistic variation, we would *hypothesize* that large ethnic populations with distinct "personalities" will distinguish themselves linguistically. Knack (1991) found that for the Jewish and Gentile populations of Grand Rapids, Michigan there were linguistic ways to mark this ethnicity which were very different from the Boston pattern. In addition to variation in the pronunciation of a particular vowel, the devoicing

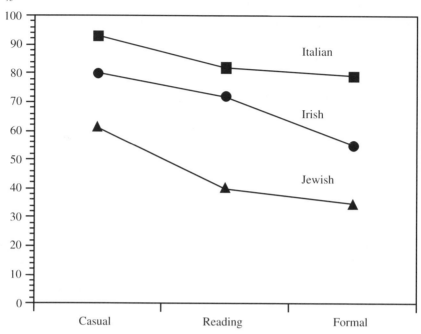

Figure 1.2 Use of new vowel [ɒ] in three speech styles for Italian, Irish, and Jewish speakers in the *short–forty* variable in Boston
Source: Adapted from Laferriere 1986

of voiced (z) to unvoiced (s) between vowels is a way to signal Jewish identity. For example, Knack found that in Grand Rapids most Gentile speakers pronounce the [s] in the sentence *She is over there* with a voiced (z), whereas Jews will *sometimes* pronounce "is" with (z) and sometimes with (s). Jewish men are much more likely to use (z), and the more integrated the Jewish males are into the social and political Grand Rapids community, the less of the (s) variant they use. Jewish women, on the other hand, use *more* of the (s) variant when they are well integrated into the community. Knack hypothesizes that this distinction between Jewish men and women has to do with the role of Jewish women as responsible for maintaining the faith, "and thus [they] have a need to persist more obviously than Jewish men in their Jewish behavior, including its linguisitic aspects. Devoiced (z), considered stereotypically Jewish, could be one of these aspects" (1991: 266).

  Some of the very earliest quantitative studies of sociolinguistic variation looked at the *walkin' and talkin'* variable. In his study of adolescent male groups in Harlem and their language behavior, Labov found this variable to be a good indicator of an individual's commitment to the vernacular culture. "Lames" in Labov's study are individuals who remove themselves from the social context of the communication networks in which they would otherwise be integrated:

> They are not hip, since they do not hang out. It is only by virtue of being available and on the street every day that anyone can acquire the deep familiarity with local doings and the sure command of local slang that are needed to participate in vernacular culture. To be "lame" means to be outside of the central group and its culture; it is a negative characterization ...

(1973: 84)

Figures 1.3 and 1.4 indicate how clearly lames use language to distance themselves symbolically: *R*-lessness is common all along the eastern seaboard, but it is a variable which shows very fine social and stylistic distributions, as is particularly salient in African American sociolinguistic marking. Labov notes that the African American communities usually show a higher degree of *r*-lessness, as well as a more distinct style shifting toward using (r) in reading styles. "In general, it can be said that the (r) variables are more important in the Black community than anywhere else as indicators of formal, educated speech. This is even more true in Black communities in r-pronouncing areas, such as Philadelphia or Los Angeles" (1973: 89). In Figure 1.3, the "1390 Lames" (a reference to the building they live in) use postvocalic (r) in greater proportions than members of

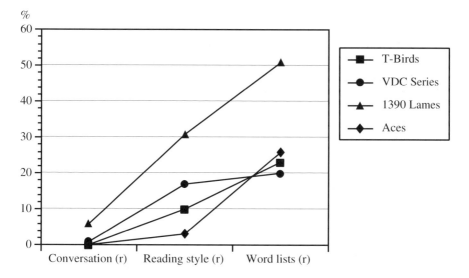

Figure 1.3 Use of postvocalic (r) by style for gang members in Harlem
Source: Adapted from Labov 1973

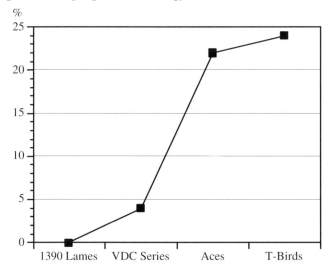

Figure 1.4 Use of *-in* for *-ing* in reading style for gang members in Harlem
Source: Adapted from Labov 1973

any of the three gangs (VDC Series, T-Birds, Aces) do, and shift more strongly toward (r) use with increasing attention paid to speech.

In a similar way, we see in Figure 1.4 that the 1390 Lames show no participation at all in the *walkin' and talkin'* variable for the most formal reading style. Of the gangs, the T-Birds approach 25 percent use of the full form *-ing* in this style.

Studies of distribution of social variants over space are necessarily more limited because of the technological challenge they represent, but when they are done they provide some interesting data, as in Bailey *et al.*'s 1993 study of the *hock–hawk* (*cot–caught*) merger in Oklahoma. In Figure 1.5 it is clear that the new vowel is diffusing in Oklahoma in a hierarchical pattern, from areas of greater population density to lesser. In addition, the younger generation is using more of the newer vowel, in a wider area. Bailey sees the interstate highway system as relevant to the spatial and temporal spread of this particular change in progress:

> Among younger generations, then, the urban/rural differences gradu-
> ally begin to level out as the use of unrounded vowels in words like
> hawk diffuses from cities to the surrounding countryside. The interstate
> highway system, which provides easy access to urban centers for some
> rural areas but not for others, seems to be a primary mechanism for
> this hierarchical diffusion ... the importance of these interstates in
> restructuring the rural population over the last three decades can hardly
> be overestimated.

> (1993: 370)

(a) Respondents born in or before 1945

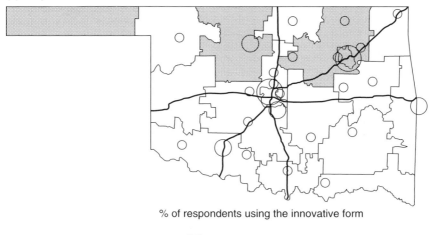

% of respondents using the innovative form

- ☐ less than 33%
- ☐ 33 – 66%
- ■ above 66%

(b) Respondents born in or after 1946

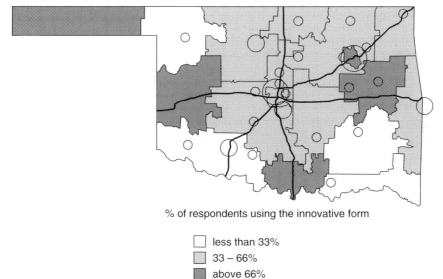

% of respondents using the innovative form

- ☐ less than 33%
- ☐ 33 – 66%
- ■ above 66%

Figure 1.5 Spatial distribution of /a/ in *hawk* in Oklahoma
Source: Bailey *et al.* 1993: 369

Figure 1.6 Use of [u] "oo" rather than [ju] "yoo" in words like *due, news, duke* (excluding *coupon*) by social class and contextual formality for 240 speakers in St. Louis, Missouri

Source: Adapted with permission from T. E. Murray (1986) *The Language of Saint Louis, Missouri: Variations in the gateway city.* New York: Peter Lang

Murray's 1986 study of 240 residents of St. Louis shows how clearly a single variable can disclose information about socioeconomic class and the effect of attention to speech. We see in Figure 1.6 that while speakers are generally unaware of the variation between [u] and [ju] in words like *duke*, the variable [u], used most consistently by the lower socioeconomic class, shows sensitivity to attention paid to speech for the middle and upper classes. This particular variable has more social currency in the south than it does in the north. A parallel study of this variable in Idaho or Maine might not be as interesting.

Yet another combination of factors relevant to the distribution of linguistic variation is seen in Wolfram's 1969 study of multiple negation among AAVE speakers in Detroit, as shown in Figure 1.7. Here socioeconomic class and gender are relevant to the degree to which an individual uses multiple negation: the higher the social class, the less likely AAVE speakers are to use this grammatical strategy; females use it less than males. Subsequent studies of this and related variables functioning in AAVE in Philadelphia and elsewhere have made it clear that there is

%

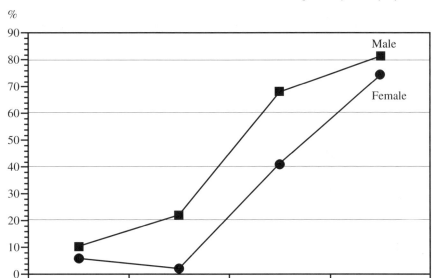

Figure 1.7 Realized multiple negation by social class and sex in Detroit
Source: Adapted from Wolfram 1969: 162

a whole range of social, stylistic, and language internal effects on these variables. These include the way individuals are integrated into communication networks in the inner city, as well as the narrative function of the particular speech act (Labov and Harris 1986).

From Detroit's AAVE speaking community to adolescent girls in the Palo Alto High School might seem a bit of a jump, but in fact Figure 1.8 indicates that what seem to be very different sets of social expectations and allegiances exert very similar pressures on language norms and function in remarkably similar ways.

The California Style Collective (CSC) study – an ongoing project – is one which departs from a socioeconomic stratificational approach to language variation, and looks at *group style* in a way which allows the examination of "production and reproduction of social meaning in variation" (1993: 2).

Preliminary study of the discourse marker *like* for one socially active teenager indicates that the variation is extremely complex. As the CSC pursue study of this particular marker, they will be looking at a variety of possible constraints on its use, from semantic effects, to topic of conversation. In the preliminary numbers shown in Figure 1.8, we see that "Trendy's" use of *like* was strongest when she was talking about the social groups she was most comfortable with and identified with most closely (a). *Like* decreased as she talked about other social groups (b), or her plans for college (c).

%

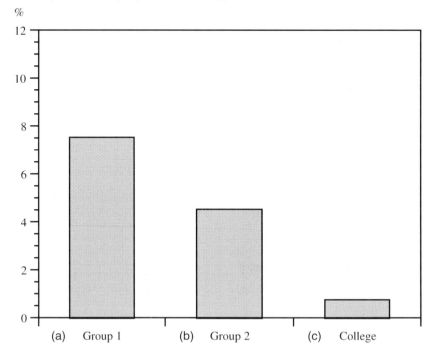

Figure 1.8 Use of the discourse marker *like* for one Palo Alto High School female ("Trendy"), by topic of conversation
Source: Adapted from California Style Collective 1993

Feagin's work in Alabama (1979) shows how complex even apparently simple points of variation can be in the way they are distributed in the community. Figure 1.9 looks at invariant *was* for a wide variety of speakers. Here it becomes clear that sex, age and socioeconomic class must be considered in tandem before it becomes possible to understand the observed distributions. Feagin found that for this variable as for most of the others she looked at, adolescent girls were the least likely to use invariant *was*, and closest in their language overall to a more standardized US English.

This is what sociolinguists do: they look at active, socially structured variation to try to understand the process of language change. How it is initiated, how it moves, what it means. We try to find universals in the power and solidarity structures which are relevant to language communities of all types, from inner-city neighborhoods to villages. But that is where sociolinguistics usually stops. Once we have understood, for example, the social correlates of *caught–cot* variation for Oklahoma – the way changes in transportation and communication have effected diffusion

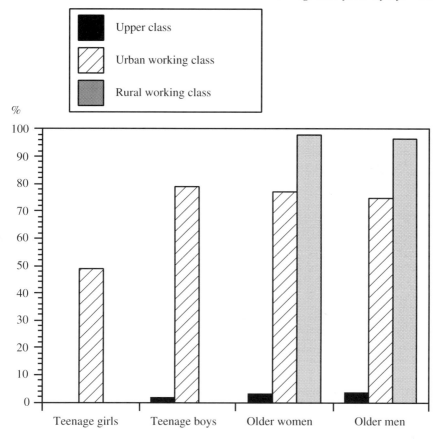

Figure 1.9 Use of "invariant *was*" by social class, sex, and age in Anniston, Alabama. Note score of 0 for rural teenagers

Source: Adapted with permission from C. Feagin (1979) *Variation and Change in Alabama English: A sociolinguistic study of the white community.* Washington DC: Georgetown University Press, pp. 204–205

of this change over generations – the job is done. We rarely ask why these facts are the way they are. We know who stigmatizes and avoids *r*-lessness, and who clings to it in spite of stigmatization, but we don't understand what underlies the process of stigmatization. Fairclough points this out as an unfortunate omission, and outlines questions he thinks should follow: "How – in terms of the development of social relationships to power – was the existing sociolinguistic order brought into being? How is it sustained? And how might it be changed to the advantage of those who are dominated by it?" (1989: 7–8).

Sociolinguists have established beyond a doubt that variation is an intrinsic and inseparable feature of the spoken language. Thus the next and logical question must be: what is a *standard language*? Isn't that term an oxymoron? And if such a language exists, what purpose does it really serve?

Because the necessity of referring to different varieties of English with specific labels cannot long be avoided, it is necessary at this point to consider the way people talk about language.

2 The myth of non-accent

The poets were not alone in sanctioning myths, for long before the poets the states and the lawmakers had sanctioned them as a useful expedient. . . . They needed to control the people by superstitious fears, and these cannot be aroused without myths and marvels.

Strabo, *Geographia*

Myth is understood broadly as a story with general cultural significance.[1] In the study of myth, veracity is secondary to the way in which a story symbolizes human experience more generally. What is particularly interesting is the way that myths are used to justify social order, and to encourage or coerce consensual participation in that order.

Standard language and its corollary, non-accent, are more usually referred to as *abstractions* than they are as myths. And in fact, this is a logical connection, as is borne out by the *Oxford English Dictionary*'s definition: "[an abstraction is] the idea of something which has no independent existence; a thing which exists only in idea; something visionary." From this follows quite neatly Milroy and Milroy's suggestion that *standard language* need not be understood as any specific language, but as "an idea in the mind rather than a reality – a set of abstract norms to which actual usage may conform to a greater or lesser extent" (1991: 22–23).[2] We can extrapolate from this position to call non-accent not any particular variety of US English, but a collectively held ideal, which brings with it a series of social and regional associations.

Nevertheless, it is useful to consider standard language and non-accent both as abstractions and as myths. It is only by doing so that we can come to understand how the collective consciousness came to be. Myths are magical and powerful constructs; they can motivate social behaviors and actions which would be otherwise contrary to logic or reason. Before we can consider the mythical and very concrete powers of a term like non-accent, however, we must first consider its opposite.

We have come a good way into our discussion without defining the term *accent*. Perhaps the reason for that is clear by now: in as far as linguists are concerned, accent can only be a fuzzy term. It is widely used by the public, however, in interesting ways. Thus we must stop to consider what we mean by accent, and how the term is put to use.

In a more technical way, accent is used to distinguish stress in words (*The accent is on the second syllable in "baNAna"*) or in sentences (*That's ANOTHER fine mess you've gotten us into!*); it can be used as a diacritic, but this is most often done in conjunction with the writing of other languages. More generally, accent is a loose reference to a specific "way of speaking." There is no official or technical specification for what this might mean in linguistic terms, but there are two widely recognized elements to what serves to distinguish one variety of a language from another in the minds of speakers:

- *Prosodic features*   The study of the phonology of a language includes consideration of intonation, or patterns of pitch contours. This includes stress patterns, both at the lexical and at the sentence level, but it also touches upon other factors such as tempo of speaking. For example, speakers of English tend to call languages or varieties of language which tend toward an up-swing in stress at the end of words *lilting*, or *sing-song*, or some Romance languages *rapid-fire*.
- *Segmental features*   We acquire, as part of our first language, the sounds of the language which fall into two major categories: vowels and con-sonants. Each of these sounds exists in relation to one another in a phonological structure. In the discussion above, it was pointed out that some speakers of US English distinguish between *Mary*, *merry*, and *marry*, or between *caught* and *cot*, while others do not, which is one indication that there are many possible phonological systems for US English.

Thus, a working definition of accent as it is used in this book follows:

Accents are loose bundles of prosodic and segmental features distributed over geographic and/or social space.

It is important to distinguish further between two kinds of accent: first language (L1) and second language (L2).

L1 accent is really no more than what we have been discussing all along: structured variation in language. Every native speaker of English has some regional variety, with the particular phonology of that area, or a phonology which represents a melding of one or more areas, for some people. In a similar way, everyone has several bundles of variants which are available to them and which they exploit to layer social meaning into their spoken language. Most usually we use geography as the first line of demarcation: a Maine accent, a New Orleans accent, an Appalachian accent, a Utah accent. But there are also socially bound clusters of features which are superimposed on the geographic: Native American accents, black accents, Jewish accents.[3] Gender, race, ethnicity, income, religion – these and other elements of social identity are often clearly marked by means of choice between linguistic variants.

L1 accent is, then, the native variety of US English spoken: *every native speaker of US English has an L1 accent*, no matter how unmarked the person's language may *seem* to be. This includes people like Connie Chung, Peter Jennings, Cokie Roberts, and Bill Moyers, prominent broadcast news and commentary personalities who are generally thought to be speakers of a Standard US English (this term will be discussed more thoroughly in chapters to come).

So where does accent end and dialect begin?[4]

This touches on one of the most intriguing and complicated questions of sociolinguistics. Why is Dutch considered a separate language from German, and Swiss German not? Why do many call the variety of English that many African Americans speak *black slang* (or a black accent) but call Cockney and Gullah dialects? Max Weinreich is widely quoted as pointing out that a language is a dialect with an army and a navy; I would like to add to that observation that a dialect is perhaps nothing more than a language that gets no respect.

If it is possible to try to distinguish between accent and language variety on purely linguistic terms, then a rough division can be made as follows:

Two varieties of a single language are divided by *accent* when differences are restricted primarily to phonology (prosodic and segmental features).

If two varieties of a single language also differ in morphological structures, syntax, lexicon, and semantics, then they are different varieties, or dialects, of the same language.

If two varieties of a common mother language differ in all these ways, and in addition have distinct literary histories, distinct orthographies, and/or geopolitical boundaries, then they are generally called different languages.

Style or code shifting is a term reflecting the speaker's ability to switch between languages or language varieties dependent on a large number of factors. It is a complicated process, and one that has been studied intensively. For our purposes, however, it is enough to say that when a speaker is shifting between two varieties of one language which are closely related, it will sometimes be appropriate to speak of "accent" and sometimes of "variety." Thus it is useful to retain the term accent to talk about phonology, but it is important to remember that this is a fluid category.

L2 accent is very different. When a native speaker of a language other than English acquires English, accent is used to refer to the breakthrough of native language phonology into the target language. Thus we might say that an individual has a Welsh accent, or a Tagalog accent, because the phonologies of those languages influence the learner's pronunciation of US English, and this is accomplished with differing degrees of success.

Thus far it has been set forth that

- all spoken human language is necessarily and functionally variable;
- one of the functions of variation is to convey social, stylistic, and geographic meaning;
- the majority of the work of variation is carried out below the level of consciousness.

Given these facts, what is non-accent? Is it what we call a standard, or mainstream spoken language? And given the fact that accent is just short-hand for variable language (which is in some ways a redundant term) what can a "standard" US English be, but an abstraction?

In spite of all the hard evidence that language must be variable and must change, people steadfastly believe that a homogenous, standardized, one-size-fits-all language is not only desirable, it is truly a possibility. This language does not exist *in fact*, but it certainly does exist as an ideal in the minds of the speakers. This takes us back to our opening science-fiction scenario, in which the positive ramifications of a world in which we are all the same size and weight are so appealing, so enticing, that we overlook the biological realities of our physical selves. Before we go on to ask how we are able to fool ourselves so thoroughly, we must first deal more carefully with the question of the mythical homogenous standardized spoken language. Until the impossibility of such a thing is established incontrovertibly, people will continue to pine after it, and, worse, to pursue it.

Let's start with an example.

James Kahakua is a native of Hawai'i and bilingual speaker of English and Hawai'ian Creole English (HCE) (commonly referred to, erroneously, as *Hawai'ian Pidgin*).[5] Mr. Kahakua, a meteorologist with twenty years of experience and considerable educational background, applied for a promotion which would require that he read prepared weather reports on the radio. It is important to note that this promotion would have entailed the reading of previously prepared weather reports, in which the syntax and lexicon of the broadcasted language would be under the direct control of the news producer.

Mr. Kahakua was not given this promotion. His employer found him unqualified to do so, not because he is incapable of reading, but because as a bilingual English–HCE speaker, he has a Hawai'ian accent.

Subsequently, Mr. Kahakua sued his employer under Title VII of the Civil Rights Act, on the basis of language traits linked to national origin, and he lost. He lost because the judge, who was not a native of Hawai'i, believed that it was reasonable to require that radio announcers speak "Standard English" (which was not defined explicitly), and furthermore, he added that "there is no race or physiological reason why Kahakua could not have used standard English pronunciations" (Matsuda 1991: 1345). The speech pathologist who testified on behalf of the employer gave the judge ammunition when she testified:

I urgently recommend [Mr. Kahakua] seek professional help in striving to lessen this handicap. . . . *Pidgin can be controlled.* And if an individual is totally committed to improving, professional help on a long-term basis can produce results.

(Matsuda 1991: 1366; original emphasis)

This is a very good – if very disturbing – example of our basic belief about language: if we want to, if we try hard enough, we can acquire a perfect language, one which is clean, pure, free of variation. Language which is not *perfect* does not have to be accepted. The judge and the speech therapist are sure of themselves: they stake their professional reputations on their statements that Mr. Kahakua could, if he wished, comply with what they see as a reasonable request of his employer. I make the claim, however, that Mr. Kahakua can no more comply with the demand that he completely lose his native phonology – his accent – than he could comply with an order of the judge to grow four inches, or, and much more controversially, than it would be possible for him to change the color of his skin.

This is a large claim, one people will not take on faith because they have been taught that the opposite is true. Putting aside the question of personal freedoms protected under the law, putting aside the issues of social identity, is it true that it is not within the power of the individual to change their language?

A linguist's first impulse is to answer this question, very simply, yes. It is not possible for an adult to substitute his or her phonology (one accent) for another, *consistently and in a permanent way.* But! The non-linguist will jump in. What about my Aunt Lillian, who came here from the Ukraine and has no accent at all? What about Eddie Murphy, who can switch from AAVE to sounding like an upper-middle-class broadcaster without a moment's hesitation? And there's Joe's wife, who just gave up her Brooklyn accent when it caused her problems in medical school.

What does it mean to lose an accent? Are we talking about replacing one way of speaking with another, or adding a new phonology to a person's existing inventory? Are we demanding that a person – Mr. Kahakua in this case – sound one way for a brief period of time, or that he always sound that way? These are important points, but before we look at them and the underlying presumptions, it is necessary to go back and consider the language acquisition process. We begin with some generalizations which are more linguistic *facts of life:*

- There is a finite set of potentially meaning-bearing sounds (vowels, consonants, tones) which can be produced by human vocal apparatus. The set in its entirety is universal, available to all human beings without physical handicap.
- Each language uses some, but not all, sounds available.
- Sounds are organized into systems, in which each element stands in

relationship to the other elements. The same inventory of sounds can be organized into a number of possible systems.

- Children are born with the ability to produce the entire set of possible sounds, but eventually restrict themselves to the ones they hear used around them.
- Children exposed to more than one language during the language-acquisition process may acquire more than one language, if the social conditioning factors are favorable.
- At some time in adolescence, the ability to acquire language with the same ease as young children atrophies.[6]
- There are as yet poorly understood elements of cognition and perception which have to do with the degree of success with which an adult will manage to acquire a new phonology, or accent.

These are very dry facts. Let's approach this in another way.

First, think of all the sounds which can be produced and perceived by the human vocal apparatus as a set of building materials. The basic materials, vowels and consonants, are bricks. Other building materials (wood, mortar, plaster, stone) stand in for things like tone, vowel harmony, and length, which are part of the articulation of vowels and consonants, but provide another layer of meaning-bearing sound in many languages. Thus far, we are talking about phonetics: the production and perception of the full set of possible sounds.

Children are born with two things: a set of language blueprints wired into the brain, which gives them some intuitive understanding of very basic rules of language; and a set of tools which goes along with these blueprints.

Now think of the language acquisition process as a newborn child who begins to build a *Sound House*. The Sound House is the "home" of the language, or what we have been calling *accent* – the phonology – of the child's native tongue. At birth the child is in the Sound House warehouse, where a full inventory of all possible materials is available to her. She looks at the Sound Houses built by her parents, her brothers and sisters, by other people around her, and she starts to pick out those materials, those bricks she sees they have used to build their Sound Houses. She may experiment with other bricks, with a bit of wood, but in the end she settles down to duplicating the Sound Houses she sees around her. She sets up her inventory of sounds in relationship to each other; she puts up walls, plans the space: she is constructing her phonology.

The blueprints tell her that she must have certain supporting structures; she does this. She wanders around in her parents' Sound Houses and sees how they do things. She makes mistakes; fixes them. In the process, she makes small innovations.

Maybe this child has parents who speak English and Gaelic, or who are natives of Cincinnati and speak what is commonly thought of as Standard

US English, as well as African American English Vernacular. The parents each have two Sound Houses, or perhaps one Sound House with two wings. She has two houses to build at once. Sometimes she mixes materials up, but then sorts them out. Maybe she builds a bridge between the two structures. Maybe a connecting basement.

The child starts to socialize with other children. Her best friend has a slightly different layout, although he has built his Sound House with the exact same inventory of building materials. Another friend has a Sound House which is missing the back staircase. She wants to be like her friends, and so she makes renovations to her Sound House. It begins to look somewhat different than her parents' Sound Houses; it is more her own. Maybe the Gaelic half of her Sound House is neglected, has a hole in the roof, a collapsing floor. Maybe she is embarrassed by the AAVE Sound House and never goes there anymore, never has a chance to see what is happening to it. Maybe in a few years she will want to go there and find it structurally unable to bear her weight.

Now imagine this.

When the child turns twenty, she notices another kind of Sound House, built by Spanish speakers, which she admires. She would like to build an extension to her own Sound House just like it. She looks for her blueprints and her tools, but they have disappeared. Puzzled, she stands on the street and looks at these Sound Houses: they are different. What is different about them? Look at that balcony. How do you build that? Why do the staircases look like that?

With her bare hands, she sets out to build an extension to her original Sound House. She sees bricks she doesn't have in her own inventory, but how to get back to the warehouse? She'll have to improvise. She's a smart woman, she can make a brick, cut down a tree. She examines the Sound Houses built by Spanish speakers, asks questions. The obvious things she sees right off: wow, they have fireplaces. The less obvious things – width of the doors, for example – slip right by her at first. She starts in on the long process. *How did you build that chimney?* she asks. *I don't know*, says her informant. *I was a kid at the time, and I've lost my blueprints.*

If she's lucky, she has a guide – an informed language teacher – who can point out the difference between the extension she is trying to build and her own Sound House. *Look*, this guide will say. *You're mixing up blue and ultramarine bricks! We use blue for this kind of wall, ultramarine for that. And you certainly can't put a pale pink brick next to a cerise one. Oh*, she says. *I hadn't noticed.* And thus she will begin to differentiate more carefully, for example between two very similar vowels which are distinctive in the language she is learning.

She works very, very hard on this extension. But no matter how hard she works, the balcony will not shape up; it is always rickety. There's a gap in the floorboards; people notice it and grin.

In absolute amazement, she watches her little sister build the exact same Sound House with no effort at all, and it is perfect. She points this out to her guide. *But your sister still has her blueprints and tools*, says her guide. Then she sees a stranger, an older man, building the same extension and he is also taking less time, just galloping through. His Spanish Sound House looks like an original to her.

Oh no, her guide tells her. *It's very good, no doubt, but look there – don't you see that the windows are slightly too close together? It would fool almost everybody, but those windows give it away.*

She digs in her heels and moves into the extension, although the roof still leaks. She abandons her original English Sound House for months, for years, she is so dedicated to getting this right. She rarely goes back to the first Sound House anymore, and the Gaelic Sound House is condemned. When she does go back to the English Sound House, and first goes through the door, it seems strange to her. But the structural heart of her Sound House is here, and it's still standing, if a little dusty.

Her Spanish Sound House feels like home. When people come to visit, they are amazed to find out that it's not her first construction. They examine everything closely. Some of them may notice very, very small details, but they don't say anything. *There's the guy down the block*, they tell her, *he's been working on the same extension for longer than you and he'll never get it right.*[7]

Adult language learners all have the same handicap in learning a second language: the blueprints have faded to near illegibility, and the tools are rusted. Regardless of how much energy and dedication and general intelligence, no one is capable of getting the blueprints and tools back, and we must all build new Sound Houses with our bare hands. When the judge claimed that there was no physiological reason that James Kahakua could not speak mainstream English, he was simply wrong.

It is crucial to point out that the structural integrity of the targeted second Sound House – which here stands in for accent – is secondary to the language learner's skill in actually *using* the target language. Accent has little to do with what is generally called *communicative competence*, or the ability to use and interpret language in a wide variety of contexts effectively.[8] There is a long list of persons who speak English as a second language and who never lost their accents. They never managed to build an English Sound House which would fool anybody at all into thinking that they are native speakers, but their ability to use English is clear. This group includes people like Henry Kissinger, Cesar Chavez, Derek Wolcott, Butros Butros Ghali, Benazir Bhutto, Corazon Aquino, and Joseph Conrad who represent the political and sociocultural mainstream, but who do it in an accented English. Do people like these choose to speak English with an accent? Have they not worked hard enough, long enough? Are they not smart enough?

The same questions are relevant to native speakers of English with marked or stigmatized regional or social accents. When we think of Ann Richards, Jessie Jackson, or Ed Koch, do we think of people who cannot express themselves? Are these people who willfully refuse to give up Texas, African American, or New York varieties of English for something less socially marked, or are they incapable of doing so?

Because two phonologies are similar, we think, it must be easier to build a second Sound House. Why can't Mr. Kahakua – who after all has an English Sound House to begin with – just make a few adjustments that will transform it into what passes as a mainstream English Sound House? If Meryl Streep can do any variety of English, why can't he?[9]

The answer is, Meryl Streep can't do it either, unless she is doing it for a short period of time and in a limited context. In the filming of a movie, Meryl Streep does her accents while the camera is running, with stops every few minutes. If she gets it wrong, they can try again. Under these favorable circumstances, many people could imitate another variety of English quite admirably – but for others, not even this is possible. There are many examples of actors criticized roundly for not pulling off an accent, in spite of expensive tutoring, and the possibility of many takes of each utterance. In either case, whether we have an English Daniel Day-Lewis who truly sounds – up on the screen – as if he were an American frontiersman, or an American Kevin Costner who tries but fails to convince us that he is English enough to be Robin Hood, we are not talking about a permanent Sound House; it is a fake store front that won't stand up to a strong and persistent breeze. And it takes an exceptional talent to achieve even this limited amount. Now, what about Eddie Murphy, or any number of other African American entertainers who seem to switch effortlessly from one variety of English to another?

Eddie Murphy built more than one Sound House *as a child*, when he had the resources and the tools to do so. He observed not just the Sound Houses of his parents and peers closely enough to duplicate them, but he paid close attention to other types of Sound Houses, and he built multiple rooms: the broadcaster room, the old Jewish male room, the southern Black evangelist room. He can move in and out of them with ease, and he does so as part of his profession. Some of these rooms are no doubt more structurally sound than others. This is not an uncommon occurrence; many African Americans grow up bidialectal. For adults, however, the option to *become* bidialectal is severely compromised.

At a sociolinguistics conference a few years ago, a colleague who works on the vowel changes known as the Northern Cities Chain Shift came to my presentation. Afterwards she said to me "You know, it was really fascinating to listen to you, – oh, and your talk was good too." The whole time I had been presenting my work, she had been listening closely to my vowels, and making notes to herself. When I was reading from prepared text, she told me, my vowels pretty much stayed put, but when I looked up from my papers and spoke extemporaneously, and with some considerable emotion, my vowels started on a steep forward slide: the chain shift in action. The more attention I pay to speech, the less I participate in the shift; this is an indication that some part of me feels compelled to move away from my background when I am speaking as an academic. But when I am involved in my subject, when I forget to monitor my speech carefully, my origins come forth: I am a native of Chicago, and a resident of Michigan, and I cannot pretend to be anything else. This has been pointed out to me by many non-linguists; people are proud to be able to listen to me (or to anybody else) for a minute and then put me on the map.

All this happens in spite of the fact that my professional training has made me aware of the way I use subtle choices available to me, and in spite of the fact that sometimes I don't particularly want to announce to the world where I am from. I have no choice but to live in the Sound House I first created as a child, which bears the structural hallmarks of the social being I am.

It is true, however, that some people are better at putting together second or even third and fourth Sound Houses. Not perfect ones, but very good imitations. The differential ability to do this is something not very well understood, but strong circumstantial evidence indicates it has nothing to do with intelligence and not very much to do with application. On the other hand, it certainly does have something to do with cognition, and – for lack of a better or more precise term – with an ear for language. Focused training, or the process of drawing the adult language learner's attention to processes he or she would not otherwise notice, can have some effect. It is possible to *adjust* an accent, to some degree. We can work on that second Sound House, with guidance. But it is not possible to substitute the second Sound House for the original. Accent reduction courses, if they are well done by persons well trained in phonology and phonetics, who understand the structural differences between the languages, may achieve that much: they might reduce an accent, but they cannot remove one.

However, accent reduction courses make an implied promise: *Sound like us, and success will be yours. Doors will open; barriers will disappear.* There are two problems here. The first is the claim that it is possible to "eliminate" an accent, which is reminiscent of magic creams to remove cellulite and electromagnetic belts to make undersized children grow. The second, almost more disturbing, implication is that discrimination is purely a matter of language, and that it is *first and primarily* the right accent which stands between marginalized social groups and a bright new world free of racism and prejudicial treatment.

A close and cynical reader of my arguments – of which there will be many – will point out that I have made two statements which seem to contradict each other. I have gone to some length to establish that all spoken language is variable, and that all language changes. Thus, the

Sound Houses we build change over our lifetimes. At the same time, it seems that I am arguing that Sound Houses *cannot* be changed. I have been critical of speech pathologists who claim this is possible. In fact, these statements are not contradictory.

A Sound House is a living, evolving product of our minds, a mirror of our changing social beings. We redecorate constantly, with a keen eye for what the neighbors are doing. Little by little, we may move a wall, rearrange the bricks, add windows. One person builds a patio, and maybe that catches on, in the same way that somewhere, one day (in a way sociolinguists have never been able to observe) the *hawk–hock* merger caught on and began to gain linguistic and social currency. Other people began to build patios, and before long, other structural changes began to follow. If you're going to build a patio, after all, you have to put in a door to get to it. Or perhaps a different analogy is needed here: we are all biologically subject to the aging process; no one is exempt from those changes over time. But neither can we willfully bring the aging process on, or stop it. Thus our Sound Houses do change over time but in ways which are out of direct control.

But can a Sound House be torn down and replaced?

The answer must be *no*. The true ability to build second and third Sound Houses *past the language acquisition stage* is undocumented. It may exist; there are certainly rumors enough of such persons, who *as adults* acquire a second variety of their native language, or another language altogether with absolute and complete native fluency. Persons who are capable of this would never let the phonology of their first language interfere with their second language, regardless of the topic being discussed, or the amount of emotion brought to the table. Such persons would have to be able to stand up to close phonetic analysis of their language – and not just by phoneticians, but also by native speakers, who are incredibly sensitive to the subtle variation in language. Perhaps most important, such persons would have to have complete control of the structured variation active in the target language.

I would hypothesize that if such persons exist at all, adults who are capable of learning to absolutely and cleanly substitute one accent for another are as rare as individuals who can do long division instantaneously in their heads, or have photographic memories. If they do exist, it would be interesting and important to study them, because it would seem that these are adults whose language acquisition function – the hard wiring in the brain – failed to stop working at the usual time.

If a person is very dedicated, works hard, and has good guidance, it may be possible to fool some of the people some of the time. The question is, *of whom do we require this trick, and why?* If a mainstream, homogenous US English is something logically and reasonably required of broadcast news reporters, why was it required of James Kahakua, and not of Peter Jennings, who speaks English with a Canadian accent? And, a more difficult question: what is right or wrong about asking Mr. Kahakua to pretend? If he is capable of faking an accent, why shouldn't his employer ask him to do this, for those few minutes he is reading the weather on the radio?

3   The standard language myth

Ah, well, the truth is always one thing, but in a way it's the other thing, the gossip, that counts. It shows where people's hearts lie.

Paul Scott, *The Day of the Scorpion* (1968)

Given uncontrovertible facts about the way language works, a spoken standardized language can only be understood as an abstraction. But it is a useful abstraction, one constructed and reconstructed on an ongoing basis with great care and attention, because it serves a number of functions.

At this juncture, it is necessary to consider in some detail exactly what this mythical beast called Standard US English is, in the minds of the people who recreate it on a daily basis.

WHAT WE CALL STANDARD US ENGLISH

People are quite comfortable with the idea of a standard language, so much so that they have no trouble describing and defining it, much in the same way that most people could draw a unicorn, or describe a being from *Star Trek's* planet Vulcan, or tell us who King Arthur was and why he needed a Round Table. For the most part these definitions will be firmly founded in the understanding that these are mythical, imaginary constructions; nevertheless, the definitions will have much in common, because they are part of our shared cultural heritage.

The way we conceive and define Standard US English brings to light a number of assumptions and misassumptions about language. *Merriam-Webster's Collegiate Dictionary* (tenth edition, 1993), which proclaims itself *The Voice of Authority*, provides a typical definition:

Standard English: the English that with respect to spelling, grammar, pronunciation, and vocabulary is substantially uniform though not devoid of regional differences, that is well established by usage in the formal and informal speech and writing of the educated, and that is widely recognized as acceptable wherever English is spoken and understood.

This definition assumes that the written and spoken language are equal, in terms of both how they are used, and how they should be used. It sets spelling and pronunciation on a common footing, and compounds this generalization by bringing in both formal and informal language use. While the definition makes some room for "regional differences" it makes none at all for social ones, and in fact it is quite definite about the social construction of Standard US English: it is the language of the educated. What is meant by "educated" is left unstated in this entry, and its implications are not fully explored anywhere else in the dictionary. What language might be spoken by those who are the *opposite* of the educated is also not made clear, but whoever these people are, they are drawn into the definition by its final component: Standard US English is *acceptable wherever English is spoken and understood.* The lexicographer assumes the consent of the non-educated, uneducated, or lesser educated to the authority of the educated in matters of written and spoken language.

Other definitions bring some important generalizations about Standard US English to the fore: *Cambridge International Dictionary of English* (first edition, 1995) also cites educated speakers as the sole possessors of the standard language, but they bring in a specific subgroup of the educated in that they assert that "most announcers on the BBC speak standard English." *Chambers Dictionary* (1994) is more specific about the path to Standard US English: "the form of English taught in schools." In 1978 the *English Journal* noted a general perception in the public of a "'standard standard'. Some people call it 'broadcast' or 'publications' standard, because most newspapers and television news shows use it."

More specific information on exactly how the lexicographer draws on the language of the educated is provided by interviews with the pronunciation editor at Merriam-Webster which appeared in various newspapers around the appearance of that dictionary's tenth edition. It falls to the pronunciation editor to decide which possible pronunciations are included in the dictionary, and how they are ordered. "Usage dictates acceptability," he is reported as saying. "There is no other non-arbitrary way to decide" (*New York Times*, July 22, 1993: C1, C8).

In order to pin down this "majority rule" the editor listens to "talk shows, medical shows, interviews, news, commentary, the weather" (ibid.) on the radio and on television. The editorial preface to the dictionary is more specific about this procedure; it lists politicians, professors, curators, artists, musicians, doctors, engineers, preachers, activists, and journalists among the type of educated person whose English is consulted as a part of this process.

> In truth, though, there can be no objective standard for correct pronunciation other than the usage of thoughtful and, in particular, educated speakers of English. Among such speakers one hears much variation

in pronunciation . . . [our attempt is to] include all variants of a word that are used by educated speakers.

(*Merriam-Webster's Collegiate Dictionary*, tenth edition, 1993: 31a)

The editors claim an objective standard (that of the language of the educated) and at the same time they acknowledge variation among educated speakers. This apparent inconsistency is resolved by the policy which includes *all variants that are used by educated speakers.* A close look at the pronunciations listed in the dictionary, however, indicates that this cannot be the case. An entry with three or more possible pronunciations is rare. If Merriam-Webster's *Dictionary* truly intends to include all pronunciations of the educated, then their definition of who is educated must be very narrow.

It must be clear that this process cannot be representative in any real way. What proportion of even the *educated* population has regular access to the broadcast media? How many of us discuss our views on the budget, on foreign affairs, or on local government in a forum which is broadcast to a wider audience? The *uneducated*, who by the dictionary definition must constitute the greatest number of native speakers of English, are even less represented.

Perhaps there is no way to write a dictionary which is truly descriptive in terms of pronunciation; perhaps it is necessary to choose one social group to serve as a model. Perhaps there is even some rationale for using the "educated" as this group. But there is nothing *objective* about this practice. It is the ordering of social groups in terms of who has authority to determine how language is *best used.*

Clearly, the rationale for this ordering derives at least in part from the perceived superiority of the written language. Persons with more education are more exposed to the written language and literary traditions; they may, in simple terms, *write* better than the "less educated." Why this should mean that their pronunciation is somehow more informed, more genuine, more authoritative, is never made clear. Definitions of standard language supplied by people who do not write dictionaries for a living echo many of the themes already established, but they sometimes become very specific, in quite interesting ways:

Standard English is . . .[1]

having your nouns and your verbs agree.

the English legitimatized by wide usage and certified by expert consensus, as in a dictionary usage panel.

what I learned in school, in Mrs. McDuffey's class, in Virginia, in the mid seventies. It really bothers me when I read and hear other people who obviously skipped her class.

the proper language my mother stressed from the time I was old enough to talk.

one that few people would call either stilted or "low," delivered with a voice neither gutteral nor strident, clearly enunciated but not priggish about it, with no one sound having a noticibly distinctive character. It is a non-regional speech but clearly and easily understood in all regions. ... Standard English uses, in general, only one syllable per enunciated vowel so most accents from the south and west are not to the pattern.

These references to the authority of educational institutions and unnamed "experts" correspond to the dictionary definitions in a fairly predictable way. Like the dictionary definitions, there is an occasional statement which makes it clear that written and spoken languages are being considered as one and the same thing when in fact they are not. What is different about these personal definitions is the willingness to identify specific grammatical and phonological points which distinguish standard from "non-standard" usage, and a highly emotional and personal element in the definitions. People feel strongly about their language, and are willing to express their opinions.

The most straightforward and unapologetically ideological definitions of standard language come from those who make a living protecting it from change: "Good English has to do with the upper classes ... with the cultural and intellectual leaders ..." (Presidential address to the Michigan Academy of Science, Arts and Letters in 1965, as cited in Finegan 1980: 174). Writers like Edwin Newman, John Simon, and William Safire have published extensively on their view of the language, how it should be spoken and written, and why their authority in these issues should not be questioned. These men, and others like them, make a good living writing about Standard English because they meet a demand:

> Aristocratic by preference, devoted to literature and the classics, and practiced in the monitored phrase, they see themselves as protectors and conservers of the durably admirable. Intelligibility is not enough; economy, exactitude, and grace are sought – and continuity with an illustrious past. And the reading public seeks their guidance and honors their judgments – at least by lip service, if not in observance. As models of sensitivity and good taste, they are salaried to be opinionated.
>
> (Finegan 1980: 160)

The social domain of Standard English has been established: it is the language of the educated, in particular those who have achieved a high level of expertise in the written language. But this simple definition of Standard English is complicated when variation over space is considered.

Dennis Preston has compiled a body of empirical studies in which he has quantified and generalized non-linguists' beliefs about the geographic distribution of a standard language. In "Where they speak correct English" (1989a), he asked seventy-six young white natives of southern Indiana to rank all fifty states as well as New York City and Washington DC in terms

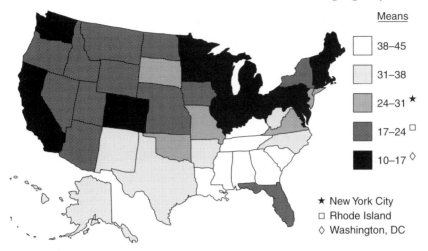

Means

38–45

31–38

24–31 ★

17–24 □

10–17 ◊

★ New York City
□ Rhode Island
◊ Washington, DC

Figure 3.1 Ratings of the fifty states, New York City, and Washington DC for language "correctness" on a scale of 1–52 (lowest = "best") by seventy-six young, first- and second-year, white undergraduates from southern Indiana
Source: Preston 1989a: 54

of "correct English," so that a ranking of 1 was where the *most correct* English is spoken, and 52, the *least correct*. Figure 3.1 provides Preston's visual representation of the means for the respondents' rankings.

If a high level of education is a primary characteristic of Standard US English, then the opinions of these college students from Indiana would seem to provide relevant information about just where that language is spoken. Preston's analysis indicated that these informants found the most correct English in five areas: North Central (including their own speech); Mid-Atlantic (excluding New York City); New England; Colorado; and the West Coast. Standard deviations indicate that the students are most consistent in their positive evaluation in the case of Michigan, Minnesota, and Wisconsin, with their agreement decreasing as they move eastward through Ohio, Pennsylvania, Maryland, Delaware, and finally Washington DC (which showed little consistency in ranking with a standard deviation of 15.67). The worst standard deviation is for New York City, which Preston hypothesizes has to do with conflicting stereotypes about the city: from the center of culture to the center of crime. Most interesting perhaps is the incredibly high level of consistency in the way these students found a lack of correct English in the south. Mississippi ranked last in terms of correct English and also was the most consistently ranked state. Preston (1989a) takes the scores for the southern states as "further proof of the salience of areas seen as nonstandard" (56).

From these various approaches to a standard US English, a picture begins to emerge. *Standard US English is the language spoken and written by persons*

- with no regional accent;
- who reside in the midwest, far west or perhaps some parts of the northeast (but never in the south);
- with more than average or superior education;
- who are themselves educators or broadcasters;
- who pay attention to speech, and are not sloppy in terms of pronunciation or grammar;
- who are easily understood by all;
- who enter into a consensus of other individuals like themselves about what is proper in language.

There are some interesting conflicts in these general statements and approaches to language. We want language to be geographically neutral, because we believe that this neutrality will bring with it a greater range of communication. The assumption, of course, is that midwest is neutral. We want it to be structured and rule-governed and clear. Something as important as language cannot be left to itself: normal people are not smart enough, not aware enough, to be in charge of their own language. There must be experts, persons in charge, structured authority. *Accent* falls into the dominion of uneducated, sloppy, language anarchists. Those areas of the country which embody these characteristics most saliently in the minds of a good many US English speakers (the south, New York City), are the natural home of accent. Everybody else speaks standard English, and as such, has no accent. A native of Mississippi or Brooklyn may have exactly the same educational background, intelligence, and point to make as their counterparts in Ohio and Colorado, but, we believe, they do so with an accent. This mindset is institutionalized in the *Oxford English Dictionary* (1989):

> [Accent is] The mode of utterance peculiar to an individual, locality, or nation, as "he has a slight accent, a strong provincial accent, an indisputably Irish, Scotch, American, French or German accent." ...
> This utterance consists mainly in a prevailing quality of tone, or in a peculiar alteration of pitch, but may include *mis*pronunciation of vowels or consonants, *mis*placing of stress, and *mis*inflection of a sentence. The locality of a speaker is generally clearly marked by this kind of accent.

(emphasis added)

The judgmental tone is quite evident even without the heavily significant choice of *mis*pronunciation, *mis*placing, and *mis*inflection. It follows from this definition that there is a correct regional pronunciation, but it is not explicitly named.

From a legal perspective, Matsuda notes the similarities between the construction of standard English/non-accent and other hidden norms codified in our legal institutions:

> As feminist theorists have pointed out, everyone has a gender, but the hidden norm in law is male. As critical race theorists have pointed out, everyone has a race, but the hidden norm in law is white. In any dyadic relationship, the two ends are equidistant from each other. If the parties are equal in power, we see them as equally different from each other. When the parties are in a relationship of domination and subordination we tend to say that the dominant is normal, and the subordinate is different from normal. And so it is with accent. . . . People in power are perceived as speaking normal, unaccented English. Any speech that is different from that constructed norm is called an accent.
>
> (1991: 1361)

The myth of standard language persists because it is carefully tended and propagated. Individuals acting for a larger social group take it upon themselves to control and limit spoken language variation, the most basic and fundamental of human socialization tools. The term *standard* itself does much to promote this idea: we speak of one standard and in opposition, non-standard, or substandard. This is the core of an *ideology* of standardization which empowers certain individuals and institutions to make these decisions.

WORDS ABOUT WORDS

It would be possible to trace the evolution of scholarly thought about the social relationship between varieties of US English solely on the basis of the terms used to draw real or perceived distinctions. The use of the terms *standard*, *standard language*, and *standard English* have remained fairly stable in the literature over time, with the occasional and more recent emergence of the term *mainstream language*. Mainstream is a term used widely in other fields, particularly in education, and has been discussed in those forums. Heath (1983) defines mainstreamers as those who

> exist in societies around the world that rely on formal education systems to prepare children for participation in settings involving literacy. Cross-national descriptions characterize these groups as literate, school-oriented, aspiring to upward mobility through success in formal institutions, and looking beyond the primary networks of family and community for behavioral models and value orientations.
>
> (391–392)

Mainstream as it is defined here (while not without problems which will be addressed below) is quite useful to the discussion at hand. The assumptions which underlie the labeling of one language as a *standard* against which other languages must be measured are largely absent. The opposite of standard appears as *substandard* or *non-standard*; these terms automatically bring with them a uni-directionality and subordination which is counterproductive to a discussion of language variation in linguistic terms.[2]

The opposite of *mainstream* is *non-mainstream*. An attempt to turn Heath's definition inside out demonstrates that the label *non-mainstream* brings some unfounded generalizations with it, if it is applied to whole language communities:

> Non-mainstreamers exist in communities which do not rely on formal education systems to prepare children for participation in settings involving literacy. These groups are illiterate, school-resistant, do not aspire to upward mobility through success in formal institutions, and they remain within the primary networks of family and community for behavioral models and value orientations.

Clearly, Heath's definition is problematic when it is thus recast. Many problems arise from the fact that the definition hinges almost exclusively on literacy and does not distinguish between spoken and written language. While the definition may work for a more general discussion of cultural and social differences between community types, it cannot serve as a basis for a distinction between *language communities*. If that attempt is made, this definition would necessarily find both Flannery O'Connor and Joseph Conrad, two of the most respected writers of US fiction in this century, to be mainstreamers – which they would clearly be, until they opened their mouths: O'Connor was a native of Georgia; her teachers at the Master of Fine Arts program at the University of Iowa told and retold stories about how impossible she was to understand when she spoke. Conrad was not a native speaker of English, and agonized all his life about speaking in public because of his accent. To *listen* to these two highly literate, highly educated persons was not to listen to speakers of Standard US English. In their lifetimes they could only be called speakers of non-standard or non-mainstream English.

Heath's definition, thus recast, proposes, for example, that all speakers of Appalachian English are resistant to formal education. That this cannot be taken as uniformly true must be clear, simply because there is movement between cultures and language communities. Not all members of peripheralized, disempowered communities find enough rewards and support in their own communities to stay within them. Many persons who function outside the mainstream embrace the goals and implied promises of participation in mainstream culture. If this were not so in terms of spoken language, then there would be no community internal discussion of language, and accent reduction courses would have no willing students.

Nevertheless, this definition of mainstreamers remains useful because it touches on two relevant points in trying to set up a reasonable way to distinguish between what is deemed socially acceptable and what is not, in terms of spoken language. First, it is clear that in this country, power and authority in language are tied inextricably to education and literacy. When Heath expands on her discussion of mainstreamers in the Piedmont, this becomes clear:

> Secondary sources, not the face-to-face network, are usually authoritative for mainstreamers. They choose their movies on the advice of the critics; they select their automobile tires on the recommendations of consumers' guides; they seek out professional advice for marital problems, and for interior decorating and landscaping ideas. An individual's assertion of formal credentials – either university degrees or public awards and distinction – makes him an authority. They formalize or "spell out in writing" rules for group activities, such as neighborhood tennis clubs, ladies' auxiliary clubs of the church. . . .
>
> (237)

Second, values of family and local networks stand sometimes, but not always, in contrast to the values of the core institutions which promote education and literacy. Thus, a more useful definition of mainstreamers and non-mainstreamers in terms of spoken language can be constructed by departing from Heath, as shown in Box 3.1.

Box 3.1

Mainstream US English speakers function in communities and institutions which rely on formal education systems to prepare children for participation in the community. Nationally, these speakers are *perceived* as living primarily in the midwest, far west, and some parts of the east and/or as upper middle class or upper class, as literate, school-oriented, and as aspiring to upward mobility through success in formal institutions. They look beyond the primary networks of family and community for sociolinguistic models and value orientations.	*Non-mainstream US English* speakers function in communities and institutions which rely less on formal education systems to prepare children for participation in the community. Nationally, these speakers are *perceived* as living primarily in the far south and inner urban centers, and/or as working class or lower class, as less interested in literacy or school, and as aspiring to local rather than supranational success in formal institutions. They tend to stay within networks of family and community for sociolinguistic models and value orientations.

Because the use of the standard/non-standard dichotomy is so firmly entrenched both in the literature and in the minds of the speakers, it is not possible to simply replace it. Where it is possible, however, mainstream/

non-mainstream will take its place. For the sake of brevity, "mainstream US English" will sometimes appear as MUSE, and its counterpart, "non-mainstream US English," as NMUSE.

A related issue is the matter of what to call specific social and regional varieties of US English. Scholarly literature has referred to the language spoken by a good proportion of the African American community (over time) as Negro English (NE), Black English (BE), Ebonics, Black English Vernacular (BEV), Black Vernacular English (BVE) and most recently, African American Vernacular English (AAVE) or African American English Vernacular (AAEV). My practice here is to use that term preferred by the African American community, which currently seems to be AAVE.

An even more complex and ideologically fraught issue is what to call those varieties of English which are not AAVE. It seems that this problem is solved by refusing to address it, for the most part. Most linguists seem to avoid the term White English Vernacular (WEV), because this sets up a racial distinction which cannot be supported by fact: there are both African Americans (and in smaller numbers) European, Latino, and Asian Americans who speak AAVE, and European, Asian, Latino, and African Americans who do not speak it. Finally, to claim that all European Americans speak mainstream US English as defined above would be to deny obvious and demonstrable truths.[3]

Mainstream English, as it is defined here, is an abstraction. It is an attempt to isolate from the full set of all varieties of US English those varieties which are not overtly stigmatized, and which find some degree of acceptance and favor over space and social distinctions. As we will see, these varieties are not coincidentially the language of primarily white, middle- and upper-middle-class, and midwestern American communities.

4 Language ideology and the language subordination model

The primary function of myth is to validate an existing social order. Myth enshrines conservative social values, raising tradition on a pedestal. It expresses and confirms, rather than explains or questions, the sources of cultural attitudes and values. . . . Because myth anchors the present in the past it is a sociological charter for a future society which is an exact replica of the present one.

Ann Oakley, *Woman's Work: The housewife, past and present* (1974)

Thus far I have established, on the basis of more than thirty years of empirical work in sociolinguistics by many scholars, that language is – among other things – a flexible and constantly flexing social tool for the emblematic marking of social allegiances. We use variation in language to construct ourselves as social beings, to signal who we are, and who we are not and cannot be. Speakers choose among sociolinguistic variants available; their choices group together in ways which are obvious and interpretable to other speakers in the community. This process is a functional and necessary part of the way we communicate. It is not an optional feature of the spoken language.

What does it mean then to ask a person to give up an accent, or to suppress it?

Given what we know about the links between social identity and linguistic variation, there can be no doubt that often when we ask individuals to reject their own language, it is not the message, but the social allegiances made clear by that language which are the underlying problem. We do not, cannot under our laws, ask people to change the color of their skin, their religion, their gender, but we regularly demand of people that they suppress or deny the most effective way they have of situating themselves socially in the world.

You may have dark skin, we tell them, *but you must not sound Black.*
You can wear a yarmulke if it is important to you as a Jew, but lose the accent.
Maybe you come from the Ukraine, but can't you speak real English?

If you just didn't sound so corn-pone, people would take you seriously.
You're the best salesperson we've got, but must you sound gay on the
phone?

Accent serves as the first point of gatekeeping because we are forbidden, by law and social custom, and perhaps by a prevailing sense of what is morally and ethically right, from using race, ethnicity, homeland or economics more directly. We have no such compunctions about language, however. Thus, accent becomes a litmus test for exclusion, an excuse to turn away, to refuse to recognize the other. Taylor describes the opposite of recognition as *misrecognition*:

> our identity is partly shaped by recognition or its absence, often by the *mis*recognition of others, and so a person or group of people can suffer real damage, real distortion, if the people or society around them mirror back to them a confining or demeaning or contemptible picture of themselves.
>
> (1994: 25)

Ideology studies are raised here in an attempt to provide a theoretical framework which makes it possible to understand how the standardization process is grounded in our culture more generally. That is, I am interested in exploring how arguments for standardization reproduce "cultural conceptions which are partial, contestable and contested, and interest-laden" (Woolard and Schieffelin 1994: 58). Thus, while there are multiple possible approaches to ideology it is used in this study to refer to *the promotion of the needs and interests of a dominant group or class at the expense of marginalized groups, by means of disinformation and misrepresentation of those non-dominant groups.*[1] A definition more specific to language issues, often called *standard language ideology* (SLI), is defined as a bias toward an abstracted, idealized, homogenous spoken language which is imposed and maintained by dominant bloc institutions and which names as its model the written language, but which is drawn primarily from the spoken language of the upper middle class.[2]

Ideology has been linked to language by many, but it was Foucault who considered the way in which discourse is "controlled, selected, organised and redistributed," or *disciplined*:

> as history constantly teaches us, discourse is not simply that which trans-lates struggles or systems of domination, but is the thing *for which and by which* there is struggle, discourse is the power which is to be seized.
>
> (Foucault 1984: 110; emphasis added)

In the simplest terms, the disciplining of discourse has to do with who is allowed to speak, and thus, who is heard. A standard language ideology, which proposes that an idealized nation-state has one perfect, homogenous language, becomes the means by which discourse is seized, and provides rationalization for limiting access to discourse. Thus Mr. Kahakua could not be allowed to be heard on the radio, because it would have been perceived as institutionalized validation of a language variety linked to a socially unacceptable set of social, economic, and racial characteristics.

Authority which is associated with education is the most often cited and best established type of rationalization in this process. Thus, it might be argued that in a culture such as ours which obliges everyone to participate in the educational system, access to discourse is at least theoretically possible: marginalized groups can, by coming through the educational system, make themselves heard in their own languages. Foucault anticipates part of this argument by pointing out the fallacy of the assumption of education as an evenly distributed and power-neutral cultural resource: "Any system of education is a political way of maintaining or modifying the appopriation of discourses, along with the knowledges and powers which they carry" (1984: 123).

In fact, access to education itself is controlled and disciplined, in part on the basis of language variety and accent; the educational system may not be the beginning, but it is the heart of the standardization process. Asking children who speak non-mainstream languages to come to the schools in order to find validation for themselves, in order to be able to speak their own stories in their own voices, is an unlikely scenario. This would be something like the fly knocking at the spider's parlor door in the hopes of a rational discussion of a possible change in the structure of the food chain. Or, as Sledd puts it unapologetically: "In a school system run like ours by white businessmen, instruction in the mother tongue includes formal initiation into the linguistic prejudices of the middle class" (1972: 319). The factual basis of Sledd's position will be explored more fully in Chapter 6.

Dominant institutions promote the notion of an overarching, homogenous standard language which is primarily white, upper middle class, and midwestern. Whether the issues at hand are larger social or political ones or more subtle, whether the approach is coercion or consent, there are two sides to this process: first, devaluation of all that is not (or does not seek to be) politically, culturally, or socially mainstream, and second, validation of the social (and linguistic) values of the dominant institutions. The process of linguistic assimilation to an abstracted standard is cast as a natural one, necessary and positive for the greater social good.

What we don't understand clearly, what is mysterious and important, is not so much the way in which dominant groups deny certain groups permission to be heard in their own voices, but more so *how and why those groups cooperate.* How do the dominant bloc institutions manage to convince whole groups of human beings that they do not fully or adequately possess an appropriate human language? And, more mysteriously, why do those groups hand over this authority? Eagleton puts a more personal face on this question when he summarizes one way ideology works:

The study of ideology is among other things an inquiry into the ways in which people may come to invest in their own unhappiness. It is because being oppressed sometimes brings with it some slim bonuses that we are occasionally prepared to put up with it. The most efficient oppressor is the one who persuades his underlings to love, desire and identify with his power; and any practice of political emancipation thus involves that most difficult of all forms of liberation, freeing ourselves from ourselves.

(1991: xiii–xiv)

A classical Marxist might look at the way language ideology works and find it an excellent example of "false consciousness," or the process by which the working class is manipulated into accepting a status quo which denies their own claims and preserves the interests of those with property and power, because it is *right* and *good* and *common sense* to do so. But this particular ideological model has limitations; its unidirectionality does not resemble the give-and-take process of standardization well enough to make it useful in this discussion.

When persons who speak languages which are devalued and stigmatized consent to the standard language ideology, they become complicit in its propagation against themselves, their own interests and identities. Many are caught in a vacuum: When an individual cannot find any social acceptance for her language outside her own speech communities, she may come to denigrate her own language, even while she continues to use it.[3]

The standard language ideology provides a web of *common sense* arguments in which the speaker of non-mainstream language can get tangled at every turn: at school, in radio news, at the movies, while reading novels, at work, she hears that the language which marks her as Asian, Muslim, or southern (for example) is ugly, unacceptable, incoherent, illogical. This is countered, daily, by her experience: she does communicate, effectively, with the people who are closest and most important to her, who mark their language similarly. She even manages to communicate with the people who are criticizing her, in spite of their complaints. The things they say about her language and her social allegiances make her uncomfortable and unhappy. The things they promise her if she were to change this behavior may be very seductive: more money, success, recognition. She may think about trying to change the way she talks, and pay some attention to grammatical points which have been brought to her attention. Her phonology – her accent – she can do less or nothing about.

This day-by-day, persistent devaluation of her social self has repercussions. It might eventually bring her to the point of resistance, on a personal level. If there is a group of people like her going through the same experience, it might bring organized resistance. There are occasional signs of this: an accent reduction class scheduled in a South Carolina school which must close because of lack of student interest (Riddle 1993); a movement to validate Hawai'ian Creole in public forums (Verploegen 1988); a group in Wisconsin which publicizes their commitment to AAVE and their wish to have it recognized for the functional language it is (Hamblin 1995); a Cambodian American who takes his employer to court for telling him that to get a promotion he must "sound American" (*Phanna K. Xieng v. Peoples National Bank of Washington* 1991, 1992).

In the rest of this book we will see that the language mainstream does not let these small acts of resistance go by unnoticed; its representatives strike back, and hard. The institutions which see themselves as protectors of the values of the nation-state wage an on-going effort to validate their favored place in that state, in part on the basis of language. This resistance and counter-resistance which pits the empowered language mainstream against small groups or individuals who struggle for recognition is an on-going process. It is reminiscent of Antonio Gramsci's recasting of Marxist social theory in terms of what he called *hegemony*, or ideology as struggle.[4]

What concerns us in the remainder of this book is the process of linguistic domination itself. The arguments which are used to legitimize the values of the mainstream and to devalue non-conforming language varieties are well established, and so accepted that they are often quite openly used as we will see here.

Before we look at specific instances of the process of misrecognition, it will be useful to focus attention on two analytical tools. The first is a working model of the way the subordination of non-mainstream language works more generally (Box 4.1). The second is a brief consideration of the way this language subordination model is realized in the uneven distribution of what will be called the communicative burden.

A MODEL OF THE LANGUAGE SUBORDINATION PROCESS

The steps in the language subordination process included in this model have been compiled from analysis of a wide range of reactions or actions of dominant bloc institutions when they have perceived a threat to the authority of the homogenous language of the nation-state. The elements in this model grew out of analysis of many kinds of public commentary on language use and language communities, but they are similar to other models of ideological processes.[5]

Mystification is a common practice in the application of any ideology. In matters of language, it is a particularly strange but obviously well worn and effective tool. The mystification process has come about as part of the same process which has extended the literacy myth to the spoken language. The claim that spoken language is so complex that mere native speakers can never sort things out for themselves is countered by the realities of a world in which people do communicate with each other in non-mainstream languages and a variety of stigmatized accents.

Box 4.1 A model of the language subordination process

Language is mystified
You can never hope to comprehend the difficulties and complexities of your mother tongue without expert guidance.
Authority is claimed
Talk like me/us. We know what we are doing because we have studied language, because we write well.
Misinformation is generated
That usage you are so attached to is inaccurate. The variant I prefer is superior on historical, aesthetic, or logical grounds.
Non-mainstream language is trivialized
Look how cute, how homey, how funny.
Conformers are held up as positive examples
See what you can accomplish if you only try, how far you can get if you see the light.
Explicit promises are made
Employers will take you seriously; doors will open.
Threats are made
No one important will take you seriously; doors will close.
Non-conformers are vilified or marginalized
See how willfully stupid, arrogant, unknowing, uninformed, and/or deviant and unrepresentative these speakers are.

The way in which authority is claimed was previewed in the average person's approach to standard language. The institutions which form the interdependent web of standardization include the educational system, the broadcast and print media – in particular the news media – the entertainment industry, the corporate sector, and, to some degree, the judicial system. Each of these institutions claims extraordinary knowledge about language and hence authority in matters of language. Each of them looks to the other for validation.

Misinformation about language provides the best examples of common-sense argumentation. Examples range from the fairly trivial ("two negatives make a positive") to the more disturbing ("Pidgin can be cured!"). In the following chapters it will become clear how much of the misinformation about language comes from ignorance of the structural and functional facts about language.

Non-mainstream accents and varieties of English can be handled in a number of ways in the subordination process. The most common one is trivialization, or humor. Some examples of this process will be seen in the chapter on the news media, where this particular method seems to be quite popular. The broadcast and print media are also prone to report about speakers of non-mainstream varieties of English who see the light and who agree to reject their accent or language in favor of the ideal of the national standard.

The promises made about the rewards of mainstream language use are usually merely implied, but there are occasions on which they are verbalized more clearly. The threats are more openly made, in which each of the dominant bloc institutions points to the next as proof that resistance is utterly useless. Persons who persist in their allegiance to stigmatized varieties of English, who refuse in the face of common-sense arguments to at least try to lose a foreign accent, will be cut off from the privileges and rights of citizenship at every turn; if they will not at least acknowledge the superiority of the mainstream language, then all the intelligence and success in the world will not open any doors.

At its most brutal, this turns into personal attacks on whole groups of people. This is often done from *within* the community, when stigmatized language or accent is used as an excuse to attack and vilify members of the in-group in ways which would never be tolerated by an outsider.[6] The most salient example of this will be seen in the way the African American community deals with the divisive issue of its own vernacular languages.

This model of the subordination process will provide a framework for the material presented in the next chapters. Before we look at the way accent shapes the lives of people, however, it is important to look at the issue of communication.

REJECTING THE GIFT: THE INDIVIDUAL'S ROLE IN THE COMMUNICATIVE PROCESS

The most common arguments for discrimination against non-mainstream accents and languages have to do with communication. *I've got nothing against [Taiwanese, Appalachians, Blacks]* the argument will go. *I just can't understand them. So maybe they can't do anything about their accent, but I can't help not understanding them either.*

Communication seems to be a simple thing: one person talks and another listens; they change roles. When the discussion focuses on accent, however, this characterization of communication becomes overly simplistic. The social space between two speakers is not neutral, in most cases. Think of the people you talked to today. Each time you begin an exchange, a complex series of calculations begins: Do I need to be formal with this person? Do I owe her respect? Does she owe me deference? What do I want from her, or she from me?

In any situation, we can, simply, refuse to communicate. In an adversarial position, we may understand perfectly what our partners, parents, friends say to us, but still respond with *I simply cannot understand you.* Magically, the listener is relieved of any responsibility in the communicative act, and the full burden is put directly on the speaker. "I can't understand you" may mean, in reality, *I dare you to make me understand you.*

Clark's cognitive model of the communicative act (which has much in common with a theory of conversational analysis) is based on a principle of *mutual responsibility*, in which participants in a conversation collaborate in the establishment of new information. This involves complicated processes of repair, expansion, and replacement in iterative fashion until both parties are satisfied (Clark and Wilkes-Gibbs 1986). In general Clark notes:

> Many purposes in conversation, however, change moment by moment as the two people tolerate more or less uncertainty about the listener's understanding of the speaker's references. The heavier burden usually falls on the listener, since she is in the best position to assess her own comprehension.
>
> (1986: 34)

When speakers are confronted with an accent which is foreign to them, the first decision they make is whether or not they are going to accept their responsibility in the act of communication. What we will see again and again in the case studies which follow is that members of the dominant language group feel perfectly empowered to reject their role, and to demand that a person with an accent carry the majority of responsibility in the communicative act. Conversely, when such a speaker comes in contact with another mainstream speaker who is nonetheless incoherent or unclear, the first response is usually *not* to reject a fair share of the communicative burden, but to take other factors into consideration.

The whole concept of units of conversation in which two partners work toward mutual comprehension assumes a certain state of mind on the part of the participants. Work in accommodation theory suggests that a complex interplay of linguistic and psychological factors will establish the predisposition to understand. Thakerar *et al.* (1982) conducted a series of empirical tests to examine accommodation behavior; they were not working directly with "accented" speech, but their findings are generally typical of such studies, which verify something known intuitively: listeners and speakers will work harder to find a communicative middle ground and foster mutual intelligibility when they are motivated, socially and psychologically, to do so. Conversely, when the speaker perceives that the act of accommodating or assimilating linguistically may bring more disadvantages than advantages, in in-group terms, he or she may diverge even farther from the language of the listener.

Two crucial elements of a successful communicative act are relevant to the rest of this book, in which we will examine how standard language ideology functions in day-to-day communications.

Degree of accentedness, whether from L1 interference, or a socially or geographically marked language variety, cannot predict the level of an individual's competency in the target language. In fact, we have seen that high degrees of competence are often attained by persons with especially strong L2 accents. Nevertheless, accent will sometimes be an issue in

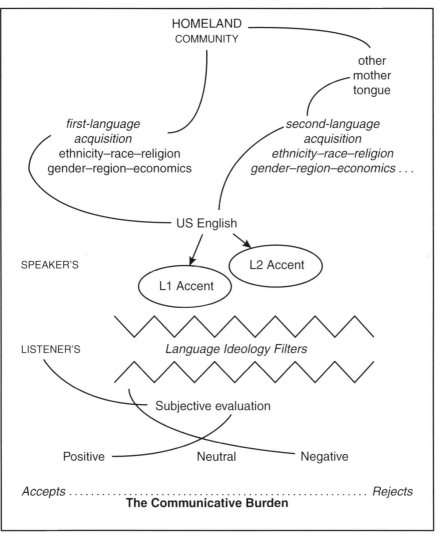

HOMELAND
COMMUNITY

other
mother
tongue

*first-language
acquisition*
ethnicity–race–religion
gender–region–economics

*second-language
acquisition*
ethnicity–race–religion
gender–region–economics . . .

US English

L2 Accent

L1 Accent

SPEAKER'S

LISTENER'S

Language Ideology Filters

Subjective evaluation

Positive ——— Neutral ——— Negative

Accepts . . . . *Rejects*
The Communicative Burden

Figure 4.1 Accepting or rejecting the communicative burden

communication, especially in the case of non-native speakers of English who are in the early stages of the acquisition process. Accent, in the general way it has been used here, can sometimes be an impediment to communication even when all parties involved in the communicative act are willing, even eager, to understand. In many cases, however, breakdown of communication is due not so much to accent as it is to negative social evaluation of the accent in question, and a rejection of the communicative burden. Figure 4.1 makes the process more visible.

When we are confronted with a new person we want to talk to or must talk to, we make a quick series of social evaluations based on many external cues, one of them being the person's language and accent. Those sociolinguistic cues are directly linked to homeland, the race and ethnicity, the social self of the person in front of us. Based on our personal histories, our own backgrounds and social selves (which together make up a set of filters through which we hear the people we talk to), we will take a communicative stance. Most of the time, we will agree to carry our share of the burden. Sometimes, if we are especially positive about the configuration of social characteristics we see in the person, or if the purposes of communication are especially important to us, we will accept a disproportionate amount of the burden.

Each of us would group the accents we come across in different configurations. For the majority of Americans, French accents are positive ones, but not for all of us. Many have strong pejorative reactions to Asian accents, or to African American Vernacular English, but certainly not everyone does. The accents we hear must go through our language ideology filters. In extreme cases, we feel completely justified in rejecting the communicative burden, and the person in front of us:[7]

> The supervisor explained that workers would . . . ask the plaintiff what he wanted them to do, and then simply walk away, unable to understand. The supervisor refused to attribute such incidents to the plaintiff's accent, but offered no other explanation. He said they just couldn't understand him "like normal people with normal language."

> I signed up for this chemistry course but dropped it when I saw the Teaching Assistant. I shouldn't have to have TAs who can't speak English natively.

> She put on a really excellent presentation to the committee, but if she had applied for a job on the phones sounding like she does, we wouldn't have hired her.

> You can speak your own language, you can have your own way, but don't force someone else to have to suffer and listen to it . . . if you want to speak Black with your friends, that's fine. But don't insult someone else's ears by making them listen to it.

The remainder of this book is about the subjugation process: how it works, why it works, and why we let it. We will see that standard language ideology is introduced by the schools, vigorously promoted by the media and further institutionalized by the corporate sector. It is underscored by the entertainment industry and underwritten in subtle and not so subtle ways by the judicial system. Thus, it is not surprising that many individuals do not recognize the fact that for spoken language, variation is systematic, structured, and inherent, and that the national standard is an abstraction. What *is* surprising, even deeply disturbing, is the way that many individuals who consider themselves democratic, even-handed, rational, and free of prejudice, hold on tenaciously to a standard language ideology which attempts to justify restriction of individuality and rejection of the *other*.

Accent discrimination can be found everywhere in our daily lives. In fact, such behavior is so commonly accepted, so widely perceived as appropriate, that it must be seen as the last back door to discrimination. And the door stands wide open.

Part II
What we sow
Institutionalized language ideology

Introduction
Language subordination at work

> To disarm the strong and arm the weak would be to change the social order which it is my job to preserve. Justice is the means by which established injustices are sanctioned.
>
> Anatole France, *Crainquebille* (1901)

In Part I of this book, I have attempted to supply some basic facts about the structure and function of language necessary to a discussion of issues of authority and discrimination on linguistic grounds. I have also outlined the ideological issues, and provided a model for the study of the language subordination process on that basis. In this section, I will apply the proposed model to specific institutional practices around language.

While "institution" is often used to refer to social relationships between individuals (*the institution of marriage*), here it is used in another sense, in which *institution* can be defined quite simply as any organization which has social and structural importance in the life of a community or society. Here, an institution is any group or collective established with a specific set of goals important to the continuation of the established social structures of the community. While many such institutions can be identified, only a subset of them are examined here: education, news media, the entertainment industry, the business sector, the government, and the legal system (which in large part exist to define and delineate social institutions). Institutions which are not included but might be are the military and specific organized religions. Because institutions provide structure in the community, they are a primary point of supra-regional and national comparison. For the moment, however, I am looking at them in relationship to each other, and how they work together. Within each of these institutions, a set of (primarily false) assumptions about language function as tools in the process of language subordination.

In the case of each institution examined here, I have only scratched the surface of the way language is used to limit or validate discourse. Because the topic is so large, and the processes so complicated, I have adopted a case-study approach in which general issues are raised, and then illustrated on the basis of a specific set of documentable circumstances or practices. It must also be pointed out that because of the parameters of a study such as this one, I must necessarily leave out the question of heterogeneity within institutions. If it seems at times that I am treating all of the news media as a monolith with the exclusive purpose of discrediting it as a whole, then I have failed in my intention to illustrate certain *kinds* of practices, rather than to provide a full and overarching understanding of the institution in all of its functions.

In Part III, I will change focus and look at how the totality of these practices in the life of a particular language community or speaker makes inroads in the way we perceive ourselves, and others.

5 Teaching children how to discriminate

What we learn from the Big Bad Wolf

> All official institutions of language are repeating machines: school, sports, advertising, popular songs, news, all continually repeat the same structure, the same meaning, often the same words: the stereotype is a political fact, the major figure of ideology.
>
> Roland Barthes, *The Pleasure of the Text* (1975)

In 1933, while the US was in the depths of a severe depression, Walt Disney's animators created a short cartoon which would make an $88,000 profit in the first two years of its release (Grant 1993: 56). Perhaps this figure is not so surprising, given the statistics of the time: by 1930 there were some 20,000 motion-picture theaters in business, serving 90 million customers weekly (Emery and Emery 1992: 265). Thus the first filming of *Three Little Pigs*, a familiar story with a message of hard work in the face of adversity, was widely seen. The theme of good triumphing over evil was clearly a timely and popular one, and it is one that has not gone out of favor: this cartoon is still shown with regularity, in part or whole, on Disney's cable television channel.

One of the topics which is often discussed in relation to this particular Disney animated short is a scene included in the original release, in which the wolf – in yet another attempt to fool the pigs into opening the door to him – dresses as a Jewish peddler (Grant 1993, Kaufman 1988, Precker 1993b). He has a hook nose, wears sidelocks and a dark broad-rimmed hat similar to one worn by some Orthodox Jews, carries his wares before him, and contrives a Yiddish accent.[1] Kaufman recounts that it wasn't until the film's re-release in 1948, fourteen years later, that Disney reanimated the scene in which the Wolf appears as a Jew. This step was taken in response to communications from the Hays Office, which brought the issue of Jewish sensibilities to Disney's attention.[2] Grant reports that Disney later admitted that the original scene was in bad taste (1993: 54); nevertheless, only the offending visual representation was changed, and much later (at a date never specified clearly), "in case the Yiddish dialect of the original scene might itself be found offensive, the dialogue was

changed as well. Now the Wolf spoke in a standard 'dumb' cartoon voice"
(Kaufman 1988: 43–44). Even when the wolf no longer appeared Jewish,
he spoke with a Yiddish accent, thus maintaining the underlying message
based in anti-Semitism and fear of the other: a link between the evil inten-
tions of the wolf and things Jewish. Grant also relates that the newer
animation and dialogue still leaned on more general stereotypes and fears:
"the disguised wolf no longer has Hebraic tones or mannerisms, instead
saying: 'I'm the Fuller brush-man. I workin' me way through college.' The
syntax alone belies that statement" (1993: 54).

Sixty years later, a similar controversy would arise over the portrayal
of characters in Disney's *Aladdin*, a movie set in a mythical Arabic
kingdom. An offending line of dialogue in an opening song, "Where they
cut off your ear if they don't like your face / It's barbaric, but hey,
it's home," was partially changed in response to complaints from the
American Arab Anti-Discrimination Committee (AAADC), but as
the representative of the AAADC pointed out, the accents of the characters remained as originally filmed. The representative

> particularly objected to the fact that the good guys – Aladdin, Princess
> Jasmine and her father – talk like Americans, while all the other Arab
> characters have heavy accents. This pounds home the message that
> people with a foreign accent are bad.
>
> (Precker 1993a)[3]

Is there truth to this supposition? What are children to take away from
the Big Bad Wolf, and from brutal Arabian palace guards? Is it significant that they see bad guys who sound a certain way, look a certain way,
and come from a certain part of town or of the world? Is this a part of
how children learn to assign values on the basis of variation in language
linked to race, ethnicity, and homeland? To make this point, it would first
be necessary to demonstrate regular patterns which are available to
children on a day-to-day basis, for as Silverstein (1992) asserts, "we are
faced first-off with indexical facts, facts of observed/experienced social
practices, the systematicity of which is our central problem: *are* they
systematic? if so, *how*?" (322).

This chapter is about the sociolinguistic aspects of the systematic
construction of dominance and subordinance in animated films aimed at
children.

It is first observably true that somehow, children learn not only how to
use variation in their own language, but also how to interpret social variation in the language of others. They do this with or without exposure to
television and film, but in the current day, few children grow up without
this exposure. The 1995 *World Almanac* reports that 98 percent of all US
households, or some 94.2 million homes, have television sets; of these,
79 percent own video cassette recorders and 63 percent subscribe to basic
cable. As seen in Figures 5.1 and 5.2, when children are not in front of

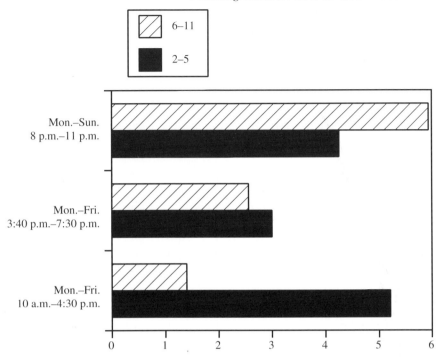

Figure 5.1 Average hours per week children watch television, by time period and two age groups

Source: 1995 *World Almanac and Book of Facts*

the television set, they are avid consumers of the products of the movie industry; in 1992 over 15 million seats were occupied by children under the age of 2; those between 6 and 11 double this number.

For better or worse, the television and film industries have become a major avenue of contact to the world outside our homes and communities. For many, especially for children, it is the only view they have of people of other races or national origins.

In traditions passed down over hundreds of years from the stage and theater, film uses language variation and accent to draw character quickly, building on established preconceived notions associated with specific regional loyalties, ethnic, racial, or economic alliances. This shortcut to characterization means that certain traits need not be laboriously demonstrated by means of a character's actions and an examination of motive. It also means that these characterizations are culture- and period-bound; in this, films have much in common with fiction, and the representation of our cultures and our selves is equally worthy of study.

It must be noted at the outset that it is not my intention to condemn out of hand all use of abstraction in entertainment film, or even

Millions

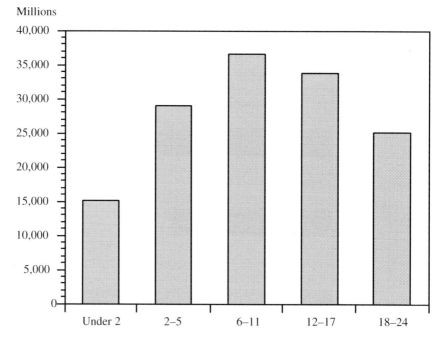

Figure 5.2 Movie theater attendance calculated for the year 1992, by age
Source: Mediamark Research 1993, vol. P13

particularly in cartoons. Some stereotyping may be inevitable. Whether or not all stereotyping has negative repercussions is a matter of interpretation; here I hope to show that while the practice is sometimes mild and no obvious or direct harm follows from it, there are always repercussions. For that reason alone, it would be good to be more generally aware of the way stereotypes function in film directed at children.

TALKING THE TALK

Any actor necessarily brings to a role his or her own native language. In many cases, the variety of English is irrelevant to the characterization and can be left alone. Often, however, the director or actor will target a particular social, regional, or foreign accent of English, perhaps because it is intrinsic to the role and cannot be sacrificed. US audiences may or may not suspend disbelief when Robin Hood speaks with a California accent, but it would be harder to cast someone with an upper-class British accent as any of the recent US presidents and not do serious harm to audience expectations and reception.

In a similar way, non-native speakers of English who come to the US to make films necessarily bring their L2 accents to their work. This accent may restrict the roles they can play, or they may have roles written or rewritten to suit the immutable nature of their accents (Arnold Schwarzenegger, Gérard Depardieu, Sophia Loren, and Greta Garbo provide examples). Actors undergo accent training of various kinds in an attempt to teach them to imitate what they need for a particular role, although we have seen that even with expensive and careful tutoring not all actors are equally capable of this task, even in the limited way it is asked of them during filming (see the discussion of the Sound House in Chapter 2).

What is particularly relevant and interesting in this context, however, is the way that actors *attempt* to manipulate language as a tool in the construction of character, whether or not they are successful. Educational programs for the training of actors for stage and screen often include classes on speech, dialogue, and the contrivance of accent. If it is possible to fool some of the people some of the time, it is still necessary to learn the skill behind this trick.

The materials used in these courses are interesting in and of themselves, because the approach often includes not just the mechanics and technicalities of one particular regional or foreign accent, but also issues of content and approach.

> Dialect actors must avoid going so far with certain speech traits that they end up creating ethnic or linguistic stereotypes . . . language or dialect background does not dictate character actions. Characters with accents must have the same range of choices available to them as characters whose speech is identical to yours.
>
> (Karshner and Stern 1990: Preface)

This is an enlightened and realistic position, certainly. Other materials prepared for actors are not always so even-handed, as seen in *Foreign Dialects: A manual for actors, directors and writers* (Herman and Herman 1943), a volume still in print:

> The Cockney Dialect: . . . The typical Cockney is often a brash little fellow. He is an inveterate heckler, and some of his favorite victims are the soap-box orators in Hyde Park. His speech is usually nasalized, possibly because of adenoid trouble which is quite prevalent in the British Isles. Often, his dialect is delivered in a whine . . . there is always a slovenliness to the pronunciation.
>
> (19)

> The Swedish Dialect: . . . the Swedes are usually more light-hearted than their Scandinavian cousins, more interested in the joys of living and eating. The Norwegians, on the other hand, are likely to be more solid and serious. The Swede likes conviviality, and the Norwegian solitary, lonely contemplation.
>
> (295)

The Polish Dialect: ... [Poles] are religious – especially the women – and devoutly Catholic. The Pole is industrious and will not shy from the hardest labor in the steel mills, foundries, and other heavy-duty jobs. He is a pleasure-loving person and it is this quality that leads him into the extremes of conviviality. He is not what may be called a thinking man ... he is slow to thought, slow to speech, and slow to action.

(351)

Sometimes, the contrivance of accent appears a logical and reasonable dramatic strategy. Often stories about people who come to the US from other countries lean hard on accent to establish the origin of the character (Al Pacino's Cuban-accented English in *Scarface*; Nick Nolte's Italian-accented English in *Lorenzo's Oil* or Marlon Brando's in *The Godfather*; the range of attempted Swedish accents in *I Remember Mama*). For films set in the southern US, actors are often coached long and hard on the acquisition of a second variety of US English (Vivien Leigh in *Gone with the Wind*); sometimes the attempt is not made at all (Clark Gable, Leslie Howard, and other men in the same movie).

Perhaps most interesting, a director often requires actors to use accents as a signal that the action and dialogue would not be taking place in English. Thus, in a Nazi concentration camp in *Schindler's List*, the commanding officer (Ralph Fiennes, who is British) speaks English with a contrived German accent to alert viewers to the fact that he would, in fact, be speaking German. There is a long list of filmed stories in which dialogue would not logically be taking place in English. Such films include *Schindler's List* (German and Polish, as well as other eastern European languages), *Papillon, Dangerous Liaisons, Impromptu*, and *Gigi* (French), *Diary of Anne Frank* (Dutch), *The Good Earth* (Chinese), *Fiddler on the Roof* (Yiddish, Russian), *All Quiet on the Western Front* (German, French), *Dr. Zhivago* and *Gorki Park* (Russian), *Kiss of the Spider Woman* (Spanish), *The Unbearable Lightness of Being* (Czech, French). Here accent becomes a signal of place and context rather than a means to quickly convey character. In such a case, it would make most logical sense to have *all* actors contrive the same French or Russian or Chinese accent.[4]

Rarely, however, is this policy consistent. In most movies, live action or animated, where accent is used as a cue to place, only some characters will speak with a contrived accent. Many possible reasons for this come to mind: Perhaps this is because not all actors are equally capable of targeting the required accent, or of temporarily disguising their own. Perhaps the director prefers no accents to partial or unbelievable ones. Or perhaps, in some cases, accent is used as a shortcut for those roles where stereotype serves as a shortcut to characterization. Actors contrive accents primarily as a characterization tool, although there is sometimes supplementary motivation in establishing the setting of the story. Below,

I will consider exactly when certain accents are contrived, and perhaps more important, when mainstream US English (MUSE) is considered acceptable, or even necessary. To do this, we will consider one body of animated film in detail.

ANIMATED FILM

In animated film, even more so than is the case with live-action entertainment, language is used as a quick way to build character and reaffirm stereotype:

> precisely because of their assumed innocence and innocuousness, their inherent ability – even obligation – to defy all conventions of realistic representation, animated cartoons offer up a fascinating zone with which to examine how a dominant culture constructs its subordinates. As non-photographic application of photographic medium, they are freed from the basic cinematic expectation that they convey an "impression of reality." ... The function and essence of cartoons is in fact the reverse: the impression of irreality, of intangible and imaginary worlds in chaotic, disruptive, subversive collision.
>
> (Burton 1992: 23–24)

There are patterns in the way we project pictures and images of ourselves and others which are available to anyone who watches and listens carefully. A study of accents in animated cartoons over time is likely to reveal the way linguistic stereotypes mirror the evolution of national fears: Japanese and German characters in cartoons during the Second World War (Popeye meets the "oh so solly" Japanese fleet), Russian spy characters in children's cartoons in the 1950s and 1960s (Natasha and Boris meet Rocky and Bullwinkle, or "beeeg trrrouble forrr moose and squirrrrrel"), Arabian characters in the era of hostilities with Iran and Iraq. In the following discussion of systematic patterns found in one specific set of children's animated film, the hypothesis is a simple one: animated films entertain, but they are also a way to teach children to associate specific characteristics and life styles with specific social groups, by means of language variation.[5] To test this hypothesis, 371 characters in all of the available Disney full-length animated films were analyzed.

DISNEY FEATURE FILMS

On the surface it is quite obvious that Disney films present young children with a range of social and linguistic stereotypes, from *Lady and the Tramp*'s cheerful, musical Italian chefs to *Treasure of the Lost Lamp*'s stingy, Scottish-accented McScrooge. In order to look more systematically at the way Disney films employ accent and dialect to draw character and

Table 5.1 The Disney films

1938	Snow White	1963	The Sword in the Stone
1940	Pinocchio	1967	The Jungle Book
1941	Dumbo	1970	The Aristocats
1941	The Reluctant Dragon	1977	The Rescuers
1942	Bambi	1981	The Fox and the Hound
1950	Cinderella	1986	The Great Mouse Detective
1951	Alice in Wonderland	1989	The Little Mermaid
1952	Robin Hood	1990	Treasure of the Lost Lamp
1953	Peter Pan	1990	The Rescuers Down Under
1955	Lady and the Tramp	1991	Beauty and the Beast
1958	Sleeping Beauty	1992	Aladdin
1961	101 Dalmatians	1994	The Lion King

stereotypes, it was necessary to analyze all released versions of full-length animated Disney films available.[6]

This body of animated films was chosen because the Disney Corporation is the largest producer of such films, and they are perhaps the most highly marketed and advertised of the field (Disney total advertising budget for 1992 was $524.6 million, some significant portion of which was spent directly on feature and animated films). Here I consider only full-length feature films (generally between one and a half to two hours in length) and specifically exclude short features, cartoons, and compilations of shorts grouped together for thematic reasons. Only fully animated films were included in the study, excluding those that combine live-action sequences with animation (*Song of the South, Three Caballeros*). Animated film created for an adult audience (the wartime film *Victory through Air Power* is one example) were also omitted. All characters with speaking roles of more than single-word utterances were included in the analysis.

A total of twenty-four films were viewed multiple times.[7] Each of the 371 characters was analyzed for a variety of language and characterization variables. The detailed linguistic description for each character consisted of a mix of phonetic transcription, quotes of typical syntactic structures, and marked lexical items. In cases where an actor is clearly contriving an accent, a decision was made as to what language variety was most likely intended to be portrayed. That is, a poorly imitated British (or other foreign) accent was still counted as such for the creators and (most) viewers. For example, in *Aladdin*, one of the minor characters, a thief, speaks primarily mainstream American, but also has some trilled r's – definitely not a feature normally associated with American English. This character's accent was still classified as mainstream American, however, since only one atypical feature appeared in his phonology. Another character whose speech exhibits features from two or more dialects is Cogsworth, the butler/clock in *Beauty and the Beast*. He speaks with a contrived British accent in which some American features crop up unpredictably; thus, though it is not an accurate imitation of a middle- or upper-class British dialect, for the purposes of this study it must be classified as such.

After a brief consideration of the findings of the quantitative analysis more generally, I will concentrate on three aspects of language use in Disney films. These are the representation of African Americans; the way that certain groups are represented (particularly lovers and mothers); and finally, using French accents as a case study, the way that even positive stereotyping can be negative and limiting.

The whole mouse and nothing but the mouse

Of the 371 characters with speaking roles in the twenty-four movies examined, 259 or 69.8 percent are male. Female characters make up the other just over 30 percent. A look at the way female and male characters are deployed, overall, indicates that within the proportions established, they are equally distributed as major and minor characters. Female characters are almost never shown at work outside the home and family; where they do show up, they are mothers and princesses, devoted or (rarely) rebellious daughters. When they are at work female characters are waitresses, nurses, nannies, or housekeepers. Men, conversely, are doctors, waiters, advisors to kings, thieves, hunters, servants, detectives, and pilots.

It is certainly and demonstrably the case that the universe shown to young children in these films is one with a clear division between the sexes in terms of life style and life choices. Traditional views of the woman's role in the family are strongly underwritten, and in Disney films, whether they are filmed in 1938 or 1994, the female characters see, or come to accept, their first and most important role in life as that of wife and mother. What does an examination of language use have to add to this observation? What do characters, male and female, speak?

For the most part (43.1 percent) they speak a variety of US English which is not stigmatized in social or regional terms, what has been called MUSE throughout this study. Another 13.9 percent speak varieties of US English which are southern, or urban, or which are associated with particular racial, ethnic, or economic groups. Mainstream varieties of British English are spoken by 21.8 percent (Figure 5.3).

While 91 of the total 371 characters occur in roles where they would not logically be speaking English, there are only 34 characters who speak English with a foreign accent. The tendency to use foreign accents to convey the setting of the story is confirmed by these distributions; there are twice as many characters with foreign-accented English in stories set in places like France and Italy.

The Lion King, set in Africa, is certainly a case of a story in which the logical language would not be English. This is acknowledged, indirectly,

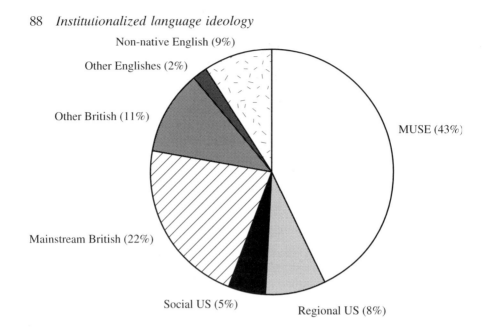

Figure 5.3 371 Disney animated characters by language variety used

in the names of the characters, many of which are derived from Swahili. The good-natured but dumb warthog is called Pumbaa, or *simpleton*; Shenzi, the name of the leader of the hyena pack, means *uncouth*. However, the only character who actually uses traces of Swahili and a contrived Swahili accent is Rafiki (Swahili, *friend*), the wise and eccentric baboon who fulfills the role of spiritual guide.

Figure 5.3 indicates that some 90 percent of all the characters speak English natively, with an American or British English accent. However, Figure 5.4 makes it clear that 60 percent of all the characters appear in stories set in English-speaking countries; thus, a significant number of English-speaking characters appear in stories set abroad (sometimes these are "Americans abroad" as in Donald Duck in search of treasure; sometimes these are characters who are not logically English speaking, given their role and the story, as in all the characters in *Aladdin*). In Figure 5.5 three *language settings* are considered: stories set in English-speaking lands, those set in non-English-speaking countries, and finally, those set in mythical kingdoms where it would be difficult to make an argument for one language or another as primary (*The Little Mermaid*, for example, at times seems to be in a Mediterranean setting). Since a contrived foreign accent is often used to signal that the typical or logical language of the setting would not be English, it is not surprising to see that the highest percentage of characters with foreign-accented English occurs in the second type of language setting. But it is also significant that even more

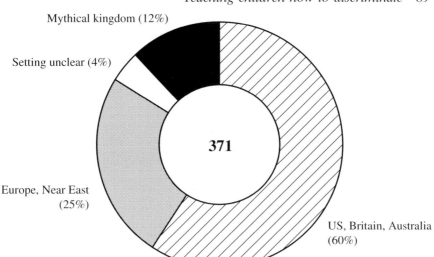

Figure 5.4 371 Disney animated characters by story setting (percentage figures rounded up)

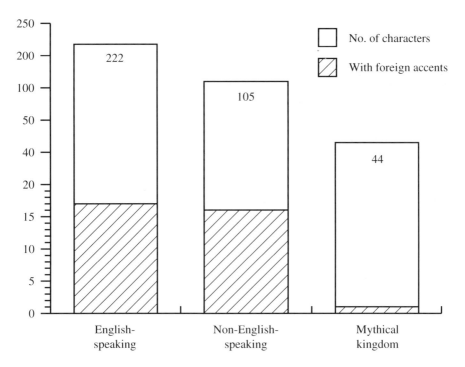

Figure 5.5 371 Disney animated characters by language spoken in the country in which the story is set, and the number of characters with foreign-accented English

Table 5.2 371 Disney animated characters by major language group and evaluation of character's actions and motivations[8]

	Motivations				
	Positive	*Negative*	*Mixed*	*Unclear*	*Total* *%*
US	122	33	11	42	208 56.1
British	53	28	11	37	129 34.8
Foreign	10	11	6	7	34 9.2
Total	185	72	28	86	371
%	49.9	19.4	7.5	23.2	100.0

characters with foreign accents appear in stories set in the US and England.

The breakdown of characters by their language variety becomes interesting when we examine that variety in relationship to the motivations and actions of the character's role. Disney films rely heavily on common themes of good and evil, and with very few exceptions they depend also on happy endings. Characters with unambiguously positive roles constitute 49.9 percent of the total; those who are clearly bad or even evil, only 19.4 percent. The remainder are divided between characters who change significantly in the course of the story (always from bad to good) and those characters whose roles are too small and fleeting for such a judgment to be made (86, or 23.2 percent of the total), as seen in Table 5.2.

Female characters are more likely to show positive motivations and actions (Figure 5.6). Unlike male characters who sometimes are bad and then become good, bad females show no character development.

The pie chart in Figure 5.7 would first seem to indicate that there is no relationship between non-native English accents and the portrayal of good and evil. There are 72 characters who are truly bad, in major and minor roles. They include the poacher and would-be child-murderer Percival McLeach in *The Rescuers Down Under* with his contrived southwestern accent and idiom ("purty feather, boy!" "I whupped ya'll!" "Home, home on the range, where the critters 'r ta-id up in chains"), and the whip-and-cleaver wielding Stromboli of *Pinocchio*, with his threats of dismemberment, incredible rages, and florid, contrived Italian accent. Of these evil 72, however, a full 85 percent are native speakers of English; almost half are speakers of US English. Bad guys with foreign accents account for only 15 percent of the whole.

Taken in context, however, the issue is more complicated. In Figure 5.8, which compares positive, negative, and mixed motivations (the marginal characters have been removed for the sake of this discussion) by major

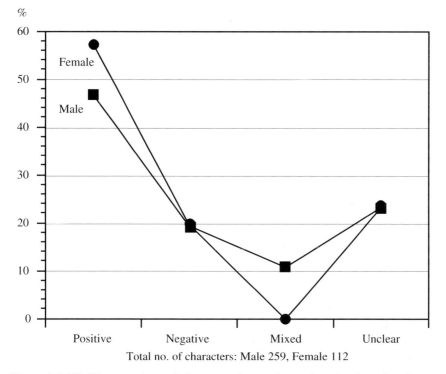

Figure 5.6 371 Disney animated characters by gender and evaluation of actions and motivations

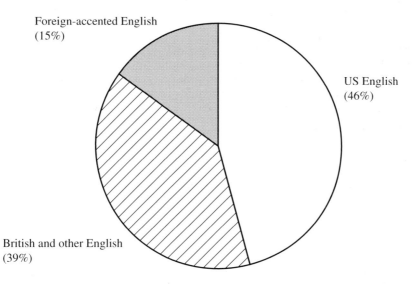

Figure 5.7 72 Disney animated characters with negative motivations and actions, by major language group

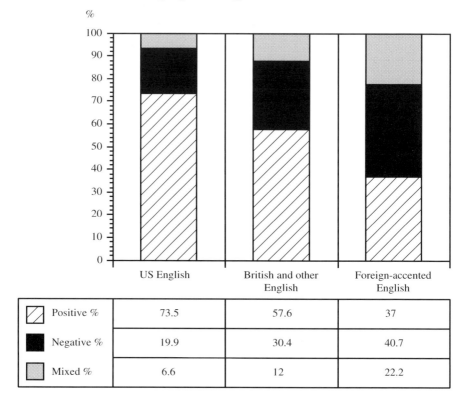

Figure 5.8 285 Disney animated characters of positive, negative, or mixed motivations and actions, by major language group

language groups, it becomes clear that the overall representation of persons with foreign accents is far more negative than that of speakers of US or British English. About 20 percent of US English speakers are bad characters, while about 40 percent of non-native speakers of English are evil.

Additional interesting patterns come forward when we examine the representation of specific languages linked to national origin, race, or characterization.

Beasts and beauties

With the 1967 release of *The Jungle Book*, the relationship between voice, language, and characterization entered a new realm in Disney film. This was the first feature in which actors were cast on the basis of voice recognition. Actors and musicians who had already established a personality and reputation with the movie-going public were drawn, quite literally, into the animation and storytelling process. This strategy was not greeted with enthusiasm by all film critics:

Animating full-bodied, expressive characters is what men like Thomas, Kahl, Johnston and Lounsberry do best. Other artists provide a hand- some backdrop and add dazzling animation effects. But breathing heart and soul into a film is not so easily accomplished. *The Jungle Book* lacked this quality, and substituted for it a gallery of characters whose strongest identity was with the stars who provided their voices. The animators enjoyed working with people like George Sanders, Louis Prima, and Phil Harris, and incorporated elements of their personalities into the animated characters. Audiences naturally responded, so the animators felt justified in continuing this practice. "It is much simpler and more realistic than creating a character and then searching for the right voice," [producer] Reitherman contended.

(Maltin 1987: 74–75)

This additional complication to the use of accent and dialect in the building of character and stereotype is relevant to a discussion of the representation of African Americans by means of language in Disney films.

Especially in more recent years, Disney has engaged African American actors to provide the voices of major characters in their animated films. Sometimes these actors speak MUSE, as is the case with James Earl Jones speaking the role of the father in *The Lion King*. Sometimes they fluc- tuate between MUSE and AAVE, drawing on rhythmic and lexical items for dramatic and comic effect. This is the case with Whoopi Goldberg's performance as one of the evil hyenas, also in *The Lion King*. Sometimes these actors seem to be using their own variety of English with little embellishment, as was the case when Pearl Bailey spoke the part of Big Mama in *The Fox and the Hound*. Table 5.3 gives an overview of all the characters in these films who use, to a greater or lesser extent, AAVE. Additional AAVE-speaking characters seem to have flitted in and out of the abduction scene in *The Jungle Book*; however, they were not included in the analysis because the speaking roles were too small to be sure of the variety of English used. It needs to be stated quite clearly that this list does not represent the sum total of all African Americans who had speaking roles in the movies examined, but only those who chose or who were directed to use AAVE for a particular part.

While the 161 MUSE speakers appear in proportions of 43.1 percent humanoid, 54.4 percent animal and 2.5 percent inanimate creatures (such as the talking teapot in *Beauty and the Beast*), all AAVE-speaking char- acters appear in animal rather than humanoid form. Given the low overall number of AAVE speakers, however, it is hard to draw any inferences from that fact. The issue is further complicated in that every character with a southern accent appears in animal rather than humanoid form. Further examination of unambiguously positive and negative characters indicates that a full 43.4 percent of 90 characters in human form show

Table 5.3 Disney animated characters who use AAVE part or all of the time

Name	Actor (where credits available)	Humanoid or animal	Film	Role evaluation	Typical language of setting
Dandy	Cliff Edwards	crow	*Dumbo*	Mixed	English
Fat	Jim Carmichael	crow		Mixed	English
Glasses	Hall Johnson Choir	crow		Mixed	English
Preacher		crow		Mixed	English
Straw Hat		crow		Mixed	English
King Louie	Louis Pima	primate	*Jungle Book*	Mixed	Hindi*
Big Mama	Pearl Bailey	owl	*Fox and Hound*	Positive	English
Scat	Scatman Crothers	cat	*Aristocats*	Mixed	French
Shenzi	Whoopi Goldberg	hyena	*Lion King*	Negative	Swahili*

*The category "typical language" is based on the country in which the story is set. Most of the movies are set in the US, thus the typical language is English. *The Jungle Book* is set in India, and *The Lion King* in Africa. The typical languages of these stories could be any one of many native languages spoken in those places; I have chosen one of the many possible languages in such cases.

negative actions and motivations while only 18.6 percent of the 156 animal characters are negative.

Perhaps more disturbing than the issue of human versus animal form is the way in the world which is cast so clearly for those African Americans who are speakers of AAVE. The stereotypes are intact: the male characters seem to be unemployed or show no purpose in life beyond the making of music and pleasing themselves, and this is as true for the crows in *Dumbo* as it is for the orangutan King Louie and his crew of primate subjects in *The Jungle Book*. Much has been made of King Louie and his manipulation of the only human being in this story; singing in the scat-style made popular by African American musicians, he convinces his audience that he has one goal in life, and that is to be the one thing he is not: a human being, a man. African American males who are not linguistically assimilated to the sociolinguistic norms of a middle and colorless United States are allowed very few possibilities in life, but they are allowed to want those things they don't have and can't be.

The two female characters are also controversial, but for very different reasons. Pearl Bailey's Big Mama must be seen as a stereotype of the loving, nurturing mammy, but one with a mind of her own. Whoopi Goldberg, who voices the part of one of the hyenas in *The Lion King*, slips in and out of AAVE for comic and dramatic effect. It must be noted that she is the only African American actor to do so in this film, a film which included – for Disney – an unusually high number of African Americans. We never hear AAVE from James Earl Jones as the King. None of the characters, whether they speak MUSE or AAVE, show any clear connection to things African, with the exception of the wise baboon, Rafiki, who occupies a special but peripheral role in the film's story.

In general, children who have little or no contact with African Americans are exposed to a fragmented and distorted view of what it means to be black, based on characterizations which rest primarily on negative stereotype linked directly to language difference.

Lovers and mothers

Romance is a major plot device in many of Disney's animated films. Of the twenty-four stories examined here, thirteen depend in part or whole on the development of a relationship between a male and a female character which has not to do with friendship, but with love and mate selection. Those characters who are young and in potential search of a mate or love interest provide some of the most interesting material in these films overall. There has been much commentary in the popular press on the physical portrayal of young men and women in extreme and unrealistic terms, for both sexes. Doe-eyed heroines with tiny waists and heroes with bulging necks and overly muscular thighs have been roundly criticized, with little effect. There is little or no discussion of the *language* spoken by lovers, however.[9]

In spite of the setting of the story or the individual's ethnicity, lovers speak mainstream varieties of US or British English (Table 5.4), with some interesting exceptions. Of the male characters in Table 5.4, only two can be said to be logically and certainly speakers of US English: Bernard, who

Table 5.4 Lovers and potential lovers in Disney animated films

Language variety	Film	Male	Female
Mainstream US	*Beauty and the Beast*	Gaston	(no mate)
		The Beast	Belle
	Rescuers	Bernard	—
	Rescuers Down Under	Bernard	—
	Cinderella	Prince Charming	Cinderella
	Sleeping Beauty	Prince Philip	Aurora
	Little Mermaid	Prince Erik	Ariel
	Snow White	Prince	Snow White
	Lion King	Simba	Nala
	Lady and the Tramp	—	Lady
Socially marked US	*Lady and the Tramp*	Jock	—
	Aristocats	O'Malley	—
Non-US English	*Robin Hood*	Robin Hood	Maid Marion
	Rescuers Down Under	Jake	(no mate)
	101 Dalmations	Pongo	Perdita
		Roger Radcliff	Anita Radcliff
Foreign-accented English	*Rescuers*	—	Miss Bianca
	Rescuers Down Under	—	Miss Bianca
	Aristocats	—	Duchess

appears twice (*The Rescuers* and *The Rescuers Down Under*), and Jock (*Lady and the Tramp*). All the other characters would be speakers of British or Australian English, or of languages other than English. The languages of the four princes (from *Cinderella*, *Snow White*, *Sleeping Beauty*, and *The Little Mermaid*) are debatable: the Disney version never specifies where these magical kingdoms are located (whether in the country of the story's origin or elsewhere).

Two of the male romantic leads speak socially marked varieties of US English: in *The Aristocats*, O'Malley (voiced by Phil Harris, a popular entertainer and singer of his day and cast on the power of voice recognition) does nothing to change or disguise his own English, which is rich in those characteristics which are often thought of as "working class" (simplified consonant clusters, double-negative constructions, and other stigmatized phonological and grammatical features). This is also the case with Jock from *Lady and the Tramp*. Both of these characters are prototypical rough lovers, men with an edge who need the care and attention of good women to settle them, and both are rewarded with such mates – females who speak non-stigmatized varieties – because they prove themselves worthy. There are no male romantic leads with foreign accents.

There is even less variation among the female romantic leads. There are no rough, working-class equivalents of O'Malley and Jock. In fact, of the seven females who speak MUSE, only one is an unambiguous case of a character who would logically speak US English: Lady of *Lady and the Tramp*. The use of a typical or logical language for the part and background of the character is clearly less important in this case than a consistent portrayal of an ideal lover and potential mate which stresses the lack of "otherness."

However, there are two female characters (one of whom occurs in two movies, *The Rescuers* and *The Rescuers Down Under*) with foreign accents, but they are both voiced by the same woman, Eva Gabor. The Gabor sisters were widely known and recognized in US culture in the 1950s and 1960s for their glamor and demanding behavior in many highly publicized affairs with rich men. They were recognizable on the basis of their Hungarian accents, and they brought with them a set of associations about sexually aware and available females that resulted in typecasting. The roles that Eva Gabor voiced for Disney were thus of elegant, demanding, and desirable females, and could be seen not so much as characters with foreign accents as one of the Gabor sisters in full costume. Perhaps Disney's hope that the public would associate the character on the screen with the public image of the actress voicing the part overrode more logical considerations. It was noted by at least one critic, however, that it made little sense to have the character of *The Aristocats'* Duchess, a pure-bred Persian cat living in France, speaking with a Hungarian accent.

Table 5.5 The language of mothers and fathers in Disney animated films

Language	Mothers	Fathers
MUSE	15	8
Socially marked US	0	0
Regionally marked US	0	1
Mainstream British	2	8
Socially or regionally marked		
British or other English	2	4
Foreign-accented English	1	1

To be truly sexually attractive and available in a Disney film, a character must not only look the idealized part, but he or she must also sound white and middle-class American or British.

In a similar way, mothers and fathers are most likely to have mainstream accents of US or British English, again with some interesting exceptions. As seen in Table 5.5, only two of these characters speak English with a foreign accent, although what would follow logically from the story setting is that eleven of these mothers and fathers would not be native speakers of English. Another thirteen characters appear in stories where the logical language might or might not be English. This applies particularly to the retelling of fairy tales in magical kingdoms (*Cinderella, Sleeping Beauty, The Little Mermaid*).[10] The two foreign accents which are evident are Gepetto's (contrived) Italian-accented English in *Pinocchio*, and once again Eva Gabor as the glamorous Duchess in *The Aristocats*. The only US-English-speaking father character with an accent which might be stigmatized is Gramps of *The Rescuers*, who is part of a larger group of stereotypical southerners with contrived accents.

Eva Gabor's voicing of the Duchess is the only instance in any of the movies where a mother takes on a romantic lead. Otherwise, in Disney movies parenthood and romance do not intersect. However, there are a great number of single-parent families overall. Of the twenty mothers, nine are widows or become widows in the course of the story, or have no husband in evidence; five are step- or substitute mothers and are unmarried; and in two cases the question of paternity is never raised, perhaps because it could not be answered in a way Disney considered suitable for children's entertainment. This is the case in *The Aristocats*, but more particularly in *The Lion King*, where Mufasa is the undisputed dominant male of his pride, and would thereby have fathered both Simba and Nala, who grow into adulthood and become mates. The fathers, in a similar way, are often widowers or simply without wives: this is the case for eleven of the twenty-two.

There are few married couples with major roles in any film. Mr. and Mrs. Darling make only small appearances in *Peter Pan*, which is also the case for the mother and father in *Lady and the Tramp* and for Colonel Hardy and his wife Winifred in *The Jungle Book*.

Perhaps most interesting is the fact that mothers who speak non-US varieties of English have a little more latitude in social and regional variation in their language. This may be because the non-mainstream varieties of British English are not poorly thought of by US English speakers, who do not distinguish, for the most part, between stigmatized varieties of British English (Geordie, Midlands, Cockney, etc.) and those with more social currency.

Lovers in Disney films marry, and sometimes at a very tender age. But young or middle-aged married couples with growing families are seldom if ever seen. And while young lovers are presented in idealized form both physically and linguistically, in later life stages these same kinds of characters are not quite so narrowly drawn. The picture of motherhood portrayed in these animated films excludes careers and work outside family and home, and clings very closely to language varieties associated with middle-class norms and values. When seen at all, mothers are presented without a hint of ethnicity, regional affiliation, color, or economics. Fathers, often comic or droll characters, have in their language (as in work, preoccupations and interests) a wider set of choices available to them.

Francophilia Limited

It is not hard to elicit stereotypes of the French, because this is not a national origin group which is seen in negative terms. Because there are good – or neutral – things to say, it is perhaps easier to say them:

> despite, or possibly because of, their civilized natures, the French people retain a childish eagerness for fun and frivolity as well as for knowledge. There is an impishness about many of them which is captivating. They are curious, like most children, and this curiosity leads them into experimenting with such things as piquant sauces for food . . . it can be said of the French . . . that when they are good, they are very, very good – but when they are bad, they are – Apaches.
>
> (Herman and Herman 1943: 143)

Aside from the clearly racist final comment which has to do not with the French, but with a Native American tribe, this view of the nation is not overtly negative. It is condescending, certainly, and narrow, but it does not call France a nation of idiots or a kingdom of evil (as the Herman and Herman volume does not hesitate to do in other cases).

There are two films which are set directly in France: *The Aristocats* and *Beauty and the Beast*, with a total of thirty-eight characters appearing in both stories. There is a wide range of characterizations, excessively evil and good, moody, generous, silly, drunken. Male characters include lawyers,

Lumiere and Feather Duster from *Walt Disney Pictures'* animated feature *Beauty and the Beast*; © Disney Enterprises, Inc.

Sebastian and Louis from *Walt Disney Pictures'* animated feature *The Little Mermaid*; © Disney Enterprises, Inc.

Table 5.6 Characters with French-accented English in Disney animated films

Setting	Character	Role	Film
France	Lumiere	maitre d', steward	*Beauty and the Beast*
	Stove	chef	
	Cherie	chambermaid	
	Unnamed	milkman	*Aristocats*
	Unnamed	chef	
Elsewhere	Louis	chef	*Little Mermaid*
	Unnamed	waiter	*Rescuers*

aristocrats, barkeepers, vagabonds, inventors, booksellers, hunters, and servants. *Beauty and the Beast* takes place in an active, busy rural village; *The Aristocats* primarily in Paris. There are children and old people, lovers and villains. Of all these thirty-eight very diverse characters, all of whom would logically be speaking French, there are a total of five who indicate this by contriving a French-accented English. In other films, two additional characters appear with French accents, as seen in Table 5.6.

Of these seven characters, one is female (Cherie, a feather duster), and her primary purpose seems to be as a romantic foil for the character Lumiere; her only line, having been pursued behind the draperies by him, is "Oh no! I've been burnt by you before!" There are other beautiful and charming women and girls in *Beauty and the Beast*, but none of them are coquettish, and none of them have French accents. The subtle but unmistakable message is quite a simple one: there may logically be thirty-eight characters before us who are French, but the truly French, the prototypical French, are those persons associated with food preparation or presentation, or those with a special talent for lighthearted sexual bantering. If a personality is established at all, there are two basic personality types available to them: irascible (the chef in *The Little Mermaid*, and his counterpart in *The Aristocats*); and the sensual rascal.

Is this a terrible picture to give children? After all, there are no truly "French" – linguistically, culturally, truly French – characters who are criminal, who threaten children, who are lazy or conniving. But there are also no French who are surgeons, rock singers, who teach school or drive a cab, or who are elderly. Rich people and aristocrats, in France or elsewhere, speak with British accents no matter what their logical language. The domain of life experience for things French is as narrow, if not as overtly negative, as that for AAVE speakers.

The cultural stereotypes for specific national origin groups are perpetuated in a systematic way in these stories created for, and viewed primarily by, children.

Summary

Close examination of the distributions indicates that these animated films provide material which links language varieties associated with specific national origins, ethnicities, and races with social norms and characteristics in non-factual and sometimes overtly discriminatory ways. Characters with strongly positive actions and motivations are overwhelmingly speakers of socially mainstream varieties of English. Conversely, characters with strongly negative actions and motivations often speak varieties of English linked to specific geographical regions and marginalized social groups. Perhaps even more importantly, those characters who have the widest variety of life choices and possibilities available to them are male, and they are speakers of MUSE or a non-stigmatized variety of British English. These characters may be heroes or villains, human or animal, attractive or unattractive. For females, on the other hand, and for those who mark their alliance to other cultures and places in terms of language, the world is demonstrably a smaller place. The more "negatives" a character has to deal with (gender, color, stigmatized language, less favorable national origin) the smaller the world. Even when stereotyping is not overtly negative, it is confining and misleading.

THAT'S ENTERTAINMENT

Disney films are not the only way in which we perpetuate stereotypes on the basis of language. The manipulation of language variety and accent to draw character is an old tool, but it is seldom a completely benign one. Stereotyping is prevalent in television programming and movies: situation comedies (*Beverley Hillbillies, I Love Lucy, Sanford and Son, All in the Family, Molly Goldberg, American Girl, Ma and Pa Kettle, Green Acres, Andy Griffith*) in particular provide numerous examples, which need to be examined more closely.

Language and accent as symbols of greater social conflict are also found in serious dramatic efforts, on television and film. The 1993 film *Falling Down* provides a disturbing example. In that film, a middle-class worker portrayed as beleaguered by inner-city life loses his temper with an irascible convenience-store clerk; the episode begins when the protagonist asks the price of an item. The following is from the script:

The proprietor, a middle-aged ASIAN, reads a Korean newspaper . . . the Asian has a heavy accent . . .

ASIAN: eighdy fie sen.
D-FENS: What?
ASIAN: eighdy fie sen.
D-FENS: I can't understand you . . . I'm not paying eighty-five cents for a stinking soda. I'll give you a quarter. You give me seventy "fie"

cents back for the phone ... What is a fie? There's a "V" in the word. Fie-vuh. Don't they have "v's" in China?

ASIAN: Not Chinese, I am Korean.

D-FENS: Whatever. What differences does that make? You come over here and take my money and you don't even have the grace to learn to speak my language ...

(Smith 1992: 7–8)

Here, accent becomes a very convenient and fast way to draw on a whole series of very emotional social issues, and all of them in a spirit of conflict, from immigration and the rights and responsibilities thereof, to greater issues of dominance and subservience, race and economics. The scene is very believable; many have had or observed such exchanges. The protagonist, clearly a man on the edge of socially acceptable behavior, is also portrayed as someone pushed to that edge by the pressures of inner-city life. He is overtly cruel and condescending and racist; but, somehow, he is also seen as not completely wrong.

In this film, a foreign accent becomes the signal of what has gone wrong with us as a nation, and his dismay and his anger, while excessive, are cast as understandable. From Charlie Chan to this owner of a corner store, our understanding of Asians – all Asians – has been reduced to a series of simple images. They are inscrutable, hard-working, ambitious, intelligent but unintelligible people, and they make us uncomfortable. I will return to the way that Asians and Asian-accent English are perceived in Chapter 11.

Even films which are made specifically for the purpose of illuminating and exploring racial and other kinds of social injustice are not free of the very subtle effects of standard language ideology. A close examination of Spielberg's *Schindler's List* (1993) shows a great deal of consistency in the use of accent: "The accents of individuals reflect their position in World War II Poland. That is, German characters are given – by and large – German accents, and Jewish characters generally possess Yiddish accents" (Goldstein 1995: 1). Even here, however, the suppression of variation for some characters has been noted, this time falling along lines not of color or religion, but of gender. In an initial exploration, Goldstein found that the more sexually available and attractive a female character was, the less distinctive her accent.

> Following this pattern, the German women who were wives and mistresses – and therefore the most sexually available women in the movie – did not have strong German accents [while] the older and less attractive Jewish women had heavier and thicker Yiddish accents ... linguistic accent seems to be part of what is deemed attractive about [some] women.
>
> (1995: 6)

These patterns held true for males as well: conservative Jews had stronger Yiddish accents; the worst of the prison guards, brutish Nazis, had the heaviest German accents (ibid.). It seems that even the highest standards in film making cannot be free of the social construction of language. And perhaps there is nothing that can or should be done about this process in its subtlest form. It is, after all, part of the social behavior which is of interest to art as the representation of the human condition.

What children learn from the entertainment industry is to be comfortable with *same* and to be wary about *other*, and that language is a prime and ready diagnostic for this division between what is approachable and what is best left alone. For adults, those childhood lessons are reviewed daily.

6   The educational system
Fixing the message in stone

"There's no use trying," she said: "one can't believe impossible things."

"I daresay you haven't had much practice," said the Queen. "When I was your age, I always did it for half-an-hour a day. Why, sometimes I've believed as many as six impossible things before breakfast."

Lewis Carroll, *Through the Looking-Glass* (1872)

Children have never been very good at listening to their elders, but they have never failed to imitate them.

James Baldwin

Built on the cornerstone of literacy, education is commonly understood to be the key to success of all kinds. We envision our school system as the place where children learn to *read and write* above all other things. Of course, schools do much more than this. The majority of children are educated in state-run and financed schools, where attendance is mandatory and the curriculum requires study of local and national history and government, among other subjects. In general, schools are seen as responsible for turning out a productive body of capable, literate citizens. Beyond that, it is the job of the educators to make sure that those citizens constitute an informed electorate, one which will accept and perpetuate the values of the nation-state.[1] The National Council of Teachers of English (NCTE) clearly links goals in literacy to those of citizenship: "Standards [in language arts education] can help us ensure that all students become informed citizens and participate fully in society" (1996: 4). The primary educational goal in our schools brings together the acquisition of *literacy* with the acceptance and acknowledgement of a *Standard US English*.

It is important to note that teaching is a difficult profession, a particularly challenging and highly responsible one. It is populated by people who are for the most part deeply dedicated, who truly wish to do well for the children in their charge. What follows in this chapter is an examination of the professed goals of educators in as far as they address language issues, and how language ideology affects those goals in both

Figure 6.1 The University of Pennsylvania Writing Center advertisement

abstract and concrete ways, in the classroom. This is not a frontal attack on the crucial but undervalued profession of teaching, but a consideration of how inequality and disadvantage are perpetuated – for the most part unwittingly – in the teaching of *language arts*.

Language ideology and policy issues in education fall into two distinct areas: language skills curricula (what to do with the child who comes to school speaking AAVE, Appalachian English, British West Indian English, Sea Islands Creole, Gullah, Mexicano English, Hawai'ian Creole English, among many others, or no English at all; the relationship between spoken language and literacy; what literatures and cultures should be represented, etc.); and a less commonly discussed or public issue, the language of teachers themselves. Here I will look at the issue of mainstream and non-mainstream language conflicts and policies, with examples from a number of school systems to see how ideology focuses and sometimes directs decision making. I will also consider the issue of the language of the teachers themselves. This second issue will be taken up again in Chapter 8, which deals with cases where teachers have sued their schools and school districts for language-focused discrimination under Title XII of the Civil Rights Act. Before we look at specific cases, however, it is important to look at some of the more general issues in education.

APPROPRIACY ARGUMENTS

Almost everyone has anecdotes about language arts instruction from their elementary school education which underscore a system-wide adherence to standard language ideology. One source of more concrete evidence is provided quite openly in texts written for teachers and children.

> Almost any sentence or sentence fragment may be acceptable in casual conversation. In more formal speaking and writing, however, nonstand-ard grammar is rarely acceptable. We need to know how to speak and write in complete, grammatical sentences that convey our thoughts clearly to others.
>
> (Ragno *et al.* 1987: T22)

> [This series of textbooks] focuses on grammar study, listening and speaking skills, and correct usage.
>
> (Strickland 1983: T21)

> Practice saying the following combinations of words. Avoid slurring any sounds, such as *whacha* for *what do you*. . . . *Whip* is pronounced *hwip*, not *wip* . . . pronounce the following troublesome words correctly. Consult the dictionary if you are in doubt. . . . Twenty-five words often misspelled because of faulty pronunciation: *busy, which, since, history* . . .
>
> (John *et al.* 1975: 28–29)

The most striking feature of these excerpts, and of many other school-related incidents around language, is an inability or perhaps even an unwillingness to keep separate the written and spoken languages. This is a problem which persists at all educational levels. Clarity of thought is linked directly to clarity of written language. The NCTE, together with the International Reading Association (IRA) regularly reviews and publishes *Standards for the English Language Arts*, a twelve-point list which emphasizes reading and comprehending skills to such an extent that spoken-language skills are referred to only three times. In this view of education, children are potentially productive members of *literacy communities* rather than language communities (NCTE 1996: 3).

In the textbook passages quoted above there is a grudging acknowledgement that languages other than MUSE exist: *Almost any sentence or sentence fragment may be acceptable in casual conversation*. This is a weak but quite clear evocation of the appropriacy arguments which are at the bottom of so many policies on language in the classroom and school. Sometimes referred to as communicative competence (a term first coined by anthropological linguists, but appropriated by educational theorists), appropriacy arguments rationalize the process by which languages of peripheralized or stigmatized groups are simultaneously acknowledged and rejected.[2] If there is no logical or reasonable authority for the identification of one variety of spoken English as superior or standard, then by extension there can be no reasonable way to declare one variety exclusively appropriate for some situations. The way that appropriacy judgements serve as a cover for culturally bound judgements of "correctness" might be made more clear by the contrast between two statements:

1 It is inappropriate for a law student to ask a question in Hawai'ian Creole English.
2 It is inappropriate for a wife to contradict her husband.

While the second statement was once unremarkable, it would now evoke resounding criticism in most quarters. The first statement might still pass without comment, although the underlying issue, silencing of voices considered unworthy or unequal, is the same. To question the first statement in the US educational system is to question the primacy of one language variety over all others.

At the same time, it is important to remember that ideologies and social strategies for the limitation of one language over another are not limited to one segment of the population. The following statements indicate that the concept of appropriacy has a wider, and quite relevant, place in the discussion of the distribution of language varieties over social space:

1 A child who is a native speaker of Hawai'ian Creole English may be criticized in the classroom for using his or her home language rather than MUSE.

2 A child who is a native speaker of Hawai'ian Creole English may be criticized at the dinner table for using MUSE rather than his or her family's home language.

Communities which employ stigmatized languages enforce their own loyalties, based on different priorities and issues of solidarity different from those of the mainstream language community. Minority-language-community ideologies are just as interesting as the ideologies and strategies of the dominant bloc institutions, and both are worthy of study. Individuals caught between competing ideologies must learn to deal with this "push-pull," a topic which will be raised at some length in Part III.

In the present discussion, I am interested in the way that appropriacy reasoning, based for the most part in common-sense arguments without factual or logical basis, functions as the mainstay of much educational policy on language instruction and use. Fairclough provides an example of such reasoning from the Cox Report on the state of English instruction in British schools, which demonstrates that use of the appropriacy argument is very widespread:

> Pupils need to be able to discuss the contexts in which Standard English is obligatory and those where its use is preferable for social reasons. By and large, the pressures in favour of Standard English will be greater when the language is written, formal and public. Non-standard forms may be much more widely tolerated and, in some cases, preferred when the language is spoken, informal and private.
>
> (Fairclough 1992a: 37)

A statement very similar in tone demonstrates how alike British and US educational systems are:

> Biloquialism calls for the learning of new, standard patterns without eliminating the old nonstandard ones. Often called bidialectalism or biculturalism (as parallels to bilingualism), this position attempts to provide mainstream linguistic and cultural resources to nonmainstream speakers, while avoiding negative attitudes toward nonmainstream cultures and dialects. The goal of this kind of instruction is to enable students to switch from one linguistic style to another, guided by a sense of appropriateness to the context in which the language is used. Since all speakers, mainstream and nonmainstream alike, shift among more or less formal styles, depending on context, to some degree, this position should be a relatively natural one. It also has the advantage of appearing to be the most reasonable position, presenting a compromise between the two more extreme positions of eradication and appreciation of dialect differences.
>
> (Farr 1991: 366–367)

On the surface, these policies seem to be conciliatory: do not deny the home language of the student; instead, redirect the student's use of that language to those environments and circumstances in which it is appropriate. At the same time, the student must be given another language – a mainstream US English – for those situations in which it will be the only socially acceptable language.

The NCTE has recently softened the language around appropriacy in its *Standards for the English Language Arts* guidelines:

> Students adjust their use of spoken, written, and visual language (e.g. conventions, style, vocabulary) to communicate effectively with a variety of audiences and for different purposes ... students develop an understanding of and respect for diversity in language use, patterns, and dialects across cultures, ethnic groups, geographic regions, and social roles.
>
> (1996: 4)

The division between public and private language is elaborated more specifically in a discussion of language "in context":

> All of us who speak English speak different varieties of English depending on whom we are communicating with, the circumstances involved, the purpose of the exchange, and other factors. Indeed, creative and communicative powers are enhanced when students develop and maintain multiple language competencies.
>
> Nonetheless, some varieties of English are more useful than others for higher education, for employment, and for participation in what the Conference on College Composition and Commmunication (1993) in a language policy statement calls "the language of wider communication." Therefore, while we respect diversity in spoken and written English, we believe that all students should learn this language of wider communication.
>
> (1996: 22–23)

While the vocabulary has changed, the message remains the same, and typically schizophrenic: appreciate and respect the languages of peripheral communities, but keep them in their place. Here, "standard" has been replaced with the longer formulation "language of wider communication." As has always been the case, the divide between socially stigmatized and sanctioned language runs along very predictable lines: non-mainstream varieties of US English should be restricted to the home and neighborhood, to play and informal situations, to the telling of folktales and stories of little interest to the *wider* world. While this kind of rationalization is used in a variety of settings and in relationship to a great many peripheralized languages (as will be seen below and in other parts of this book), it is perhaps most often evoked in educational debates around AAVE. Drake examines the history and motivation of educational bidialectalism for blacks and notes both the commonly cited logic for this stance and the underlying rhetoric:

> The teacher grants [the validity of AAVE in communicative terms] yet assigns the use of standard to all socially important roles, telling the students in effect: "Your native dialect is fine for home use and for activities in the ghetto, but when you try to achieve anything in school or in the larger culture, use the standard I'm trying to teach you." This "separate but equal" doctrine is a familiar one to Blacks, and we may be sure that many read the covert message it bears.
>
> (1977a: 94)

Unfortunately, it seems that few do in fact recognize the "separate but equal" message embedded in appropriacy arguments. This is partially because for many individuals, it is not readily apparent that the two varieties of English are in fact equal in linguistic terms. With both feet firmly planted on the false assumptions of the standard language ideology and the literacy myth, the teacher is adamant in the need to weed out the bad language and replace it with the good. To give children what they really need, these educators believe, they must supply them with a currency they don't have: Standard English, which is defined only by default; it is not what these children speak. What is more disturbing than this reliance on the idealized Standard, however, is the way in which non-mainstream languages are devalued. Both the British and the US policies draw strong distinctions: Standard English is preferred, obligatory, appropriate, widely used, while the Other Languages are narrow, inappropriate, and even *tolerated*. Farr (1991) labels *appreciation* of such languages as an extremism. Fairclough points out particularly this formulation in the Cox Report ("Non-standard forms may be much more widely tolerated") as the stroke which "lifts the veil on a tradition of prescriptive bigotry towards non-standard varieties which is largely absent from the Report" (1992a: 37).

Prominent school adminstrators are not hesitant to put forward appropriacy arguments in public, as was the case with the head of the Philadelphia School Board, an African American woman, in explaining why it was necessary to "drum Standard English into the heads" of AAVE speakers:

> In the process of young people applying for jobs, employers would ask them a question which would elicit a response, "I bees ready for coming here next week." This ... um ... utilization of the word and insertion of *bees* is rampant and I think really throws an employer off in terms of what the young person's talking about. "Uh, now that you're finished with me I *bees* going home." ... If we relegate them only to that narrow, limited, provincial dimension of life and language, we do them a disservice because I see that they will not go beyond the

borderlines of their immediate neighborhood. And we have no right to do that to any child.

(McCrum and MacNeil 1986, broadcast)

The misinformation used here is not uncommon: while AAVE invariant "be" is one of those points of contrast between AAVE and other varieties of English which elicits a lot of negative response, it is quite silly to claim that it would cause a breakdown in understanding among speakers of English. What this administrator is saying, however, is that employers would have a negative emotive reaction to this usage which may well cause them to reject their fair share of the communicative burden. This is almost certainly true. From this, her logic follows, it is necessary to eradicate this grammatical feature and all of AAVE in favor of the language – and the prejudice – of the employer. Here AAVE is narrow, limited, provincial – by which she means restricted to inner-city Philadelphia. This kind of appropriacy rhetoric can be found again and again across the country in arguments for the subordination of languages and language varieties out of social favor. Sometimes the argument is that the subordinated language must be eradicated (as in the Philadelphia case); at other times the message is softened by arguments for supplementation in the form of an uneven bilingualism, a separate-but-equal language policy which relegates home languages to the peripheral and disposable.

In contrast, a Massachusetts teacher of Puerto Rican students makes no economic argument at all, but one which is purely ideological:

> These poor kids come to school speaking a hodge podge. They are all mixed up and don't know any language well. As a result, they can't even think clearly. That's why they don't learn. It's our job to teach them language – to make up for their deficiency. And, since their parents don't really know any language either, why should we waste time on Spanish? It is "good" English which has to be the focus.
>
> (Walsh 1991: 107; cited in Zentella 1996: 8–9)

In this second approach, a teacher has effectively summarized all of the conclusions drawn from Bernstein's theories of restricted and elaborated codes: speakers of non-mainstream language don't possess sufficient human language to think or reason, and must be helped to overcome these language and cultural handicaps. The fact that Bernstein's theories and the resulting pedagogical innovations based on them were thoroughly and resoundingly debunked as long ago as 1969 with Labov's "Logic of Non-Standard English" is an indication of how seductive such rhetoric can be in an educational setting. Is it not easier to approach language as a one-size-fits-all proposition? If there is only one proper language for the children in our care, and only one proper variety of that language – which happens to be the teacher's language – then it becomes easy, even prudent, to dismiss the work that comes along with making teaching a dialogue rather than a lecture.

Yet another variation on the complex set of rationalizations around subordinating language is seen in the essay "Standard English vs. 'The American Dream'" (Winsboro and Solomon 1990) which consolidates appropriateness and economic arguments with assimilationist rhetoric:

> While we must continue to manifest pluralistic approaches to integrating Black English into the curriculum, as necessary, we must simultaneously teach those who speak with a dialect that a realistic chance of success in American society is frequently based on mastery of Standard English.
>
> Studies consistently demonstrate that educators manifest a generally negative reaction to the "less familiar dialect" in favor of Standard English. Black educators themselves have long recognized the possible socioeconomic disadvantages of speaking a black dialect in a predominantly white society.
>
> There is empirically based evidence of teacher bias against black students, and it is obvious that listeners may not limit their criteria for judgment strictly to quantifiable data. Furthermore, if students are labeled as less capable and are then treated as such, they will probably begin to display characteristics of those who indeed are less capable of speaking and writing formal English. Unfortunately, the subjects of this pattern are the most likely candidates for code expressions such as "slow learner," "learning disabled," "intellectually impaired," or "not a strong potential candidate."
>
> Evidence clearly suggests that speakers of Black English are presented with more obstacles to success than are speakers of Standard English. This phenomenon permeates the educational institutions and lay communities as well. It affects not only speakers of Black English, but ultimately society at large, for it is often a perceived lack of effective communications that can deprive society of contributions from all its members. Conversely, it is not in society's best interest to eliminate nonstandard dialects, for that would destroy an important cultural heritage of 12 percent of the American melting pot.
>
> On the other hand, a realistic appraisal of the American Dream reveals that upward mobility is the fountainhead from which most societal successes flow. This vertical mobility process itself is most likely to occur when speakers of Black English complete an education and aculuration process through which they acquire and manifest speech patterns perceived by the dominant group as being necessary for, and indicative of, its high standards of achievement. In short, the mastery of Standard English almost uniformly is a prerequisite to upward mobility because those who shape our society historically have exercised a tight control over entry to prestigious and remunerative positions. . . . *Today's educators may find it prudent to move toward a greater appreciation for the sociocultural limitations of Black English.* Much of

our nation's future depends on our ability as a people to confront antipluralist views and to convert these views into new positive streams of cultural awareness and achievement. This will occur most readily as educators at all levels strongly promote both intercultural standards and a meaningful approach to "making it" in American society. This is a sensitive and controversial issue for educators, yet it is an approach that will give students an education that is not only inspiring but truly "realistic" as well.

(51–52; emphasis added)

The reasoning here is unapologetically racist. Teachers discriminate against AAVE speakers; this is a sad but demonstrable fact. Another fact, and one which is hard to counter: in such an atmosphere of rejection, no child can thrive. But the conclusion which comes from these two facts, while presented as common sense and logical, is in fact logical only in as far as one accepts the underlying premise of linguistic superiority and the primacy of economic motivations.

FACT: Language A and Language B are equal in linguistic and cultural terms.
⇓
FACT: Language B is rejected by teachers and employers.
⇓
FACT: Rejection has a negative effect on the speakers of Language B.
⇓
CONCLUSION: Language B must be discarded in favor of Language A.

The teachers writing this essay never even discuss an alternate conclusion: *Teachers and employers must learn to accept Language B*. The facts of language subordination are inviolate: The teacher discriminates because the employer does; the child pays the price of that discrimination by accommodating and assimilating. The only way to achieve pluralistic goals, we are told, is to make everyone alike. In any confrontation between the powered and the disempowered, it is never the disempowered who must give way in the resolution of conflict. This essay, with its melting-pot images (diversity in; homogeneity out), tries to straddle the fence, praising the ideals of multiculturalism and pluralistic educational values, while it rejects diversity.

A wide variety of rationalization strategies for the peripheralization and exclusion of non-mainstream language are commonly heard in educational settings. The fact is that these tactics work, and they work well.

THE RESULTS OF APPROPRIACY ARGUMENTATION

By the time they finish their elementary education, most children are firm believers in the appropriacy argument. If they are native speakers of a language other than MUSE, they will willingly tell anyone who asks what is wrong with their own language and that they are uncomfortable with it. "The more you get into [learning MUSE]," says a student in South Carolina, "the more I realize not how bad I sound but how much better I could sound." (ABC Evening News, December 15, 1991). "I don't want my accent to hurt my self-esteem anymore," says a native speaker of Spanish. "I know I can get my point across in English, but I don't want to feel uncomfortable every time I say something" (Hernandez 1993: 1). In a series of studies using matched-guise testing, Carranza and Ryan (1975) showed that African American, Anglo, and Hispanic students all found Spanish-accented English to be lacking in prestige and inappropriate for a classroom setting; in Ryan *et al.* (1977) "Small increments in accentedness were found to be associated with gradually less favorable ratings of status, solidarity, and speech characteristics" (summarized by Eisenstein 1983: 173).

In the teaching of language, there is a very striking division between educational psychologists and theorists, on the one side, and boards of education and classroom teachers on the other. The NCTE circulates a publication list to its 90,000 members which includes titles such as *Kids Come in All Languages* (Spangenberg-Urbschat and Pritchard 1994) and "Students' Right to Their Own Language" (NCTE 1974). For the most part these are well-balanced reports on those factual issues which should be clear to every teacher involved in language instruction. In spite of the availablity of such resources, however, the language arts classroom is one of the best places to watch the way the languages outside the mainstream are subordinated by means of misinformation, trivialization, and a carefully constructed set of threats and promises.

It must be pointed out, however, that on occasion discussions around appropriacy are not ideology motivated, but have to do with factual observations of how the social contract around style switching in the community is coded. If one child threatens to break another child's head for the sin of touching a toy, I may tell the child that both the language and the wish that it expresses are inappropriate – by which I mean, unacceptable. I do not doubt that these are the true feelings of the child, but I will try to redirect her anger in a way which is not destructive. If one person addresses a lover in an intimate situation in the same way he or she would in a boardroom discussion of a financial policy, this is either humor or – as the lover might well perceive it – inappropriate to the situation. Again, the lover would reject or correct language that makes him or her uncomfortable because the associations it brings forth conflict with the setting and mood.

Appropriacy must be accepted on some level in education, but it is crucial that we recognize and *acknowledge* the value system underlying the messages we give children. Is it appropriate to speak Louisiana Creole in an interview? We can state with some certainty that the employer will have a negative reaction toward this language, but to call the use of the language inappropriate is to become complicit in the process of rejection.

It is not so much the term "appropriate" which is the problem but the way it is used, sometimes very subtly, to support and propagate ideological ends.[3]

In the following sections, I will look at two sets of issues. The first has to do with attempts to suppress minority languages and varieties of English in the schools, and the political aspects of those attempts. The second concerns measures to keep teachers with stigmatized accents out of the classroom.

GOOD ENOUGH ENGLISH

In the second half of the last century, the government was hard-pressed to find some kind of lasting resolution for the ongoing conflicts with the continent's indiginous peoples. Disease, warfare, and systematic routing had reduced the great variety of native cultures to a handful. Tribes that were not wiped out entirely wcre decimated often to less than 10 percent of their original numbers (Stannard 1992). By the mid-nineteenth century, the Native American diaspora and the accelerated western push by European Americans had increased pressure to find a lasting solution. A remedy was needed which moved beyond the writing of treaties which the US government drew up and signed, but ignored at whim.

In a series of policy statements written between 1868 and 1887, the Federal Commissioner of Indian Affairs put down a very clear strategy which involved moving away from traditional warfare to a policy which depended on forcibly breaking up family and tribal units to speed up the process of assimilation. Very astutely, the commissioner pinpointed the matter of language as crucial. Without tribal languages which functioned as the primary marker of social identity and provided a cohesive force in the face of so much turmoil, the indiginous peoples could be more easily drawn into the fold:

> The white and Indian must mingle together and jointly occupy the country, or one of them must abandon it . . . by educating the children of these tribes in the English language these differences would have disappeared, and civilization would have followed at once. Nothing then would have been left but the antipathy of race, and that, too, is always softened in the beams of a higher civilization . . . through sameness of language is produced sameness of sentiment, and thoughts; customs and habits are molded and assimilated in the same way, and thus in process of time the differences producing trouble would have been gradually obliterated . . . in the difference of language to-day lies two-thirds of our trouble . . . schools should be established, which children should be required to attend; their barbarous dialects should be blotted out and the English language substituted. . . . The object of greatest solicitude should be to break down the prejudices of tribe among the

Indians; to blot out the boundary lines which divided them into distinct nations, and fuse them into one homogeneous mass. Uniformity in language will do this – nothing else will. . . . There is not an Indian pupil whose tuition and maintenance is paid for by the United States Government who is permitted to study any other language than our own vernacular – the language of the greatest, most powerful, and enterprising nationalities beneath the sun. The English language as taught in America is good enough for all her people of all races.

(Atkins 1887 as reproduced in Crawford 1992: 48–49)

Reading this passage, one might be pacified, somewhat, by its date. This was written over a hundred years ago, the argument might go. Surely, we must have a more democratic and fair-handed approach now. Are we not making slow progress on the rights of the continent's indigenous peoples?

In fact, at least in matters of language in some school districts, there does seem to be some progress in the way the indiginous peoples have claimed the right to determine educational language policies for themselves. New Mexico, in particular, has instituted procedures by which state educational adminstrators work together with tribal authorities to set up bilingual education policies acceptable to the tribal administration. This would seem to be a necessity in a state where 56 percent of the population between 5 and 17 years of age are non-native speakers of English (based on the 1980 census; Waggoner 1988: 90). As a part of these policies, the New Mexico Department of Education has worked together with the Pueblo Indian community, for example, to establish an assessment protocol for those Pueblos who teach in the bilingual education program (Sims 1992). Because each tribe has a different set of views on bilingual education, each designs its own program.[4] In a similar way, there are healthy and growing immersion schools for the Kanien'kehaka (Mohawk) – primarily in Canada – where policy and curriculum are directed exclusively by and for that language community.

But these are questions of bilingualism, it must be pointed out, and since the first boarding school for Native Americans was opened at Carlisle in Pennsylvania, the language issue for Native Americans has become complicated by the development of distinct varieties of *English*, distinct both from tribal languages and the English of non-Native Americans. Thus, much like Mexican Americans, Native Americans are confronted with educational challenges of two types: bilingualism, and bidialectalism. Leap (1992) makes the salient point that for each Native American tribal language there is a distinct and functioning variety of English with phonological, morphological, syntactic, and discourse features specific to it (Box 6.1). This variety of English must be taken into consideration in the classroom, and *not just as an object to be replaced with another, less socially stigmatized and mainstream English*:

Whatever the connection between English and ancestral language fluency, we can understand why community members might want to retain control over a nonstandard, community-based English code, and why they might be reluctant for fluency in standard English to replace such language knowledge. Indian English, in each of its many occurrences, is closely tied to the "package" of historical, political, and psychological experiences that define tribal and community identity in contemporary American society. Fluency in these codes offers speakers a powerful means of representing and renewing these themes in every facet of daily experience.

(146)

Box 6.1 Some features of Indian English from the Northern Ute Reservation

---

- Devoiced (or "whispered") vowels in middle and final word position
- Tense marked only once per clause (e.g. on the helping verb or the main verb but not on both elements)
- Right-to-left arrangement within sentence-level constructions (e.g. the pronouns precede rather than follow their antecedents)

Source: Leap 1992: 144

The underlying motivations of language education policies are rarely overtly or obviously racist or eurocentric, and it is precisely for that reason that they work so well. Few would try to argue that there are unwritten policies which have as their goal the removal of children from their homes in order to raise them in boarding schools where they will learn to be "real" Americans. It would be difficult to show proof of conspiracy plots to turn Mexican children in Texas, Chinese children in San Francisco, Arabic children in Detroit, or AAVE-speaking children in Baltimore into something better by removing them from their families bodily or even emotionally. Those who insist on an educational policy which targets a standardized English for all children do so, they say quite clearly, for the children's welfare and future. We would like to believe that the more these children willingly submit to mainstreaming, the better the mainstream will treat them. The circular and faulty logic is rarely challenged.

The most commonly heard position on this issue of the appropriate language of education was summarized quite saliently by William J. Bennett, who served as Secretary of Education in the late 1980s:

Our origins are diverse. Yet we live together as fellow citizens, in harmony. ... Each of us is justly proud of his own ethnic heritage. But we share this pride, in common, as Americans, as American citizens. To be a citizen is to share in something common – common principles, common memories, and a common language in which to discuss our common affairs. Our common language is, of course, English. And our common task is to ensure that our non-English-speaking children learn this common language. ... We expect much of [our schools] – to impart basic skills, to help form character, to teach citizenship. And we expect our schools to help teach all of our students the common language that will enable them to participate fully in our political, economic, and social life.

(Bennett 1988 as cited in Crawford, ed., 1992: 358)

While there is neither time nor space to explore bilingual education in this volume, this is the place to focus on at least one aspect of this very complex and emotional issue. The debates around bilingual education seem to pose very simple questions:

- Should children be required to learn English, and learn in English, regardless of their own home languages and the primary languages of their communities?
- Can one policy – based on allegedly common views of the responsibilities of citizenship – be just for all students in all schools, whether the student is a native speaker of Navajo, Arabic, or Spanish?

These are crucial issues, but ones which seem to have found no resolution in spite of many years of debate and experimentation. However, one basic question has not been raised in this debate:

If by magic it were possible to make every school-aged child in the nation instantaneously bilingual, equally proficient in English and in their native language, would the problem of language in the school go away?

To begin considering the underlying complexities of this question, let's look at a policy proposed by the Board of Education of the State of Hawai'i in 1987, called *Standard English and Oral Communication*:

Standard English [shall] be the mode of oral communication for students and staff in the classroom setting and all other school related settings except when the objectives cover native Hawaiian or foreign language instruction and practice.

(cited in Sato 1991: 653)[5]

The issue here is not whether English should be the language of instruction, or the target of language instruction; the school board takes that as given. The issue is, instead, *which* variety of English is good enough for education. Not surprisingly, Standard English is not defined. Neither is the targeted *unacceptable* variety of English defined, but it could have been. Multiple newspaper accounts of the controversy which ensued from this proposal did not hesitate to name it:

Panel wants pidgin kept out of schools
Panel urges pidgin ban in schools
Board votes 7–4 to keep pidgin out of classroom[6]

Thus this proposal would have had the effect of outlawing Hawai'ian Creole English, or Pidgin, in the schoolroom. It would have, in addition, barred the language from playgrounds at recess, gymnasiums during basketball practice and cafeterias during lunch. It would have restricted the English spoken by the children and many of the teachers to one variety, "Standard English." While it is not possible to define what is meant by standard English – except by exclusion – it is possible to define Hawai'ian Creole English, and to get an idea of the people who would have been affected by such a policy.

Hawai'i is as multilingual a place as one could find in the United States. In addition to English, there are Hakka, Cantonese, Japanese, Korean, Tagalog, Ilocano, Cebuano, Hiligaynon, Portuguese, Spanish, and Samoan language communities which have been flourishing for many generations. There are also populations of immigrant workers.

The aboriginal Polynesian language of Hawai'i (*'Olelo Hawai'i*) was once the only one spoken in the islands; when Hawai'i came under the control and rule of the US, 'Olelo Hawai'i was systematically suppressed and finally outlawed. In 1978 'Olelo Hawai'i regained its status as one of the official languages of the state.[7] During the time that 'Olelo Hawai'i first came under attack and began its struggle for survival, another language took root and flourished. In the first decades of exchange between westerners and Hawai'ians, a pidgin, or contact language developed which was English based, but which drew heavily on the native 'Olelo Hawai'i and the Pacific Rim and Asian languages of immigrant fieldworkers. In time, this pidgin acquired native speakers and thus a new language came into being, which is called Hawai'ian Creole English (HCE), or more widely (and erroneously) *Pidgin*. It is also called *Da Kine*. The original pidgin language has become eclipsed by its logical evolution to HCE, a language which has continued to change and develop, as in the normal life cycle of all human languages. So that while 'Olelo Hawai'i was in true danger of extinction at several points and its ultimate fate is not yet clear, HCE is a healthy, but socially stigmatized, language spoken by some 600,000 people. Of these, 100,000 to 200,000 do not speak any other variety of English. This means that of the almost 1.3 million inhabitants of Hawai'i as of 1990, almost half speak HCE to some degree, and somewhere between 10 and 30 percent speak it as a primary language (Grimes 1992).

As is the case with creoles, HCE exists in various forms along a contiuum of most to least similar to the base language – in this case, English. On that end of the continuum where HCE has more in common with English, it is used in a wide variety of public settings; Grimes reports that it is commonly heard in the judicial system and is used there by officers, jurors, plaintiffs, and defendants, that it is used by some on radio and TV in public service announcements, and that there is a "growing body of serious literature, including poetry" (ibid.). In its basilectal form (where there is the least mutual intelligibility with English), HCE is spoken widely by persons of all ages and races, but it is more common among the poor and working class, which accounts in part for its stigmatization.[8]

The proposal by the school board in 1987, then, would have taken this well-established language spoken natively by more than half a million people and banned it from the school system and from the social life of all students in as far as that social life was connected in any way to schooling. Why was this language, of all the many languages spoken in Hawai'i, singled out for exclusion? While in Arizona legislatures may be debating bilingual education for native speakers of Apache and Spanish, and the role that English should play in the education of those children, in Hawai'i it occurs to the school board to ban a language which, on one end of the continuum, is mutually intelligible with English. Why?

During extensive public debate of this issue, a Honolulu newspaper conducted a survey of 986 graduating high-school seniors on this topic, and that report reveals how socially complex HCE is, and how closely tied it is to issues of economics and class:

> Whereas only 26 percent of the private school students surveyed felt that HCE use should be allowed in school, 54 percent of the public school students supported this area. . . . Comments ranged from "Pidgin English fosters illiteracy" "Pidgin is a lazy way to talk; it promotes backward thinking"; and "Correct English will get you anywhere" to the polar opposites of "banning pidgin would violate our freedom of speech"; "Pidgin is a natural language"; and "it's our way to make Hawai'i different from anywhere else in the United States."
>
> (Verploegen 1988 as cited by Sato 1991: 654; further citations omitted)

On Hawai'i's Waianae Coast, one of the areas of greatest concentrations of native Hawai'ians and of HCE speakers, an elementary school teacher further clarifies the connection to race. A native speaker of HCE herself, she does not hesitate to draw battle lines, with emotion and clarity:

> What we're finding is that children who appear to be pidgin speakers to the max, meaning it appears they can't speak anything else, those same children are sitting in front of the TV set every night or reading standard English, right? They are surrounded by it. These kids are bilingual.
>
> We'll never give pidgin up. We won't give it up because it means something to us. It means we're not holy, we're not standard English – we are people of color. We won't give up pidgin because we love it.
>
> (Drummond 1990, broadcast)

By legislating language in the schoolroom, the School Board hoped also to legislate world view, and a choice for status over solidarity.

Once again it becomes clear that the process of standardization and language subordination is concerned not so much with an overall homogeneity of language, but with excluding only *certain types* of language and variation, those linked to social differences which make us uncomfortable. By the simple expedient of substituting one language for another, we hope to neutralize social conflicts grounded in race, ethnicity, and social class. If this could be achieved, "Nothing then would [be] left but the antipathy of race, and that, too, is always softened in the beams of a higher civilization," hypothesized the Commissioner of Indian Affairs. While his methods would be seen as unacceptable today, the underlying sentiment remains.

In another state, this one in the southwest where native speakers of Spanish and a number of Native American languages attend schools, a proposal was put forth at a State Board of Education meeting in 1987 which echoes in many ways the actions of the Hawai'ian school board. This proposal was for a new competency standard which, had it been implemented, would have required that seventh graders "speak expressively through appropriate articulation, pronunciation, volume, rate, and intonation" before they were promoted to the eighth grade.[9]

In this case, the professional educators and administrators approached the issue by posing a number of thoughtful questions for themselves, questioning first the parameters of what would constitute "appropriate" accents:

> Can we establish an acceptable standard for children in all school districts in [the state]? Can we be assured that Hispanic, Native American, and Asian students will not be retained because of what may be considered an "unacceptable" pronunciation? What happens to children who do not master this competency? When will they receive needed attention to academic skills and conceptual development?

Administrators consulted a range of specialists in language and linguistics as well as education, and came to the conclusion that this proposed policy was ill conceived, summarizing their position quite simply: Accent is a minimal type of competency in relation to conceptual development and language use. "Rather, let us teach children to use language to expand intellectual development, to appreciate the richness of expression, and enrich lives by knowing what words to choose and use rather than how to pronounce them."

While this case took a reasonable ending, similar legislation and policies continue to be debated in other states. Stalker (1990: 64) reports that in the 1980s, bills requiring school systems "to determine which students do not use standard English, and to provide remedial work for them" were submitted multiple times and rejected each time, but *only because funding for testing and remedial work was not available.*

It is worthwhile to consider the mindset that allowed the question to be raised at all. We want the children of the United States to have a thorough command of English, but it is more than that. We are not satisfied with English as it lives and breathes, English with a Cuban accent, the English spoken off the coast of South Carolina, or Hawai'ian Creole English. We want good English, the one correct English. In the face of huge amounts of factual evidence that a homogenous and monolithic variety of perfect English does not and cannot exist, we still pursue this mythical beast as if it were the solution to all of our societal ills. One Good English, we feel, is the right of our school children, and the responsibility of their teachers.

TEACHER TALK

Formal expectations about teachers' language skills are easy enough to document. Each state has a complex administrative body which is responsible for reviewing and licensing teachers, and each publishes those guidelines openly. Guidelines for Michigan, New Mexico, California, and New York, for example, all have similar language about the native language skills of any teacher, which include phrases such as "demonstrates excellent skills of pronunciation and grammar" and "carries out instruction in content areas of the curriculum using a standard variety of the native language" (New Mexico guidelines effective July 1, 1989). Whether or not this latter expectation is realistic or enforceable is never addressed.

While the official pronunciation and accent test once administered by New York City to prospective teachers is no longer used, such policies have been employed elsewhere: in the 1970s, speakers of Chicano English were still failing the speech test required for teacher certification in California (Peñalosa 1981: 8). These tests may no longer be used (in part because of protections provided under Title VII of the Civil Rights Act, as seen in Chapter 8), but the mindset remains. Informal guidelines which are used to winnow teachers with stigmatized social and regional accents out of the teaching force are difficult, but not impossible, to document. In a telephone interview, a high-level administrator in a major eastern school district was quite candid, speaking on the matter of accent in the teaching force. He noted that in the evaluation of potential employees, there are different sets of expectations, so that

> if you are interviewing for a laboratory specialist who has no contact with the students, then you have lower expectations. An African-American accent would be more acceptable in a phys ed teacher for example than it would be in a teacher of speech.
>
> (Director of Evaluation Programs, interviewed June 1994)[10]

These issues rarely come to the attention of the public, unless the media takes interest in some particular case, as in the 1992 controversy around teachers with foreign accents in Westfield, Massachusetts, a town of about 36,000 people and a broad ethnic mix.[11]

In July of that year, a petition signed by 403 residents was presented to the school board in protest at a decision to reassign two bilingual education teachers to positions as regular classroom teachers. The petition specifically addressed the issue of accent, urging that no teacher be assigned to first- or second-grade classrooms "who is not thoroughly proficient in the English language in terms of grammar, syntax, and – most important – the accepted and standardized use of pronunciation."

George Varelas, the mayor of Westfield and simultaneously the chair of the city's school committee, had spearheaded the effort behind this petition, promoting it vocally with the press. Mr. Varelas is himself a native speaker of Greek and speaks English with that accent, but he found this proposal to the school board a compelling one.

> "Persons like myself – and I cannot be confused with someone from Boston or Alabama – should not be in a self-contained classroom for a full year teaching 5- and 6-year olds the multitude of phonetic differences that exist in the English language," the Mayor said in an interview. "I would only impart my confusion and give them my defects in terms of language".
>
> (Associated Press 1992: 12)

A debate ensued between Mr. Varelas and Piedad Robertson, a native of Cuba, former kindergarten teacher and at the time of the petition the Massachusetts Secretary of Education. Ms. Robertson openly called for the rejection of the petition: "instead of fostering the acceptance of cultural diversity, [it] would appear to encourage bigotry, racism, and discrimination."

In the end, the school board voted down the petition quite resoundingly, but whether or not this was out of conviction of the wrongness of the proposal or the fact that the State Attorney General had pointed out that it would violate Title VII of the Civil Rights Act, is unclear. What remains after the issue was resolved are a number of unsettled questions. Commentators on the fracas observed that the parents feared not so much that the teachers would be incomprehensible, but that their children would pick up the teacher's accent.

In linguistic terms, this fear has no foundation. Children learn their phonologies first from their families and then from their peers, and that process is largely finished by the time they get to school. Phonetics and phonology do not pass from adults to children like viruses. A teacher provides a language role model, certainly, but of a different type: with schooling the lexicon and stylistic repertoire expands, but these are additions to the basic structure or the *grammar* of language, which is well established by age 6. In terms of the Sound House analogy used in Chapter 2, a child has already constructed a Sound House by the time he or she enters school. If any major remodeling is done (and it can still be done at this age), the moving of walls or the addition of a staircase, it is done out of wanting to imitate the Sound Houses of other children. In contrast, the stylistic effects of certain grammatical strategies and lexical items might be seen as interior decorating with drapes and carpets, fabrics and colors, and will be greatly affected by the acquisition of literacy and hence by interaction with the teacher. Accent is not an issue; communicative effectiveness may be, but that is true whatever the native language of the teacher.

While these fears are easily addressed, the underlying issues remain. There is a strong resistance in the US to teachers with foreign accents, and nowhere is that resistance so loudly voiced as in the university setting. Most large research universities with graduate programs employ graduate students to teach, or assist in teaching, large introductory courses in their areas of expertise and scholarship. This is both a reasonable part of the training of future teachers and an economical necessity in larger institutions. Many of these graduate students come from outside the US, and speak English as a second language – an issue which has become one of the most contentious ones on large campuses. Emotions on the matter of graduate student instructors in the classroom sometimes run very high:

A more recent experience concerns my daughter, a recent graduate of the engineering college. Most of her undergraduate experience was with TAs, many of whom were ill equipped to communicate the language let alone ideas. For $10,000 a year in out-of-state tuition we expected more.

(from a letter to the "Alumni Voices" section of the University of Michigan *LSAmagazine*; Spring 1993)

The ONE problem with Ann Arbor (aside from construction, too many coffee shops, Graduate Student Instructors who don't know how to speak English . . .

(Jones 1996: 14B)

Of course it's hard to understand them, and of course I resent it. Why can't I get what I pay for, which is a teacher like me who talks to me in my own language that I can understand?

(from a questionnaire distributed annually to incoming students in a linguistics course, Fall semester 1995)

The issues raised here, directly and indirectly, have to do with unmet student expectations. One set of expectations has to do with the contract between student and university, both formal and implied. Whether or not that contract is fairly interpreted to include student preferences on the nationality or ethnicity of instructors and faculty cannot be taken up here. What is relevant to this discussion are the issues of accent, comprehensibility, and communication.

In response to complaints from the student body on this issue, the university administration has taken a number of steps to ensure that graduate student instructors are indeed prepared to teach in English:

> The Center for Research on Learning and Teaching, in cooperation with the English Language Institute, also provides extensive training for international teaching assistants (those from other countries), including a three-week intensive workshop. International TAs must successfully complete the workshop and also must pass an oral proficiency screening before being allowed to teach. This is a significant change from not so long ago, when written exams were used. Those who don't pass the oral screening continue to take English classes until their English is acceptable. In fact, the University of Michigan now has the toughest standards in the country for international teaching assistants, and its training and screening programs have served as a model for many other universities.
>
> What must be said additionally about our international teaching assistants is that as a result of the training and screening program, what once was a serious problem has now become a potentially rich resource for our students. These courageous and committeed graduate students have often had to battle significant odds to come to this country. They are brilliant scholars and experienced teachers who provide a wonderful opportunity for [our] students to have sustained contact with someone from another country. In the long run, undergraduates can benefit enormously from this group of teachers if they put aside stereotypes and biases. Powerful evidence of the quality of international teaching assistants is that last year two of the Rackham Teaching Awards went to international TAs.
>
> (Dean Edie Goldenberg, University of Michigan *LSAmagazine*,
> Spring 1993: 3)

Box 6.2

Problem	Proposed solution
Graduate student speakers of English as a second language have special hurdles to deal with in order to become effective classroom teachers.	Increased and more diligent screening and training of non-native English-speaking graduate student teachers.
Undergraduates have stereotypes and biases which, if not put aside, interfere with a potentially positive and valuable learning opportunity.	None.

In this open letter to the student body, the dean draws up a set of problems and proposals, as shown in Box 6.2. While the university recognizes its responsibility in screening and training non-native speakers of English who will be given teaching responsibilities, there is no parallel recognition of the need to educate undergraduates to discern between real communicative difficulties and those stemming not from language, but from stereotype and bias.

It should be stated that these issues are also relevant for non-native English-speaking lecturers and professors: a Ph.D. cannot render anyone accentless. Undergraduate complaints, however, focus almost exclusively on graduate student teachers, which indicates that the underlying issues are complicated by the power and authority structures of any university setting. Undergraduates who come into the university system directly from high school are often very unclear on the organization of the faculty and the degree system; they might not even realize what roles a graduate student instructor plays. As a body, graduate student teachers seem to occupy a role in the minds of the undergraduates which is both subordinate and superordinate: because they teach, evaluate, and grade, they have a significant amount of power. Conversely, because they are themselves still in training and perhaps close in age to their undergraduate students, they may be perceived as socially subordinate in ways which clash distinctly with the power of the red pen and gradebook. If we add to this equation differences of race, ethnicity, national origin, academic expectations, and language, undergraduate willingness to challenge the graduate student's authority seems to rise exponentially.

A small body of research has been established which moves beyond the anecdotal data usually called forth in this debate. A few studies have concentrated on the undergraduate's ability to distinguish between accents and make fair assessments of English proficiency. Orth (1982) found that undergraduates were not very good at making such assessments; their evaluations of non-native English-speaking instructors were biased by the grades they anticipated receiving from the instructor. Rubin and Smith (1990) found that students were not always able to distinguish between different levels of accentedness; regardless of the correctness of the perception, however, it served as a very good predictor of how the student rated the teacher. Thus, if students assessed an instructor with a very slight Cantonese accent as *highly* accented, they also found that person to be a poor teacher. In another study that drew a great deal of attention, Rubin (1992) used an interesting technique to see how students' expectations of foreign instructors played into their attitudes and learning experience.

In that study of how expectations built around accent and race affected student perceptions and performance, sixty-two undergraduate native speakers of English participated. Each undergraduate listened to a four-minute lecture on an introductory topic, prerecorded on tape. There were two possible lectures, one on a science topic and the other on a humanities topic. While listening, the students saw a projected slide photograph which was meant to represent the instructor speaking. *Both of the recordings* heard were made *by the same speaker* (a native speaker of English from central Ohio), but there were *two possible projected photographs*: half of the students saw a slide of a Caucasian woman lecturer, and the other half saw a woman similarly dressed and of the same size and hair style, but who was Asian. Both were photographed in the same setting and in the same pose, and in fact no difference was registered between the Caucasian and the Asian photographs in terms of physical attractiveness.

Immediately after listening to the four-minute lecture, each student completed a test of listening comprehension, and then a testing procedure which was designed to test homophily, which in effect asks the respondents to compare the person speaking to themselves and to judge the degree of similarity or difference. This measurement has been found to be very useful in studying communicative breakdown across cultural boundaries. Studies indicate that students "respond more positively to teachers of optimal homophily" (Rubin 1992: 513). There were other items included in this questionnaire which asked the students to rate accent (*speaks with an American accent . . . speaks with an Asian accent*), ethnicity, and quality of teaching.

Figures 6.2 and 6.3 indicate that students clearly perceived the difference in ethnicity in the slides they looked at. As hypothesized, the Asian instructor was perceived to be more "Oriental/Asian" than was the Caucasian instructor, regardless of the subject of the lecture. What Figures 6.2 and 6.3 also show very clearly is that perceived ethnicity on the basis of the photograph did have a great deal of influence on the way students evaluated language. Depending on the slide projected, the students evaluated the same native speaker of US English as having more or less of a foreign accent. To put it more bluntly, some students who saw an Asian were incapable of *hearing* objectively. It can be stated with absolute certainty that the prerecorded language they listened to was native, non-foreign-accented English; students looking at an Asian face, however, sometimes convinced themselves that they heard an accent. Here it becomes clear that the students' negative preconceptions are at work.

Even more interesting is the fact that overall, students scored lower in the comprehension test when they *believed that the lecturer was Asian* (Figure 6.4). Not only were some of these students incapable of hearing objectively when confronted with an Asian face, their block extended to the way they absorbed and understood factual material. This was more extreme in the case of the science lecture, something not totally unpredictable. Rubin notes that

> For many undergraduates, introductory courses in mathematics and the natural sciences have reputations as extremely inhumane courses designed to winnow out marginal students. And it is well known that

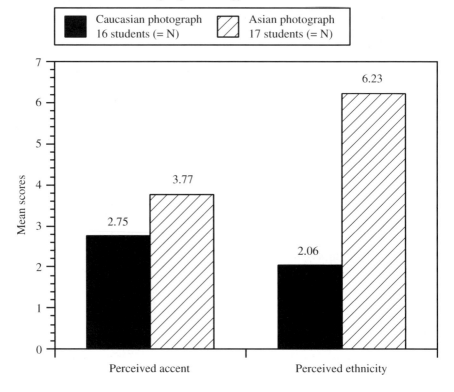

Figure 6.2 Student evaluation of lecturer's ethnicity and accent, recorded humanities lecture
Source: Rubin 1992

> [non-native English-speaking graduate student teachers] are dispro-
> portionately assigned responsibility for such high-anxiety classes.

(1992: 512)

Thus it seems likely that preconceptions and fear are strong enough moti-
vators to cause students to construct imaginary accents, and fictional
communicative breakdowns.

The proposed rationale for the rejection of instructors with foreign
accents in teaching must be carefully examined:

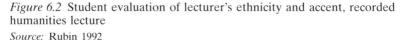

ACCENT → COMMUNICATIVE BREAKDOWN →
POOR CLASSROOM/LEARNING EXPERIENCE

Rubin's study indicates that whether or not an instructor actually does
need further training in English may be irrelevant, if racial and ethnic
cues are more important than degree of accentedness. If any cue is enough
to shift the communicative burden entirely to the other party, the formula
takes on another dimension:

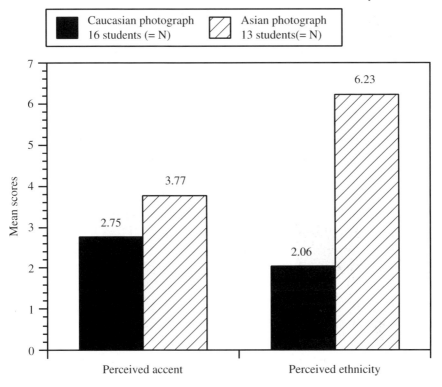

Figure 6.3 Student evaluation of lecturer's ethnicity and accent, recorded science lecture

Source: Rubin 1992

INSTRUCTOR'S *PERCEIVED* ACCENT → STUDENT'S NEGATIVE EXPECTATIONS
↘
COMMUNICATIVE BREAKDOWN → POOR CLASSROOM EXPERIENCE

Of course, it *is* possible that a true communicative breakdown may cause difficulties between a non-native speaker of English and a student. One important difference remains, though. A student new to the lecture hall has no way of knowing whether or not the person teaching the course is going to be a good communicator and dedicated teacher, but *the native language of the instructor is incidental to this question.* Native speakers of English are usually given the benefit of the doubt; some turn out to be good teachers, and others do not. However, non-native speakers of English – specifically, speakers of Asian, African, and South American languages – are often not given a chance at all.

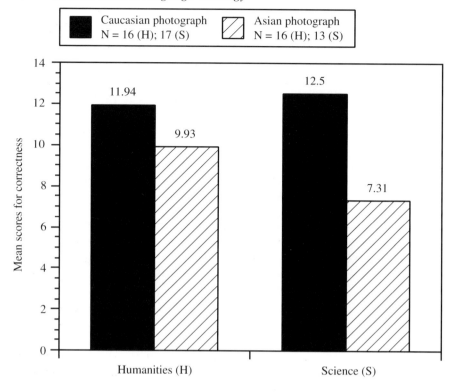

Figure 6.4 Student comprehension scores, by ethnicity of slide viewed and subject of lecture
Source: Rubin 1992

While universities and colleges across the country are trying hard to deal with the complicated issue of graduate student instructors who are not native speakers of English, it seems that any policies to address the question of quality of classroom instruction must have a broader view. Other studies have indicated that in addition to language instruction, foreign students need help in acclimating to a very different academic and social culture, in a variety of matters. Language is of primary importance, and deserves careful attention. In addition to the training of the foreign students, it must be noted that our own students have to be educated about matters of language and communication in the classroom, and be taught to take a reasonable amount of responsibility for a successful educational experience.

SUMMARY

Educators have a difficult job. We want them to provide our children with a great variety of skills, from reading and writing to job training. Furthermore, we entrust them with teaching our children the basics of good citizenship and responsible behavior as social and sexual beings; we charge them with occupying and entertaining, even on occasion with passing on parenting skills. On top of all these expectations, we want the teacher to give our children that mythical perfect spoken language we call Standard English, a language which is grammatically homogenous and accentless. Whether or not the child can do anything constructive with that language is in many instances secondary to the social construction of accent.

Teachers have responded to these expectations by developing authority structures around language – written and spoken – which are projected as absolute and inviolate. We trust their intuitions and whims above all others. This authority is sometimes abused. Teachers are for the most part firm believers in a standard language ideology which rejects or marginalizes those varieties of US English which are markedly non-middle class, non-Middle American, and colorless. Arguments for this overt limitation of discourse which affects huge numbers of children are usually based in economics. If asked about a wider possible view, and policies of acceptance, every teacher will point to the other institutions which support and propagate a standard language ideology. Employers have expectations, they will argue. There will be repercussions.

But the teachers themselves are capable of seeing this circular logic:

> Since English teachers have been in large part responsible for the narrow attitudes of today's employers, changing attitudes toward dialect variations does not seem an unreasonable goal, for today's students will be tomorrow's employers. The attitudes that they develop in the English class will often be the criteria they use for choosing their own employees. English teachers who feel they are bound to accommodate the linguistic prejudices of current employers perpetuate a system that is unfair to both students who have job skills and the employers who need them.
>
> (National Council of Teachers of English 1974: 14)

Are there no examples of educators with more informed and enlightened approaches to diversity in language? Teachers who strive to teach children to read and write, and at the same time respect the wholeness of the home language and the social facts attached to it? Teachers who question underlying assumptions? Of course there are. We have seen a native-speaking HCE teacher in Hawai'i who takes a firm stand. At a college in the midwest, there is at least a single English teacher who does not find it necessary to eradicate one variety of English to teach reading and writing in another. The *Chicago Tribune* found this method so remark-able that it ran an article on the approach, and highlighted a classroom practice of "[not] scold[ing] black students ... when they said 'ax,' rather than 'ask' ..." (Warren 1993: 2). At Stanford, a group of linguists and educators have taken another hard look at the issue of using the dialect as a departure point for teaching AAVE speakers how to read the written language (Rickford and Rickford 1995). In New Mexico, the Hopi Nation oversees the training and evaluation of bilingual teachers who come from the community and teach in the community, so that the experiences of Luther Standing Bear, a Sioux enrolled in an English Only boarding school, do not have to be repeated: "How hard it was to forego the conso-lation of speech" he wrote in his autobiography (Standing Bear 1928, as cited in Reyhner 1992: 44).

These stories of teachers and administrators who resist the process of language subordination are rare. What our schools do, for the most part, is to insist that some children forego the expressive power and consolation of speech in that variety of English which is the currency of their home communities. This gesture of denial and symbolic subordination is projected as a first and necessary step to becoming a good student and a good citizen.

7 The information industry
Selling America to Americans

I therefore claim to show, not how men think in myths, but how myths operate in men's minds without their being aware of the fact.

Claude Lévi-Strauss, *The Raw and the Cooked* (1964)

In the past twenty years, the services of the print and broadcast news media have become more widely and consistently available. Cable television and computer technology have expanded the scope of the industry, so that the amount of information available to the consumer has become overwhelming. At the same time, consumers of these products have begun to look more closely at what is available. Increasing critical awareness of the workings of the information industry has spawned a great deal of scholarly and more general investigation and, of course, further publication and discussion in and out of public forums. Consumers and journalists themselves are concerned about the lack of objectivity in reports about minority groups or anti-abortion activists on television news; about the demagoguery of radio talk-show hosts; about the way newspapers structure our understanding and interpretation of world events, in part by simply not bringing things to our attention.

It is indisputable that the mass media plays a major role in the communication and transmission of social values, and the propagation and defense of national culture. There was open public debate around this very issue with the earliest advances in broadcast technology, when educators and broadcasters struggled for the right to shape the public mind with the new powerful technology. Spring (1992) documents this long and complicated public debate, one result of which was the formation of a Federal Radio Education Committee that met for the first time in a national conference in 1936:

> At the first session of the conference, Anning S. Prall, Chairman of the FCC, argued that educational goals should be combined with the basic structure of the American broadcasting system by developing radio as a form of democratic propaganda. After noting the sinister connotation

of the word "propaganda," Prall told his audience, "Yet propaganda, radio's greatest function in Germany and Russia, can spread the ideas and ideals of America, can 'sell' America to Americans, and thus forge a weapon of national unity that no other agency can create. Why cannot propaganda be used for good as well as for evil ends?" Answering his own question, Prall argued that educators would be the best people to assure that propaganda on radio could be for "good" ends.

(108)

Spring concludes that the arguments put forth for commercially controlled radio broadcasting based on democratic ideals were spurious:

Public school leaders had once dreamt of creating a national culture through public schooling, but radio and televison might have proved more influential. Broadcasting helped create a shared national culture by establishing a common knowledge of consumer items and a shared experience of sponsored radio and television entertainment.

(109)

While teachers were disappointed at the lack of control they had over the content of public broadcasting and with the commercial focus of radio, it is clear that the culture of radio and later, television, sought to sell more than cars and cigarettes. Today, it is not hard to document news stories of various kinds about a wide variety of subjects which start something like this:

In the past 50 years, there's been a kind of homogenization in America. With the proliferation of fast food chains and mega department stores, Main Street in Boaz, Alabama looks pretty much like Main Street in Watkins Glen, New York.

(National Public Radio News, September 4, 1994)

This mantra of cultural homogenization, a world in which we are all the same because we buy the same things and eat the same food, is repeated so often by the media that it has come to be accepted as a common-sense truth. The irony of this plaintive cry is that the news media is financially dependent on *selling* a homogenous national culture; if successful (whether in real or perceptual terms) the media mourns its own success.

In a 1988 study which looks at a variety of political issues and how they were reported in the mainstream print press, Herman and Chomsky demonstrate the way in which the news media uses propaganda to "inculcate individuals with the values, beliefs, and codes of behavior which will integrate them into the institutional structures of the larger society" (1988: 1). In this work they provide a propaganda model composed of a number of *news filters* which expose the ideological underpinnings of news reporting. Herman and Chomsky use "propaganda" in the sense of systematic distribution of disinformation. In matters of language we can also speak of propaganda, albeit of a more subconscious and subtle variety. In as much as language about language is factually incorrect or misleading, it becomes self-referential propaganda: it serves as both the vehicle of disinformation and its object. This process is a difficult one to look at closely, for while it is not so hard to reconstruct the motivations for the media's positive representation of the Gulf War, given the corporate structure and economic dependencies of broadcast and print journalism, the motivations that underlie the limiting of discourse are not always so close to the surface. The data is often fragmentary, as in the following examples:[1]

> [national television news] The idea is to teach them how to speak English so that it sounds like English, and not, as Henry Higgins might put it, like warmed-over grits. Think of them as prisoners – prisoners of their own accents.
>
> (CBS Evening News, October 10, 1984)

> [newspaper editorial] We like Hahn, 34, who was born in South Korea and whose positions on controlling growth are much like our own. Unfortunately, we think his heavy accent and somewhat limited contacts would make it difficult for him to be a councilman.
>
> ("For Santa Clara County," *San Jose Mercury News*, October 18, 1988: 6B, as cited in Matsuda 1991: 1346)

> [newspaper article] No matter how qualified a person is, a voice twisted by regional or ethnic influences can be a stumbling block socially and professionally. If others can't understand you or your words are too richly flavored with down-home spice, you could find all your skill and intelligence thwarted by a telltale tongue.
>
> (Kerr 1994)

> [national television news] For all the damage now being done to the English language there are people who continue to care about its health. Dr. Grammar is one of them.
>
> ("Dr. Grammar," NBC, April 26, 1993)

Newspaper headlines alone are sometimes quite sufficient evidence of a particular slant on language issues: "Bad English spoken here" (McKenzie 1992); "Language is the guardian of culture" (Nenneman 1992); "Speak English, troops" (Hamel and Schreiner 1989); " 'Black English' not spoken here" (Jarrett 1979a); "Oy gevalt! New Yawkese an endangered dialect?" (Sontag 1993).

Language is one area in which the news media representatives vigorously advance the notion of homogeneity, directly and indirectly. The process of linguistic assimilation to an abstracted standard is cast as a natural one, necessary and positive for the greater social good. The people who bring us our news claim authority in this process, although with different areas of focus. Print journalists have always taken a special

Figure 7.1 Newsweek advertisement. Reproduced with permission

interest in preserving and promoting a standard written language, and this with some justification, as we have seen in earlier chapters. In this process, superior access to information is linked to superior knowledge of the language in which it is shared. Many of the mass market books available on language are written by newspaper journalists, which makes a great deal of sense if someone is looking for guidelines on the writing of English. At times, however, print journalists will venture out of the realm of the written language and into the spoken, which we will see in the next chapters, apparently because they see little important differentiation between the two. They also often fail to distinguish between objective reporting on matters of language which are of public interest (English Only legislation; bilingual education, etc.) and providing subjective commentary.

The broadcast news industry takes a proprietary interest in the spoken language. It promotes its own language as the only possible language of an educated, informed mainstream. It is in part by means of claiming authority in matters of spoken language that it establishes itself, over and over again, as an important public institution – and one as crucial as the educational system to the well-being of the nation-state. This role of the broadcast journalist was seized very early in the evolution of the technology. In developments better documented in England than they were in the US, the managing director of the British Broadcasting Company (BBC) voiced opinions in 1924 which seem to still be widely held today:

> One hears the most appalling travesties of vowel pronunciation. *This is a matter in which broadcasting may be of immense assistance.* . . . We have made a special effort to secure in our stations men who, in the presentation of programme items, the reading of news bulletins and so on, can be relied upon to employ the correct pronunciation of the English tongue. . . . I have frequently heard that disputes as to the right pronunciation of words have been settled by reference to the manner in which they have been spoken on the wireless . . . *our responsibilities in this matter are obvious*, since in talking to so vast a multitude, mistakes are likely to be promulgated to a much greater extent than was ever possible before.
>
> (*Broadcast over Britain*, 1924, as cited in McArthur 1992: 109–110; emphasis added)

Any successful entrepreneur will validate the simple fact that the first step in any venture is either to find a hole in the market – a real need which has not been filled – or to create a need in the mind of the public for a new product. Some place along the way such a need for a better, more efficient language was created in the minds of English speakers (and speakers of many other languages).[2] This followed not because speakers of English were suddenly no longer able to communicate with each other, but because they were told that they would soon not be able to communicate with each other if they didn't do something about their language, given the new technology and the demands that technology put on spoken language. The parties sounding these dire proclamations were, not coincidentally, the ones with the cure to sell – those right-thinking and right-speaking individuals who were able to set the public on a straight and narrow path. The authority to do so is given to "those who set the style [in speech] . . . the cultured, those who have traveled, the politically powerful, the educated, the wealthy, the socially influential, and the professional users of speech" (Kanter and West 1941: 261).

Radio news and other broadcasts began at about this same period in the midwestern US. The National Broadcasting Company (NBC) also took it upon itself to codify spoken US English for its announcers and for the public at large, although the rigor and organization of the BBC effort was never matched. There is also a more democratic approach, at least on the surface: "From a realistic point of view, that pronunciation is best that is most readily understood, and that pronunciation is most readily understood that is used by most people" (Ehrlich 1951: ix). From this follows a discussion of how many people speak each of the three varieties of US English, as defined and identified by NBC: "(a) New England or Eastern, (b) Southern, (c) Western, Middle Western, or General American" (ibid.).

Of course, this overly simplistic regional division cuts the pie so that the largest numbers fall to (c), which is from the outset seen as "General American," or unmarked. Thus, NBC concludes:

> When a broadcaster speaks over a powerful station or nation-wide hook-up, he desires to use a pronunciation that is most readily understood by the majority of his listeners. In such an event, the broadcaster would be well advised to use a pronunciation widely known among phoneticians as "General American," the standard presented in this book.
>
> (ibid.)

The logic here is quite straightforward. In order to be most effective, the medium demands clarity of spoken language; clarity of spoken language follows from good pronunciation; there is one ideal pronunciation which is accessible to all Americans. To underscore the validity of this claim, the author draws in two kinds of authority: majority rule (in that most of the US lives in the midwest), and the ubiquitous advertising and marketing claim EXPERTS AGREE (here without the amusing qualification "three out of four" or "nine out of ten"). As is normally the case when authority is claimed in this manner, the identity and credentials of the experts are left conveniently in the shadows.

But if logic is going to be used in an effort to lend authority to one variety of English over another, and to the broadcasters for identifying and promoting that variety, then this is not enough.

> Whenever a group of model speakers is used for purposes of reference and standardization, variant pronunciations are likely to arise. These must often be resolved by arbitrary decision if only one pronunciation for each word is wanted. ... Because this manual presents a recommended pronunciation, it will doubtless find dissenting readers. Consequently, it may be considered a thesis for discussion among those intelligent and informed people who are concerned about the welfare of the spoken word. Criticisms, judgments, and suggestions are hereby solicited, especially from those readers who have more than a bowing acquaintance with the study of pronunciation. It is anticipated that changes will be made, for only by keeping a constant watch over current standards of speech will audience and broadcaster alike be assured of a dynamic oral language to serve a great democracy.
>
> (Ehrlich 1951: x–xi)

The NBC *Handbook of Pronunciation* began by limiting appropriate language to one region, the mid- and far west. It now becomes more narrow. While variation within this regional area cannot be overlooked or denied, and some of it is not even wrong, variation must still give way to one correct pronunciation for each word. Why this is necessary is never addressed, with the exception of the note that "inconsistencies in pronunciation irritate some listeners" (Ehrlich 1951: x). There is a tacit acknowledgement that while this is the right goal, it is not realized in the best of circumstances: there are "large numbers of professional broadcasters and laymen in America who use excellent pronunciation even though they may not always be consistent" (ibid.).

This last formulation is particularly interesting. We began with a nation of English speakers who showed regional differences; now we have "professionals" and "laymen." This subtle but effective move toward authority is further bolstered by the identification of those with the right to voice their opinions: those *intelligent and informed people who are concerned about the welfare of the spoken word.*

In a series of small steps, we have seen spoken language transformed from the possession of many to the responsibility of few, from a universal human characteristic to a specialized and endangered tool. The need for an approach to language which will minimize the technical problems of broadcasting has turned into an arena for who has a right to make decisions – and enforce them – about how English should be spoken, and who deserves to be heard.

We will see that things have not changed much in the fifty years since NBC first sought to assume this kind of authority. In an examination of the current state of affairs, I will look at both print and broadcast journalism. Television and radio form natural, but not identical, allies in the approach to matters concerning spoken language. Newspapers and magazines focus primarily but not exclusively on the written language. In all cases, information about language comes in two forms: direct commentary in focused news reports, or indirect commentary made in the course of other reports or observations. The second type of information is useful in the examination at hand, but it is also the most difficult kind of data to document consistently.

In the next part of this chapter, I will present and analyze two case studies: accent-reduction schools, and regional dialects, as they are treated in both the print and the broadcast news media directly and indirectly.

THE SEDUCTION OF ACCENT REDUCTION

The news media has topics which seem to be of steady and ongoing interest to it, and these are brought to the public's attention on a regular basis. One such area is that of accent reduction, or a concentrated effort to take a person who speaks English with a stigmatized regional, social, or foreign accent, and replace it with one which is favored.

Accent reduction is marketed and sold by individuals who own their own businesses, or, more rarely, in courses organized by local schools and colleges. College courses to reduce accent are found primarily in the New York area and in the southern States. Speech or accent reduction provided privately is expensive: one Chicago-based company estimated a one-on-one instruction program of thirty lessons (forty-five minutes each) at a tuition of $750, excluding materials or tapes.[3] These businesses claim that their clients are primarily professionals who have experienced discrimination on the basis of language in their work. Actors are also ready clients. Because these businesses are dependent on finding a new clientele, they function in the public eye and use a variety of advertising strategies.

The business of accent reduction is to be kept clearly distinct from speech pathology, in which professionals are trained to deal with people who, as a result of a stroke or other physical or developmental impairment, have difficulty in the production of speech sounds. Children born with cleft palates, for example, need the help of a speech pathologist to learn how to produce certain speech sounds. People who call themselves accent-reduction specialists may in fact have been trained as speech pathologists, but they serve another function entirely. The distinction between physio-logical dysfunction and normal heterogeneity of phonology (accent) seems to be unclear in the mind of the public more generally and the news media in particular, as typified in a *New York Times* headline: "Where to Drop a Lisp or Pick Up an Accent: Speech Therapist Tells How It's Done" (August 11, 1993, City section: B4).

In any city of average size, there will be a few people who have hung out a shingle and sought clients with the claim that they can teach them to lose one accent and acquire another: some may be speech pathologists; others are not. There is no regulation or licensing for such businesses, in the same way that an individual can claim to have developed a miracle diet and charge money for it. Professionals who are honest with them-selves and their clients may still have a legitimate service to offer people who have acquired English as a second language and who would simply like to come *closer* to a native pronunciation of US English. Actors often need to learn how to simulate another accent, in a contrived setting and for short periods of time. These are not unreasonable goals, and they are often pursued by well-meaning individuals.

Figure 7.2 provides an example of accent-reduction advertising which is primarily reasonable in its claims, in that it targets "improved" articu-lation; the end in sight is "increased options." There is still a certain amount of disinformation in this advertisement, however, in that the repre-sentation of Gullah might be challenged on factual grounds.[4] In contrast, the advertising copy in Figure 7.3 promises *elimination* of accent, both regional and foreign, with no qualifications or small print, which is an insupportable claim.

SPEECH EMPOWERMENT

First of a Three-Part Series
... ... Shows Speakers of
Black English Dialect How
to Speak Standard English
for Business and Increase
Options for Greater
Success.

With This Program
You Will:

–Boost Self Esteem with a
Brief History of Gullah –
considered the "Mother" of
Black Dialect in America –
Tracing Its Origin Back to
West Africa Today!

–Use 3rd Person Singular
Verbs with 100% Accuracy.

–Improve Articulation
and Pronunciation of Words
Often Mispronounced.

–A "Must Have" for
Libraries, Linguistics,
English and Speech
Departments, and
Multicultural Programs.

Figure 7.2 An accent-reduction advertisement with somewhat reasonable claims

The providers of these services are often quite willing to take a public
stance on issues of multilingualism and accent:

It is absolutely wrong to discriminate on the basis of accent. However,
I think this country would be much better off if everybody spoke the
same language and if communication was as clear as possible. ... If we

---

SPEECH IMPROVEMENT SERVICES
The Speech Professionals

Regional and Foreign Accent Elimination
All Stage Dialects for all Acting roles
Highly effective short term programs
Consultants to the major acting schools and agents
State Licensed Speech Pathologists

Figure 7.3 An accent-reduction advertisement with less reasonable claims

were all clearly communicating – this doesn't mean behaving the same – we'd be much better off as a society. I'm not denying heritage, but I think that speech impediments make a person feel bad about him or herself. Speech differences [can foster] misinterpretations. Accents divide people.

(Schanberg 1993)

The fact that this accent-elimination specialist does not think accent discrimination is allowable, but then promptly refers to accents as "speech impediments," makes his own stance clear, and also contributes to an understanding of the media's (and public's) confusion on these matters.

In a similar way, a teacher of a college-based accent-reduction course in Manhattan provides a rationalization for the services she offers. When asked by the reporter "Is this another step in the homogenization of America?" she answers:

I'm not on a search and destroy mission to eradicate accents. You know most of the country speaks General American, and we want *to fit in.*
(CBS Evening News, October 10, 1984)

Having asked the difficult question which addresses individual freedoms and the relationship of language and accent to identity, the reporter has also solicited the standard response, which is quite simply that homogenization is a good thing. The issue of whether or not the goal is realistic or attainable has never been raised, but the ideal – linguistic assimilation to MUSE norms – is seen as an appropriate price to pay in order to *fit in.*

The media likes accent reduction, and it does not seem to distinguish between reasonable claims about language and more outrageous ones. In fact, journalists seem to be so clearly enamored of the idea of accent reduction and assimilation to a homogenous MUSE that they are willing to write and broadcast stories about these efforts on a regular basis.

There follows a discussion of three news reports on accent reduction: a CBS Evening News human-interest report on accent-reduction classes at a college in the south; excerpts from an *American Demographics* article on similar classes for non-native speakers of English in California; and a newspaper article about accent-elimination services available in New York City.

Institutionalized snickering

Text 1 ABC Evening News, December 15, 1991

ANCHOR: Don't ask me why, but you know and I know the rest of the country 1
   tends to snicker when they hear a strong southern accent, which can make
   the speaker feel a little self-conscious. So what do you do about it? Well
   you can ignore it or get annoyed, or like some Greenville, South Carolina
   students, if you can't beat 'em, you can join 'em. Here's Al Dale. 5
[film clip: *My Fair Lady*, "The Rain in Spain Stays Mainly in the Plain"]
AL DALE: Henry Higgins had Eliza Doolittle and Dave F. has Mary M.
STUDENT: There is a tall willow outside my window [pause, due to dissatisfaction
   with her pronunciation. Repeats:] M*aaa*.
TEACHER: Ok, try it again. 10
AL DALE: At South Carolina's Greenville Tech, F. teaches a popular course
   called "How to Control Your Southern Accent." Not how to lose it, just
   how to bring it under control.
TEACHER: A communication problem is when someone starts paying more attention to how you're saying something than what you're saying. 15
[film clip: *Cool Hand Luke*, "What we've got here is failure to communicate."]
AL DALE: In movies and on television, southern accents are often used to indicate villainy or dim-wittedness.
[television clip: *Andy Griffith Show*. Man fooled into believing that dog can talk.]
AL DALE: That attitude irritates Bill J. who signed up for the course because he 20
   does business on the phone with northerners.
STUDENT: They will make fun of you, and 'listen to this guy', you know, 'put
   him on the loudspeaker.'
AL DALE: In the offices?
STUDENT: Yeah, you know they want everybody to hear. 25
STUDENT: The more you get into it, to me, the more I realize you know not
   how bad I sound but how much better I could sound.
AL DALE: Other students on campus say sounding southern is just fine.
STUDENT: Don't see any reason changing it now.
STUDENT: Somebody was going to judge me on the way I spoke then I would 30
   judge him as being close-minded.
AL DALE: Students in the class say they're not trying to deny their heritage.
STUDENT: I don't feel comfortable with the way I speak. I feel like I should do
   better.
[film clip: *My Fair Lady*, "The Rain in Spain"] 35
AL DALE: Just as it did for Eliza Doolittle, what worked for these students is
   practice . . .

STUDENTS: "pepper . . . hanger" "sister, remember" "I can't follow the minnow in the shallow water."
STUDENT: You've got it, by Jove.   40

Text 2 American Demographics (print news journal), January 1989: "Speak English, Troops"

Speech pathologists trained to combat foreign accents are doing big business in 1
multi-ethnic California . . .
    The influx of Asian and Hispanic immigrants has created strong demand for
English-language training and accent-modification courses. Many foreign born
professionals believe that their accents impede their careers, and they are prepared 5
to pay hundreds of dollars to free their English from traces of their homelands.
. . . A person with a heavy accent may start his or her career in a technical job
where few speaking skills are required, but advancement usually brings a greater
emphasis on communication. An employee who is difficult to understand may be
shrugged off as stupid or simply passed over in favor of someone who speaks 10
clear English.

Text 3 Providence Journal-Bulletin, April 1994: "Voice of success silences dialect," by Bob Kerr

You're ambitious. You're also smart, resourceful, attractive and considered a good 1
person by close friends. But you can't catch a break on the career ladder. Every
time you open your mouth to make a point in your favor, people's lips tighten
and their brows wrinkle.

Hit could be yer haksent   5

No matter how qualified a person is, a voice twisted by regional or ethnic influences can be a stumbling block socially and professionally. If others can't understand you or your words are too richly flavored with down-home spice, you could
find all your skill and intelligence thwarted by a telltale tongue.

Program helps people shed telltale tones   10

It isn't fair. It might even be considered another sad sign of the times, further
evidence that we are becoming less and less tolerant of natural differences. But
as the world shrinks and the information highway extends farther into once remote
places, uniformity becomes a business asset. If you talk with distinction, you could
go places. . . . There is a program to eliminate American regional accents, Asian, 15
Indian and Middle Eastern accents and Spanish accents. The goal is something
called standard American English.
    "We take a speech pattern and ask what is different from national expecta-
tions," [S.C.] said. "Even the untrained ear can pick up on an accent."
    There is, he added, a "national aesthetic" in language that is showcased in the 20
national media, where no one who is anyone betrays where he or she came from

when they speak. The way you speak is one of the standards by which others judge your intelligence, he said, even if it is sometimes misleading.

... [S.C.] recommends that people record their attempts to reach totally unremarkable speech habits. He says it is also important to "self-correct" in conver- 25 sation.

"The average person cringes when he hears himself on playback," he said. "They never realize their accent is so different from their expectation."

These three reports deal with different aspects of accent reduction or change: a broadcast news report on a college course in South Carolina, a newspaper article on a speech pathologist who advertises accent removal of all kinds, and an excerpt from a journal article on similar services offered to Asian and Hispanic immigrants in California. In spite of the different focus of each of these pieces, and the differences in tone, there are some striking similarities. One notes the repeated use of war or conflict metaphors: "if you can't beat 'em, you can join 'em" (1.5); "Speak English, Troops" (2.0); "to combat foreign accents" (2.1); and beyond that, the simple and very expedient use of social and peer pressure, without any attempt for logic or justification: "Don't ask me why, but you know and I know the rest of the country tends to snicker when they hear a strong southern accent" (1.1); "Every time you open your mouth to make a point in your favor, people's lips tighten and their brows wrinkle" (3.2); "An employee who is difficult to understand may be shrugged off as stupid" (2.9). These are *post hoc* rationalizations, for which no one takes direct responsibility; they are put forth as self-evident.

An accent-reduction teacher justifies the endeavor using the communicative burden argument: "A communication problem is when someone starts paying more attention to how you're saying something than what you're saying" (1.14). This is a demonstration of that logic discussed in the section "Rejecting the gift: the individual's role in the communicative process" in Chapter 4, in which in a communicative act, one person rejects out of hand his or her portion of the responsibility for a successful exchange. The right to do so is couched in arguments based on economic expediency, business need, and logic, although the logic is never explicitly explored.

"Many foreign born professionals believe that their accents impede their careers, and they are prepared to pay hundreds of dollars to free their English from traces of their homelands" (2.4) is another statement in which true agency is neatly sidestepped. Professionals who speak English with a foreign accent are often discriminated against not on the basis of performance or ability, but simply on the basis of accent and the social identities linked to accent; this is demonstrated clearly in Chapter 8. This report presents a picture of foreign professionals functioning in a communicative vacuum: their lack of success is of their own making, and (according to the text) they perceive themselves as solely responsible for the communicative breakdown which contributes to their failures. In fact, the foreign professional and his or her ability to speak English is only part of the success equation, something many foreign professionals are well aware of. The native US English speaker, the person with the power to limit access based on subjective evaluation of accent rather than performance, is left out of the article's representation of this process in an effort to shift all responsibility to the person with the socially stigmatized accent. And once again we note the metaphor of struggle and liberation: English must be "freed" from negative influence. In a similar way, a picture is evoked of an accent which is a living being, a difficult one in need of taming: "Not how to lose it, just how to bring it under control"(1.12).[5]

The media draws a clear distinction between acceptable English and what is not acceptable. There is little or no hesitation in making value judgements about specific varieties.

Mainstream US English
- good communication
- clear English, talking with distinction
- uniformity: a business asset
- goal: standard American English
- "national aesthetic" equals national media, "where no one who is anyone betrays where he or she came from when they speak"

Non-mainstream US English
- accents impede communication
- strong, heavy accents; voice twisted by regional or ethnic influences: a telltale tongue
- goal: control an accent
- goal: combat foreign accents
- goal: eliminate American regional accents, Asian, Indian, and Middle Eastern accents and Spanish accents

While disinformation is easily documented in these news reports, it is the nature of the disinformation which is revealing. We hear here from news media representatives that their own language is the right and proper model, the "national aesthetic," and that these persons, particularly those in broadcast news media, speak a homogenous English which does not betray (and one notes the value-laden nature of that particular lexical choice) their regional origin. In fact, broadcast news journalists do speak US English with the same range of social, regional, and stylistic variation that every other speaker uses. What this means, then, is that not all variation is unacceptable or forbidden or stigmatized: it is only those variants associated with groups out of favor which must be addressed. "Asian, Indian, and Middle Eastern accents and Spanish accents" are not acceptable; apparently French, German, British, Swedish accents are, regardless of the communication difficulties those languages may cause in the learning of English.

In New York, the accent-reduction teacher tells the reporter that people there want "to fit in"; but the fact is, those speakers do fit into their settings, in linguistic terms. What she seems to be saying is that a language which "betrays" a New York origin is a liability, whereas one which indicates the midwest is not. The subtle argument is not for overall linguistic assimilation to a perfectly static US English, but to a language which is generally midwest and middle class.

In the news items under examination, many common-sense arguments and assumptions about southern varieties of US English are openly voiced. Here I am more concerned with the strategies used to subordinate non-mainstream language more generally; in Part III there will be a more careful look at the social construction of southern US English, in part on the basis of these excerpts. Here I would like to look at one broadcast news report on one language in some depth, to explore the subtleties of the subordination process.

When is a language not a language?

One sure way to draw the media's attention to a subordinated and stigmatized variety of English is to give that language some print or broadcast coverage which is not directly or overtly negative. In other chapters of this book, there will be such examples of critical reaction by journalists to the positive portrayal of language variation. Here, I turn to a single broadcast report apparently produced in response to the success of a number of popular press books for tourists on "Pidgin," or Hawai'ian Creole English (HCE). In addition, news coverage on HCE and other language issues from within Hawai'i are touched upon in the chapters on ideology in education and in the legal system.

Nationally broadcast network news has long used the last few minutes of airtime to bring stories called *human interest*. These reports often deal with topics which are amusing or inspiring, or with an obvious and unapologetic lesson in citizenship and morals. Commentaries on language often come in this packaging. One such report aired on July 3, 1983 under the title *Pidgin language fad is used as defense against tourists in Hawaii* (Judd Rose on location in Honolulu, Hawai'i, Sam Donaldson in Washington DC, ABC).[6]

While this news report employs most of the steps in the language-subordination process outlined earlier (mystification, the claiming of authority, disinformation, trivialization, and marginalization and/or villainization) the two primary tools are authority and trivialization. There are two broadcast journalists (anchor and reporter) involved. The anchor – a role well known to the viewing public, and already credited with a great deal of authority – presents basic background information in an introductory or framing statement. Here, one of the nation's best-known news broadcasters, Sam Donaldson, immediately sets the tone by drawing up language right-and-wrong battle lines: *Not everyone speaks the King's English in this country or for that matter the King's Spanish, Italian or German, but most people try.*

The King – the ultimate symbol of paternal and political authority – has one kind of language which is correct, regardless of the nation in question. In a confident manner, Donaldson lists some primary transgressions against "King's English": split infinitives, verb agreement, who versus whom. He constructs this "good" language as one which is the logical goal and responsibility of good citizens, in turn defined as those who try, even if they do not always succeed, to achieve this goal of perfect language. To this point, the authoritative stance is accompanied by a paternalistic smile, but the final statement is more formal, and draws a contrast between those who are willing to try to speak "good" language and those who are not: *Not so, some people in Hawaii. There . . . some people try not to speak any recognizable language at all.* Thus, he seems to conclude, those who do not try for this one perfect language are willfully pursuing a non-language, one unworthy of recognition.

Following from this introduction drawing primarily on unsubstantiated authority, the reporter begins the story with a war metaphor, in which *conquerors* (or tourists) *have landed.* Here, the original colonization of Hawai'i is drawn upon, and for humorous effect, trivialized. In a disarming way, stereotypes are used first for these conquerors: we see various shots of American tourists, overweight and dressed in strange combinations of color and pattern, festooned with cameras and standing unknowing and unseeing in the middle of a paradise, covered with suntan lotion and yawning. The main purpose of this metaphor seems to be to set up a conflict between the tourists and the locals, a plot which is often seen in movies about occupied Japan or Asia, in which the civilizing influences of the Western forces must first contend with the stereotypical crafty Oriental. In this case, the locals have an unusual weapon, the whole focus of this news report: Hawai'ian Creole English, or as it is called in this story, Pidgin.

The next large portion of the report is an attempt to define HCE in very specific social terms. Here, misinformation is the primary tactic, underscored with authority: *Pidgin is a decades old blend of oriental languages and teen slang: the King's English, it is not.* Not only is the first part of this statement absolutely false, it is also phrased to combine mystification ("the orient"), and marginalization ("teen slang"). By appealing once again to the "King's English," the opening position statement is reiterated: the object of this report is, from the very beginning, a non-language. To illustrate this fallacious definition, speakers of HCE are presented as evidence. We see three dialogues, each of them between two persons:

1 Two local men are interviewed while they lie in the sun ("Pidgin is sort of a like a secret code that only us can understand.").
2 A staged dialogue: two younger men are looking into the ocean, evaluating the conditions for surfing ("Ou look good today, yea.").

3 In a second staged dialogue, a young couple argue in a parking lot ("Hey you think I dumb or what?").

Here HCE is the language of the young, the unemployed, the over-wrought and emotional, the fun-seeking, the beach boy, and the teenager: people who are believed to have no serious purpose in life. The fact that this is a language spoken by judges and cooks, young and old, is not made clear. As there are no adults speaking HCE, the viewers may well assume it is a language of youth and will pass with maturity, like pimples or an obsession with loud music. In a similar way, the only uses for HCE are trivial, humorous, or, in the case of tourists, obstructionist. As a language which typifies *good grammar gone to grief*, it can have no serious purpose. From this report, there is no way to know that a significant body of poetry and prose has been produced in HCE, and that there is a strong and productive oral storytelling tradition. There is no way of knowing if the reporter is unaware of the range and social complexity of HCE; perhaps he is ignorant of these facts, or perhaps he is purposefully choosing to undercount and misrepresent the language and its speakers – not an unknown strategy in news reporting.[7]

Having established a narrow and erroneous definition of HCE, the reporter finally reveals the motivation for the report: a series of popular press books have been written about HCE, and they are selling well, engaging positive reaction or attention not from HCE speakers, but from the mainstream and the wider world: *Pidgin . . . has become respectable with the island's mainstream . . . a full-blown fad. It's due to this book, a tongue-in-cheek pidgin dictionary, the work of a beach boy from the shores of Nebraska.*

The book that the reporter refers to is the first in a series entitled *Pidgin to the Max*. The author, Douglas Simonson, is indeed not a native speaker of HCE, but his mass-market books have found a wide audience, a fact reiterated with considerable emphasis in the advertising copy for the series:

> *Pidgin to da Max* is the best-selling book ever published in Hawaii. It's also the best-loved book ever created for and about Hawaii. . . . First published in 1981, *Pidgin to da Max* has sold well over 150,000 copies to date. The book is an illustrated dictionary of Hawaiian pidgin – an insider's dictionary.
>
> (http://www.aloha-hawaii.com/peppo/home.html)

While the advertising claims must not be taken at face value (for this World Wide Web text is marked clearly as advertisement, with forms for ordering the book and its sequels), the news broadcast is assumed to be more neutral. Nevertheless, the claims about the book made by the author are echoed by the reporter, as if this were the only study ever undertaken of the language.

In fact, HCE has been extensively studied by linguists, some of whom are natives of Hawai'i. But no mention is made of this body of literature; instead, Simonson is presented as the only authority, at the same time openly acknowledging that he is not a native speaker. The reporter is willing to rely on the authority of this *beach boy from the shores of Nebraska*, a character presented in this broadcast as someone as light and frivolous and trivial as the native speakers he writes about. In a similar way, the contrast between the blond author and the dark-skinned HCE speakers is never commented upon, just as the exploitative nature of these books is kept far from the discussion. They have come to the attention of the reporter not because of their accuracy, but because of their popularity and the fact that they have made a profit.

While the trivialization approach is maintained throughout the report, there is also a tone of disapproval. Especially displeasing, but cast in a humorous light, is the attention of the local Hawai'ian government to HCE: *Even the Hawaii House of Representatives got into the act, passing a resolution that encouraged use of pidgin.* The reporter interprets the interest of the Hawai'ian government as a lark, a joke. This cannot be a serious effort on their part to preserve a language spoken by many of the people they represent; it must be seen as a diversion in the otherwise serious undertakings of the legislature. The viewers have no way of knowing that the issue of recognition of HCE in education and public forums has been discussed at great length and with utmost seriousness by the legislature on many occasions.

From here, the report moves unapologetically to the uncloaked: a local comedy club, and humor directed by the insiders toward the insiders, for the appreciation of the outsiders. This is a big step in the process of trivializing the language of so many. Locals become complicit in the subordination process in order to add another layer of authority to external censor and ridicule.

In his summary, the reporter draws parallels between HCE and other stigmatized and trivialized varieties of US English. He calls HCE a Pacific version of Valley-Girlese. It has become, for him – and now, for his viewers – the language of those social groups who have not quite found their way into the real, adult world. The final trivialization is the reporter's summary statement in his own native MUSE. While he is speaking, his words appear at the bottom of the screen as subtitles, translated into HCE. This role reversal, in which the "understandable" language is translated into the secondary or peripheralized language, draws further on the contrast between "real" languages which have written forms, and "non-languages" which do not have established orthographies. We will see similar tactics employed to subordinate southern US varieties of English in Chapter 10.

This report on HCE, which is meant to amuse but also to inform, has another set of underlying motivations which are subtle but effective. Most mainland US residents have never had any contact with HCE or its speakers, and perhaps had never considered that such a language might exist. In fact, most mainlanders would have very few associations about Hawai'ians at all, and if there are stereotypes in place, they would be for Hawai'ians of a different age and place, the subject of many movies on colonization of the islands. However, as a result of this brief but well-produced and quite engaging report, new stereotypes have been established for a large portion of the population, in a devastatingly effective manner.

SUMMARY

The individuals who provide us with information and news on a daily basis in print and broadcast forums have an unusual amount of power and control in the lives of the public. They are given free admittance to our homes, to bring to us their factual knowledge about the workings of the world. This process involves choosing among those pieces of information to share, and presenting them in a form which is accessible and understandable. The translation process from raw material to finished news report involves news filters of all kinds, many of which we are not immediately aware of when we take in the information over our dinners. The politics and cultural preconceptions which shape the news and the presentation of the news include ideas about language, and the importance of language. The process of language standardization is one which is implicitly and explicitly supported by the information industry, for practical reasons. In practical terms, it is useful for them to have authority in issues of language, which is their primary tool. This authority was assumed long ago, but it is necessary in this social contract – as in others – to remind all parties of the terms.

We concede to the information industry, particularly to the broadcast news industry, authority in the spoken language. We identify journalists and broadcasters as our role models; we allow them to chide us when our language differs from those varieties of English they speak, or think they speak. They have convinced us that they have the right to do this, and we do not challenge that right.

8 Language ideology in the work-place and the judicial system[1]

The stranger within my gate,
He may be true or kind,
But he does not talk my talk –
I cannot feel his mind.
I see the face and the eye and the mouth,
But not the soul behind.
The men of my own stock,
They may do ill or well,
But they tell the lies I am wonted to,
They are used to the lies I tell;
And we do not need interpreters
When we go to buy and sell.

Rudyard Kipling

In 1965, at the age of 29, Sulochana Mandhare left her home in the Maharashtra region of India and came to the United States. At that point in her life, Ms. Mandhare – a native speaker of Marathi – had been studying English for almost twenty years.

Ms. Mandhare speaks in a soft voice and an English which is characterized by full vowels in unstressed syllables, distinctive intonation patterns, aspirated fricatives and stops, and a lack of distinction between initial /v/ and /w/. She is an intelligent and articulate woman, and she tells her story in a clear and completely comprehensible accented English.[2]

After some time in the US, Ms. Mandhare relates, she decided to continue her education. She had arrived with undergraduate degrees in both liberal arts and education, but she returned to school and in 1972 completed a master's degree in education at New Orleans's Loyola University; in 1979 she was certified as a school librarian after completing a program at Nichols State University. After working for one year as an elementary school librarian, Ms. Mandhare applied for and was given a job as a librarian at a school serving kindergarten through second grade in the Lafargue, Louisiana school district, for the 1980–1981 school year.

Ms. Mandhare speaks of that year as a happy and successful one. Her responsibilities were to oversee the small library, read stories to the children, and introduce them to using the library, and she enjoyed this work. Therefore, when in April 1981 she was told that her contract would not be renewed because of her "heavy accent, speech patterns and grammar problems," and in spite of her excellent skills as a librarian (*Mandhare* 1985: 240–241), she was stunned and angry.[3] She investigated her options, and because she understood that the Civil Rights Act prohibits national-origin discrimination in the work place, she filed suit. This civil action was decided in Ms. Mandhare's favor; the decision was reversed by the US Court of Appeals in favor of the school board.[4]

Ms. Mandhare's case, and other cases like hers, are important because they provide real-life examples of how the language subordination process works, even when there are measures to combat it. We will return to her case later in this chapter.

LANGUAGE-FOCUSED DISCRIMINATION AND THE CIVIL RIGHTS ACT

Some types of language-focused discrimination have been illegal *in the work place*[5] since 1964, when Title VII of the Civil Rights Act of 1964 (42 United States Code §§2000e–2000e-17 (1982)) was passed into law.

Title VII provides recourse for workers who are discriminated against on the basis of race, color, religion, sex, or national origin.[6] However, it wasn't until 1980 that the Equal Employment Opportunity Commission (EEOC), a body created by Title VII, directly addressed trait-based discrimination.[7] In their *Guidelines on Discrimination Because of National Origin*, revised on a regular basis, the EEOC currently defines national-origin discrimination

> broadly as including, but not limited to, the denial of equal employment opportunity because of an individual's, or his or her ancestor's place of origin; or because an individual has the *physical, cultural or linguistic characteristics* of a national origin group.
> (United States Equal Employment Opportunity Commission 1988: §1606.1; emphasis added)

The spirit of the law is clear: an employer may not reject a job candidate, fire or refuse to promote an employee because that employee externalizes in some way an allegiance to another culture.

In the case of racial discrimination "It is clearly forbidden by Title VII to refuse on racial grounds to hire someone because your customers or clients do not like his race" (Matsuda 1991: 1376, fn 169; citations omitted). Similarly, a qualified person may not be rejected on the basis of linguistic traits that the employer or the employer's customers find aesthetically objectionable. In contrast to racial discrimination, however, an employer has some latitude in matters of language: "[a]n adverse employ-ment decision may be predicated upon an individual's accent when – but only when – it interferes materially with job performance" (Civil Rights Act of 1964, §701 ff., 42 United States Code Annotated (USCA) §2000e ff.).[8]

Title VII is very limited in its scope. Under the law as it currently stands, discrimination on the basis of *regional* origination is not covered. An accent must be directly traceable to a specific national origin to be eligible for Title VII protection.

Raj Gupta, former Attorney Counsel to the commissioner of the EEOC, states that there are forces within the EEOC who would like to see the definition of language-focused national-origin discrimination made more comprehensive (personal communication). So, in his example, a person from Appalachia would have recourse under Title VII because the features of Appalachian English are directly traceable to a number of dialects in Great Britain.[9]

THE LEGAL PROCESS

Alleged language-focused national-origin discrimination cases usually begin when an individual files a complaint with the EEOC (or a similar agency on a state or local level). The employee may then file a civil action in the trial courts, in which he or she claims that civil liberties (as set out in the Civil Rights Act of 1964) have been violated.

In some instances, these cases are brought to the courts not by the individual or group of individuals with the same complaint, but by a private agency acting for the injured party, such as the American Civil Liberties Union (ACLU), or by a government agency, such as the EEOC. This action may be initiated at the state level, as many states have adopted civil liberties legislation patterned on the federal statutes.[10]

An individual claiming language-focused discrimination must first prove a *prima facie* case of disparate treatment in four steps: establishment of identifiable national origin; proof of application for a job for which he or she was qualified, and for which the employer was seeking applicants; that he or she was rejected in spite of adequate qualifications; and that after such rejection, the job remained open and the employer continued to seek applicants with the Plaintiff's qualifications. After a *prima facie* case has been established, the burden shifts to the employer to rebut presumption of discrimination by articulating some legitimate, non-discriminatory reason for the action; if the employer does this, the burden shifts back to the Plaintiff to show that the purported reason for the action was a pretext for invidious discrimination. The Plaintiff can show the employer's pretext directly, by demonstrating that the employer was more likely motivated by discriminatory reasons, or indirectly, by showing that the proffered reason is unworthy of credence (Civil Rights Act of 1964, §701 ff., 42 USCA §2000e ff.).

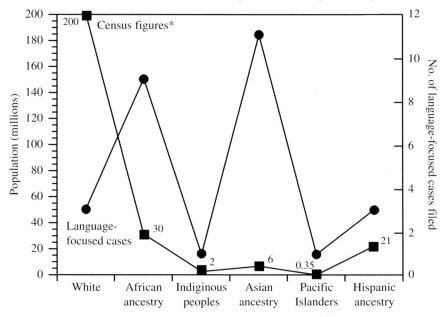

Figure 8.1 US population by race and relative number of Title VII language-focused complaints tried, 1972–1994. (Figures rounded. "Hispanic" may be any race)

Source: 1990 census

DISCRIMINATION IN THE WORKPLACE

In an excellent study of language and discrimination in the workplace in Great Britain, Roberts *et al.* (1992) provided numerous examples of discrimination focused on language, and directed toward ethnic and racial minorities. No such systematic and well-documented study exists for workers in the United States, although this is an area of great importance. The evidence of discrimination provided here is limited to specific instances which have found their way into the legal system.

Table 8.1 provides a breakdown of twenty-five language-focused national-origin discrimination cases heard in the federal and state courts and by the EEOC since 1972. Further excluded or missing are: cases which concerned the English Only question (for example, *Garcia (b)*); cases in which language-focused discrimination played a minimal role in the Plaintiff's arguments (*Garcia (a)*, *Bell*, and many others). In some of the cases included, both racial and national-origin discrimination were at issue. In most of the cases, accent, language use and communication figured prominently in the testimony, argumentation, discussion, and final opinion.[11] Figure 8.1 recasts these figures into a graph which includes total populations for each of the groups represented.

Table 8.1 Distribution of twenty-five language-focused discrimination cases in the courts/EEOC hearings by plaintiff's national origin, 1972–1994

Plaintiff's national origin	No. of cases filed	Court found for	
		Plaintiff	Defendant
ASIA, PACIFIC RIM			
Philippines Lubitz, Fragante, Carino	3	1	2
Vietnam Tran	1	0	1
China Ang, Hou	2	0	2
India Duddey, Mandhare, Patel	3	1	1
Cambodia Xieng	1	1	0
Korea Park	1	1	0
	11	4	6
CARIBBEAN/WEST INDIES			
Dominican Republic Meijia	1	0	1
Haiti Stephen	1	0	1
Cuba Rodriguez	1	0	1
	3	0	3
CENTRAL/SOUTH AMERICA			
Venezuela Dercach	1	0	1
Bolivia Ipina	1	0	1
	2	0	2
EASTERN EUROPE			
Armenia Vartivarian	1	0	1
Poland Berke	1	1	0
Ukraine Staruch	1	0	1
	3	1	2
AFRICA			
Nigeria Dabor	1	0	1
Liberia Andrews	1	0	0
Ghana Kpodo	1	0	0
	3	0	1
OTHER			
African American Sparks, Edwards	2	2	0
Hawai'ian Creole Kahakua	1	0	1
	3	2	1
Totals	25	7	15

Note: Discrepancies between the number of cases filed and those resolved for plaintiff or defendant are usually the product of an out-of-court settlement.

How widespread is language-focused discrimination? The General Accounting Office of the United States Government (GAO GGD 90–62 Employer Sanctions: 27) conducted a carefully designed statistical study of a stratified random sample of employers nationwide, and reported that 10 percent of their sample, or 461,000 companies employing millions of persons, openly, if naively, admit that they "discriminated on the basis of a person's foreign appearance or accent" (ibid.: 38). In hiring audits specifically designed to detect discrimination on the basis of accent (telephone inquiries about advertised jobs), such discrimination was found to be prevalent (ibid.).[12] This type of behavior was documented again in *Carroll*, when an employment agency receptionist was directed by her manager to screen all persons inquiring over the telephone: to those who did not "speak right," the job was closed. Carroll was also told to make notations about the caller's speech and accent (*Carroll*: 1173).

There are a number of possible reasons for the low number of documented cases, some of which include: employers who discriminate may do so in a non-blatant way; the persons discriminated against are so accustomed to this treatment that they no longer react; if they are aware of the treatment, they may not know that they have legal recourse, or how to pursue it; complaints are handled internally and resolved before litigation becomes necessary. Of course, many discriminated against on the basis of language may not find anything surprising or wrong about that fact. This is, after all, not the only society in the world that promotes a standard language ideology.

The bulk of the burden seems to fall, predictably, on the disenfranchised and the unassimilated. Cutler claims that the manner of enforcement of Title VII "permits an employer to reject qualified applicants of a particular national origin as long as he hires more assimilated applicants of the same origin instead" (1985: 1164; footnotes omitted).

Once cornered in a courtroom, what do the employers offer in the way of excuse? The approaches taken by defendants range from the naively and openly discriminatory to the subtle:

[I]n offering examples of Mr. Dercach's communication problems, Mr. M. explained that workers would ask Mr. Dercach what he wanted them to do, and then simply walk away, unable to understand. Mr. M. refused to attribute such incidents to Mr. Dercach's accent, but offered no other explanation. He said they just couldn't understand him "like normal people with normal language."

(*Dercach*: 899)

After listening to the transmission described by Dispatcher M. as *jargon*, . . . Rodriguez claims that during [a telephone] conversation Sgt. M. told him to "speak English like in Queens, New Jersey, not Little Havana." Sgt. M. testified that he could not recall ever having talked to Rodriguez.

(*Rodriguez*: LEXIS)

Managerial level employee LS told Xieng he was not being promoted because he could not speak "American."

(*Xieng* 1991: Appeal Court Opinion: 5)

the complainant's supervisor had removed her because of concern about the effect of her accent on the "image" of the IRS, not any lack in either communication or technical abilities.

(*Park*: EEOC press release dated June 8, 1988)

the ability to speak clearly is one of the most important skills . . . we felt the applicants selected would be better able to work in our office because of their communication skills.

(*Fragante* 1989: 598)[13]

So the court has before it a Plaintiff who claims that his or her basic civil liberties have been violated, and an employer who claims the right to make appropriate business decisions. How do courts handle this conflict? What factors, legal and otherwise, play a role in the decision-making process?

Some of those factors have to do with technicalities of the law and standards for evidence: in *Vartivarian*, for example, the Plaintiff presented only double hearsay: "X said Y was angry because a person with an accent [Plaintiff] had been hired behind his back" as evidence; there was no direct testimony or way to corroborate her claims.

In some cases one must assume that sometimes a Plaintiff will claim language-focused discrimination when in fact none has taken place. Or, there may be clear evidence of language-focused discrimination which the court overlooks because there is, in addition, a *bona fide* reason to deny employment. In *Dercach*, the court felt that blatant language-focused discrimination could not mitigate the fact that the Plaintiff, while hard-working and knowledgeable, was insufficiently literate. Because the job required close work with a written code book, and the ability to write multiple reports on a weekly basis, the court found for the Defendant.

The courts have stated that "[t]here is nothing improper about an employer making an honest assessment of the oral communications skills of a candidate for a job when such skills are reasonably related to job performance" (*Fragante* 1989: 596–597). Matsuda calls this the *doctrinal puzzle of accent and antidiscrimination law*: Title VII disallows discrimination on the basis of accent when it correlates to national origin, but it allows employers to discriminate on the basis of job ability. Employers claim that "accent" impedes communication, and thereby poses a valid basis for rejection; the courts are especially receptive to this argument (Matsuda 1991: 1348 ff.).[14]

Further, employers point out, the decision-making process in business hiring and promotion practices is often unavoidably subjective in nature. The courts have supported them in this:

It does not follow, though, that ethnic discrimination is the only explanation why Plaintiff was not promoted. Other plausible explanations
may exist. For instance, Nasser may not have chosen to promote
Plaintiff simply because he personally did not like her. While making
allowance for this kind of decisional criterion would arguably call into
play the "business judgment" rule enunciated in *Williams*, the court
does not reach its conclusion on the basis that it cannot review
Defendant's proffered reason.

(Vartivarian: 6558)

But how can the courts distinguish between an *admissible* business judgment based on business necessity or personal preference and *inadmissible*
considerations based on race or national origin? Is it simply a matter of
presentation of the right arguments by the employer? Cutler has pointed
out that employers are favorably predisposed to potential employees who
are "like" them, and less disposed toward potential employees who are
"unlike" them. Because the courts fail to recognize this fact, and refuse
to reject the validity of the personal preference rationale, "Title VII
becomes a statute which, at best, coerces job applicants to assimilate and,
at worst, keeps them jobless" (Cutler 1985: 1166).

I proceed from the point at which the Plaintiff and the Defendant have
made their cases, and the court must now decide whose argumentation
better fulfills the requirements set forth by the law. It is possible to
trace the influence of the standard ideology through much of the court's
deliberations.

STANDARD LANGUAGE IDEOLOGY IN THE COURTROOM

In the opinions put out by the courts there are a range of approaches
toward communication and accent. One assumes that the courts are unbi-
ased, and sometimes there is evidence of that:

> Accent and national origin are obviously inextricably intertwined in
> many cases. It would therefore be an easy refuge in this context for an
> employer unlawfully discriminating against someone based on national
> origin to state falsely that it was not the person's national origin that
> caused the employment or promotion problem, but the candidate's
> inability to measure up to the communications skills demanded by the
> job. We encourage a very searching look by the [trial] courts at such
> a claim.

(Fragante 1989: 596)

> Testimony of both Plaintiff's and Defendants' witnesses have convinced
> the Court that the Plaintiff's accent was a major factor in the
> Defendants' evaluation of his supervisory abilities . . . a trait related to
> national origin must be of an immutable nature in order to come within

Title VII protections. . . . An accent would appear to approach that sort of immutable characteristic . . .

(*Carino*: 1336–1337)

Plaintiff's accent did not interfere materially with his job performance, nor would it have interfered materially with his job performance . . . if he had been promoted . . .

(*Xieng* 1992, Supreme Court Opinion: 2)

But at the same time, and sometimes *in the same cases*, it is clear that the courts are willing to depend on their own often factually incorrect understanding of language issues:

Fragante argues the district court erred in considering "listener prejudice" as a legitimate, nondiscriminatory reason for failing to hire. We find, however, that the district court did not determine Defendants refused to hire Fragante on the basis that some listeners would "turn off" a Filipino accent. The district court after trial noted that: "Fragante, in fact, has a difficult manner of pronunciation . . ."

(*Fragante* 1989: 597)

The judge discounted the testimony of the linguist who stated that Hawai'ian Creole pronunciation is not incorrect, rather it is one of the many varieties of pronunciation of standard English. *The linguist, the judge stated, was not an expert in speech.*

(Matsuda 1991: 1345–46, including quotations from *Kahakua* 1987b: 22–23; emphasis added)[15]

During the Vietnam conflict, Mr. Tran worked as an interpreter for the US forces. That has misled him to believe that his English is better than it is in reality. Occasionally Mr. Tran's spoken English is readily understood, while at other times it is understood only with difficulty and sometimes not at all.

(*Tran*: 472)

The judges who wrote these opinions were willing to depend on their own expertise in matters of language in a way they would never presume to in matters of genetics, or mechanical engineering, or psychology. In *Kahakua*, the judge heard testimony of expert witnesses and then chose to give credence to that witness whose testimony most closely matched his own personal opinions on matters of language use. In none of these cases was there any attempt to assess the communication demands of the job in a non-prejudicial way, and *intelligibility* was a matter of opinion only.

How do some plaintiffs manage to win? *Xieng* provides an example of a successful case.

Phanna Xieng is a Cambodian American who worked for Peoples National Bank of Washington. Mr. Xieng was repeatedly denied a promotion although he had an excellent work history, high marks in his reviews, and had been filling in on the very position he applied for over an extended period of time. There were documented comments from his superiors concerning his accent as the primary stumbling block to his promotion. In this case, the court could not overlook the fact that Mr. Xieng could carry out the job he claimed he could do, in spite of his accent, precisely because *he had already been performing well at the job*. It might seem that being on the inside – already employed by the Defendant – provides an employee with a valid language-focused discrimination complaint with some strong evidence, but there are many other cases of denied promotion which were not so successful as *Xieng*.

Is it the case, then, that the Plaintiff's chances of winning a language-focused discrimination case depend to the greatest degree on the integrity and objectivity of the judge hearing the trial? Unfortunately, it is not so easy as this. Below it will become clear that for some areas of employment, even the most open-minded of courts still are subject to the unwritten laws of the standard language ideology.

EDUCATION-RELATED CASES

I consider here four cases in which educators sued their respective schools or school systems for racial and/or language-focused national-origin discrimination:

Sparks: an African American who was dismissed from her job as a school teacher

Hou: a native of China and professor of mathematics who was refused promotion

Edwards: an African American whose teaching contract was not renewed

Mandhare: a native of India who was denied reappointment to her position as a librarian at a K-2 school.

Ms. Sparks and Ms. Edwards won their cases; Ms. Mandhare won at trial court but lost on appeal; Dr. Hou lost his case.

Academic institutions were meant to be included within the scope of Title VII; nevertheless, the "trend in many courts has been to exercise minimal scrutiny of college and university employment practices, due, in large part, to the subjective factors on which many academic employment decisions are based" (*Hou*: 1546). They will intercede, but seem to do so with considerable forbearance for the opinions put forth by school administration. In addition, the courts have shown reluctance to reverse administrative decisions (*Hou*: 1548).

This deference for academic decision making was the downfall of *Hou*. The judge pointed out that "The issue of accent in a foreign-born person of another race is a concededly delicate subject when it becomes part of peer or student evaluations, since many people are prejudiced against those with accents" (*Hou*: 1547), and then went on to approve the loophole used by the institution:

We find that comments about Dr. Hou's accent, when made, were directed toward the legitimate issue of his teaching effectiveness. Teaching effectiveness, as the testimony at trial indicated, is an elusive concept (evaluation of teaching ability [is] necessarily [a] matter of judgment). Teaching effectiveness does, however, include the ability to communicate the content of a discipline, a quality which should be carefully evaluated at any college or university.

(ibid.; citations omitted)

There was never any discussion of appropriate, non-prejudicial assessment of Dr. Hou's communicative competence or intelligibility. The defense depended *exclusively* on anecdotal evidence provided by the defendant, and this satisfied the court.

[The college records showed that] He is at a decided disadvantage in the classroom because of his natural accent ... he has a difficult time overcoming this handicap. The obvious grammatical errors on his application attest to his communication problems ...

(ibid.)

The question must be, then, why other education cases prevailed where *Hou* could not. I consider *Sparks* and *Edwards* before a discussion of *Mandhare*.

Sparks and *Edwards* were built primarily on racial discrimination. In many pages of correspondence on the matter of Ms. Sparks' dismissal, the school administrator (Mr. Griffin) commented only once on the language issue: "Mrs. Sparks has a language problem. She cannot help the negro dialect, but it is certainly bad for the children to be subjected to it all day" (*Sparks*: 437). In *Edwards*, the discussion of language use is limited to general comments: "The plaintiff's contract was not renewed allegedly because of complaints received from parents and students. ... Several complaints concerned students' alleged inability to understand the plaintiff's 'black accent' " (*Edwards* Federal Reporter: 496).

In both these cases, the opinions indicate that the heart of the matter was racial discrimination. In other words, if the accent issue had never been raised in *Sparks* or *Edwards*, these Plaintiffs would still have won. This was fortunate for the courts, as it relieved them of the trouble of dealing with the matter of language and accent. In discussing the language-focused discrimination portion of *Sparks*, the court limited its comments to one short footnote: "With no disposition to be unkind, we question, based on the spelling and composition of the two letters ... the ability of Mr. Griffin to diagnose a 'language-problem' " (*Sparks*: 442). The letters written by Mr. Griffin regarding the dismissal of Ms. Sparks and referred to by the court were, in fact, poorly written and contained many spelling and/or typographical errors; nevertheless, the court is clearly uncomfortable chiding an educator, in this case an administrator with advanced

degrees, in matters of language use: "with no disposition to be unkind."
More importantly, the court never addressed the *content* of Mr. Griffin's
complaint (Ms. Sparks' "negro dialect" and its appropriateness for the
classroom); it addressed only the superintendent's qualifications to make
judgments on that dialect, *given his poor letter-writing skills.*

Would the court have thought seriously about this criticism if Mr. Griffin
had written elegant, grammatically appropriate prose? If he had argued
that Ms. Sparks' teaching effectiveness was compromised by her language
use? It seems likely that the school system could have found a line of
argumentation which would have pleased the courts; they failed to do so
in this case.

The court neatly sidestepped the "concededly delicate subject" of
language-focused discrimination for *Edwards* as well: "The district court
stated in its opinion that it was 'apparent' that the plaintiff could be easily
understood and that there was no evidence the plaintiff made grammatical
errors rendering her speech difficult to understand" (*Edwards* Federal
Reporter: 496).

In these two cases, the schools were deservedly punished for racial
discrimination; for language-focused discrimination, they were slapped on
the wrist.

It is worthwhile to look at how race and national origin intersect in
cases involving persons of African origin. Table 8.2 breaks down the nine
examined language-focused cases which were filed by such persons. The
two successful cases were brought by African Americans, native speakers
of English who also speak AAVE. The others were brought by persons
who speak English as a second language. This is some indication that there
are more negative feelings about persons who have recently immigrated
from Africa than there are about US residents who are native speakers
of English, even if the variety of English in question is stigmatized. There
is little work done on the way ethnic and national origin differences
may cause strife within the African American community, but that such
problems exist is a matter of record. I will look at this topic briefly in
Chapter 9.

I return now to the case of Sulochana Mandhare, with whom I began.
Earlier it was established that Ms. Mandhare's contract as a school
librarian was not renewed after that first year because her duties were

Table 8.2 Title VII cases won and lost by persons of African descent, by
country of origin, 1972–1994

Country/countries of origin	Cases lost	Cases won
African countries	5	0
Caribbean countries	2	0
United States (African American)	0	2

thought to be compromised by her heavy accent, specifically because her "problems with speech and grammar made it difficult for her to be understood by students and teachers ... plaintiff would do an excellent job at a school where her speech, grammar and story telling would not be so critical" (*Mandhare* 1985: 238).

The official published summary of the case indicates that Ms. Mandhare then met with the superintendent of schools and on the advice of her supervisor requested a transfer to Thibodaux Junior High School, as a librarian.[16] The school board refused to reappoint Ms. Mandhare to this requested new position; testimony revealed that in their private and public deliberations, Ms. Mandhare's foreignness and accent had been discussed.

The trial court was very firm in this case: Ms. Mandhare had been discriminated against, and she must prevail. However, the school's initial decision that the Plaintiff could not teach young children because of her "heavy accent and speech patterns and grammar problems [which] prevented her from effectively communicating with primary school students" (ibid.) *was never questioned*. The court took this claim on faith, and instead stated:

> Defendant's contention that its legitimate reason for plaintiff's termination or non appointment was that she had a communication problem because of her accent which prevented her from effectively communicating with primary school students is a feigned contention. Plaintiff was not being considered for a position which would require such communication. She was to be appointed librarian at a Junior High School, a position for which it was established that she was eminently qualified.
>
> (ibid.)

It is important to remember that in this case, as in every other case discussed, no effort was made to make an objective assessment of the communication skills required for the job, the Plaintiff's speech, the quality of her interaction with children or her intelligibility. The administrators found the Plaintiff's accent difficult; they decided not to reappoint her to her job in the grade school. This alone would have made them the focus of the court's scrutiny (although not necessarily to the Plaintiff's favor), but they redeemed themselves in the court's eyes: they praised the Plaintiff's industry and skill, and they went out of their way to locate a position in a school where her accent would *neither offend nor inconvenience*. The court could then focus on the school board, which refused to give the Plaintiff this new job. The validity of the initial firing was never challenged. Thus everyone (except the school board) was happy: the administrators were left intact as arbiters of the standard language ideology and lionized for their largesse; the court was not forced to challenge those educators on the factual basis for their decisions about appropriate language; Ms. Mandhare was to be reinstated as a librarian, in a junior high school.

The question remains: were Ms. Mandhare's civil rights protected? Were her best interests really served? Put more controversially, if Ms. Mandhare had been forbidden to ride public transportation, and challenged that restriction, should she then have been pleased to be offered alternate transportation, in the form of a bicycle, a Mercedes-Benz, or another, different but equally functioning, bus?

Ms. Mandhare did not really want the transfer to another school in a school district which had treated her so badly; she wanted back pay, which she did not get. Whether or not she would have been satisfied with the new position was never established, because the trial-court decision was reversed by the US Court of Appeals for the Fifth Circuit:

> The district court's determination that the Board had intentionally discriminated against Mandhare is clearly erroneous. The court focused on the wrong issue. It premised its conclusion on the Board's refusal to follow LeBlanc's recommendation that Mandhare be transferred to a junior high librarian position. That was not the issue as framed by the unamended pleadings and pre-trial order. Mandhare's action asserted discrimination in the Board's refusal to reemploy her as elementary school librarian, not their failure to create and transfer her to a junior high position.
>
> (*Mandhare* 1986: 5)

The terrible irony of this reversal should be clear: Ms. Mandhare was originally protesting *her dismissal* on the basis of language-focused national-origin discrimination; the judge in that first case chose not to deal with that delicate issue, but to bypass it completely by focusing on the possibility of a position in another school. This gave the appeal court an out, which it took. The appeal court accused the trial court of focusing on the wrong issue and *on that basis* it reversed the decision.

In the end, both courts were satisfied to let the school administrators and school board exclude on the basis of accent. In the analogy above, the first court offered Ms. Mandhare a Mercedes-Benz when all she wanted to do was ride on the bus. The appeal court said that the court had been wrong to offer Ms. Mandhare a Mercedes-Benz that didn't exist and that no one was obliged to buy for her; it did not even question why she had been forced off the bus in the first place, and it certainly didn't offer her the opportunity to get back on, or compensate her for her trouble.

The appeal court filed the reversal on May 2, 1986, six years after Ms. Mandhare was denied renewal. The failure of the American judicial system caused her untold emotional anguish, financial difficulty, and was detrimental to her health. Today, she works as librarian for a private school in her home town of Thibodaux, but she will carry this experience with her for the rest of her life.

BROADCAST-RELATED CASES

The Kahakua and the Staruch cases both have to do with the broadcast media, specifically with radio broadcast. These cases are clearly very different from the other cases presented here because they involve de-contextualized communication, in which heavier burdens are placed on the speaker.[17] Nevertheless, they provide interesting insight into the court's deliberations on matters of language.

We considered Mr. Kahakua's case briefly in the first chapters, but it is worthy of a closer look in this context. Mr. Kahakua is a native of Hawai'i, a bilingual speaker of Hawai'ian Creole and English; as a meteorologist with twenty years of experience and considerable educational background, he applied for a promotion so that he could read weather reports on air.

Mr. Staruch, a native of western Ukraine, wanted to read news on the air, for the US Bureau of Information, *in his native tongue*. This time, the Plaintiff was penalized for speaking Ukrainian with a stigmatized regional accent of that language.

Both lost their cases.

If the courts are deferential to academic institutions in matters of internal administration and language use, they seem to be even more willing to defer to the standards of the broadcast media, even when those standards involve blatant language-focused discrimination. The arguments put forward by employers in these cases and accepted by the courts involve the following elements:

1 *Refusal to acknowledge accent as an immutable characteristic of national origin* (misrecognition)

   The court added, "there is no race or physiological reason why Kahakua could not have used standard English pronunciations."

   (Matsuda 1991: 1345)

2 *Allowing direct and non-factual association of negative social values with stigmatized linguistic variants* (disinformation)

   the agency contended that the appellant's accent was undesirable ... found to lack authority, friendliness, clarity and other qualities desired in a broadcasted voice.

   (*Staruch* 1992, EEOC Hearing Opinion)

   [The judge said] The white candidate was selected because he had "better diction, better enunciation, better pronunciation, better cadence, better intonation, better voice clarity, and better understandability."

   (Matsuda 1991: 1345, citing from *Kahakua* 1987b)

3 *Willingness to allow the media to set its own standards on the basis of personal preferences, even when those preferences necessarily involve language-focused discrimination* (claiming authority)

the judge credited the testimony of speech experts that . . . "Standard English should be used by radio broadcasters."

(ibid.)

The agency stated that the appellant's voice was not suitable for broadcast purposes . . . Appellant's voice was described as having a definite Western Ukrainian accent. As in the United States, where national network news is broadcast in "television accent" rather than the regional accents sometimes heard on local broadcasts . . .

(*Staruch*: ibid.)

4 *Lack of concern with established facts about language structure and use, or with consistent, non-prejudicial evaluation of language skills* (disinformation)

[An external review found him] . . . "not persuasive"; his pronunciation as "often incorrect," delivery "dull" and "sounding strange to the listener."

(ibid.)

I [expert witness "speech consultant"] urgently recommend he seek professional help in striving to lessen this handicap. . . . *Pidgin can be controlled.* And if an individual is totally committed to improving, professional help on a long-term basis can produce results.

(*Kahakua* 1987b: Excerpts of the Record: 31, as cited by Matsuda 1991: 1366; original emphasis)

The *Staruch* decision has to do with the limited scope of Title VII: the EEOC commissioners who heard the case accepted the argument that Ukrainian speakers who had evaluated Staruch's speech didn't like his *regional* accent.

The courts clearly have bought the argument that in broadcast media, language-focused discrimination is nothing more than good business practice; that is, mainstream language use is a *bona fide* occupational qualification. Kahakua's attorney, Richard Hearn, has put this more succinctly: The employer didn't want Kahakua on the radio, because Kahakua didn't sound white (Drummond 1990).

Of course, the behavior of the courts follows logically if one accepts the premise that the media appropriately embodies the standard language ideology, and should be entrusted with both the preservation and propagation of that standard, and the exclusion and disempowerment of those who do not subscribe to it.

SUMMARY

If ideology is most effective when its workings are least visible then the first step must be to *make visible* the link between the enforcement of standard language ideology and social domination. The educational system is the obvious point of departure, but that system is itself part of the problem. Given the way the schools, media, and employers work together to promote language ideology, the education of the public is both a lonely and a difficult – but certainly not an impossible – task.

Beyond education, linguists have hard-won knowledge to offer which would be of some assistance in the difficult questions faced in matters of language policy, but that knowledge is often not sought; if sought, it may be summarily rejected; in either case, it is often hotly resented. Nevertheless, there are good reasons to persevere. This type of behavior causes real harm to real individuals, and it deserves attention.

In the judicial system, there may be some lessons for linguists to learn from psychologists and psychiatrists, whose contributions to trial law are better established, although the effectiveness and value of those contributions are often challenged (Faust and Ziskin 1988). While the overall quality of contribution of psychologists in legal cases is still being debated, some issues have been clarified as a result of that body of testimony. The law now defines and takes seriously such human conditions as battered-woman syndrome, clinical depression and post-traumatic stress syndrome.

Conversely, while the courts have called on linguists to address technical matters of authorship and identification to be used as evidence,[18] they are less interested in a linguist's definition of communicative competence or assessment of intelligibility, as was seen in *Kahakua* and *Fragante*, because these are areas they deem within their own powers of reasoning and expertise.

Xieng provides an interesting illustration of the status of linguistics in the courts: there was no expert testimony at all on the pivotal matter, which was the employer's claim that Mr. Xieng's accent was too strong and impeded communication. However, a psychiatrist was called, who then argued and convinced the court that there did exist a "causal relationship between the [employer's] national origin discrimination and Xieng's severe emotional distress and depression" (*Xieng* 1991: *Findings of Fact*: A13).

Psychologists ask themselves a two-part question to determine the quality of their forensic contribution: (1) can we answer questions with reasonable accuracy? (2) can we help the judge and jury reach a more accurate conclusion than would otherwise be possible (Faust and Ziskin 1988: 31)? That is, does the subject lie beyond the knowledge and experience of the average layman, and can the expert inform without invading the province of the jury by expressing a conclusion as to the ultimate issue?

For most of the cases presented here, a list of questions could have been put to linguists which would have met both of these basic criteria. Questions about the process of standardization, differences between spoken and written language varieties, cultural differences in discourse style and structure which may cause processing difficulties, second-language acquisition and accent, subconscious social evaluation of active variation, and change over time and space could be answered with reasonable accuracy. We *could* provide the judge and the jury with information and knowledge beyond that of the average layman, but the issue is this: we cannot make them *want* that information, no matter how factually correct or how strongly supported by empirical evidence.

Linguistic contributions to the legal process are not valued because ideology intervenes in a way that it does not in matters of mental health. A judge may have no personal investment in accepting evidence linking systematic, long-term physical abuse and violent behavior; he or she is more likely to have a strong personal reaction when asked to reconsider the assumptions underlying the standard language ideology.

Fairclough, who acknowledges this somewhat depressing state of affairs, also points out that "resistance and change are not only possible, but are continuously happening. But the effectiveness of resistance and the realization of change depend on people developing a critical consciousness of domination and its modalities, rather than just experiencing them" (1989: 4).

Some of the discussion around language standards is so emotional in tone that parallels can be drawn to disagreements between scientists and theologians over the centuries. In our own time, in the courts, science and rational inquiry have come up against public opinion based on personal preferences and intuition:

> the real problem faced is not legal but sociological. In the centers of population men have gone on assuming certain bodies of knowledge and certain points of view without realizing that they were living in a different world from that inhabited by a considerable portion of their fellow-citizens, and they have been unconscious of the danger which threatened them at the inevitable moment when the two worlds should come in conflict.
>
> (*Nation*: July 22, 1925: 28; cited in Caudill 1989: 23)

This editorial was written at the height of the Scopes Trial, in which fundamentalists and empiricists argued the very definition of truth. It was a trial surrounded by sensational journalism and followed with great interest by many people. Scopes, a science teacher who taught the theory of evolution in a state which forbade him to do so, lost his case and was fined $100.

But something else, something perhaps more important, was won. Before the trial, one might gather that the majority of American citizens had never come in contact with evolutionary theory. After the trial, many of those people were thinking about their own beliefs, about science, and about the nature of authority and its relationship to knowledge. Whatever an individual's personal beliefs, after the Scopes Trial it became increasingly difficult for anyone to dismiss out of hand the facts put forth by scientists. Today, more than seventy years later, evolution is taught in all public schools and most private ones.

The Scopes Trial involved free speech, educational policy, and a range of sociological issues. When the topic is discrimination on the basis of language, the stakes are very different. *Mandhare, Hou, Xieng, Kahakua,* and the other cases like them test an even more basic freedom: the individual's right to be different:

> The way we talk, whether it is a life choice or an immutable characteristic, is akin to other attributes of the self that the law protects. In privacy law, due process law, protection against cruel and unusual punishment, and freedom from inquisition, we say the state cannot intrude upon the core of you, cannot take away your sacred places of the self. A citizen's accent, I would argue, resides in one of those places.
>
> (Matsuda 1991: 1391–1392)

It would seem that linguistics and language-focused discrimination have yet to meet their Scopes Trial.

Part III

What we reap

Consent manufactured

Introduction
Our naked skins

> We live in an atmosphere of shame. We are ashamed of everything that is real about us; ashamed of ourselves, of our relatives, of our incomes, of our accents, of our opinions, of our experience, just as we are ashamed of our naked skins.
> George Bernard Shaw, *Man and Superman* (1905)

All human beings living in contact with other human beings construct and project their social identities with the help of language variation. At the same time, speakers are constantly bombarded with messages from and about the people around them, again at least in part by means of the structured heterogeneity basic to language. In the previous sections, we have seen that for some speakers, this natural and unavoidable feature of spoken language becomes the focus of censure and correction. The varieties of English which are singled out for this attention are linked to specific regional varieties of English, or to accents with links to other national origins, homelands, races, ethnicities, or social class.

Systematic disciplining of speakers who do not willingly attempt to assimilate to a set of abstract language norms is well documented. Those institutions which promote an idealized nation-state and its abstracted standard language have been seen to work together and support each other in this goal. Educators point to the expectations of the business sector; the judicial system points back to the educational system. The broadcast and print media, as well as the entertainment industry, reinforce the message in a variety of ways.

It would be useful, at this juncture, to remind ourselves that standard language ideology is concerned not so much with the choice of one possible variant, but with the elimination of *socially unacceptable* difference. This is externalized in the targeting of particular variants linked to specific social identities. The subordination process seeks to limit access to discourse on the basis of language, silencing many before their message can be heard. Gramsci's definition of hegemony (1985), in which ideology is equated with an ongoing struggle, is useful here: institutionalized language policies insist in the first line on elimination of subordinated language varieties, but when resistance arises, they cope by giving in a little to retain a lot. *Yes*, the argument goes, *we concede that your language is perfectly adequate and viable and equal. But*, they continue, *let's put it (and you) over there, out of view, where unacceptable otherness can be ignored.* This is the basic conflict that speakers of those stigmatized varieties must confront and resolve.

We have seen in the previous chapters the ways that the dominant institutions structure arguments for assimilation. Here we will look at how individuals see and evaluate speakers of stigmatized languages. Of particular interest is how the basic conflict between the assimilatory message of the dominant institutions and personal experience is resolved. If an individual chooses to assimilate, how is this action justified? How and why do some individuals resist linguistic assimilation?

Of the many social and regional varieties which have suffered the same fate to a greater or lesser extent, I consider two in detail here. In Chapter 9 I look at AAVE, and in Chapter 10, the totality of languages known simply as southern US English. In Chapter 11 there is a brief look at the issue of foreign-language accent for Latinos as well as for Asian Americans. It must be brief, because each of these groups would require an entire volume to explore the complexities of language and accent for them.

AAVE and southern US English provide an interesting contrast. In many ways they could not be more different, and some will say that this juxtaposition is perhaps less than politically astute, given the historical relationship between race, geography, and extroverted racism. In fact, language subordination tactics are surprisingly consistent and successful across racial, socioeconomic, and regional lines, although resistance takes different forms in each of these populations. It will become clear that ideology functions more consistently and more forcefully in the case of AAVE, but the tactics are similar in both cases.

One matter must be taken up briefly at the start, which has to do with terminology.

Sometimes scholars use the term *linguistic insecurity* to describe how speakers of peripheralized languages subordinate and devalue their own language in line with stigmatization which originates outside their communities. This term was coined by Labov in his analysis of social variation in New York City, as an explanation of his finding that "New Yorkers hear themselves not as they actually sound, but rather in accordance with the norms they acknowledge" (1982a: 332). He points out that linguistic insecurity is something which developed together with a "doctrine of correctness."[1]

Linguistic insecurity, which in other places Labov notes could be termed "linguistic self-hatred" at its severest, is put forth as an explanation for hypercorrection, which in turn is defined in his work as the errors speakers make when they attempt to target norms, or to use rules, which are not native to their own variety of the language, as in *Whom did you say was calling?* In his work in New York, centered on socioeconomic class, Labov explores only one direction of this process, where speakers of (what he calls) non-standard varieties target the language norms of higher classes.[2]

Linguistic insecurity or self-hatred, along with another term, "covert prestige," are simply ways of observing that stigmatized language communities have different scales of value when it comes to the evaluation and choosing of language variants, and that they are often caught between community internal values and values external to their home communities. If in observing the behaviors of speakers of peripheralized languages we find this conflict, it is not enough to conclude that they seem to want to command the mainstream language, or that they choose not to because their own language has community-based prestige. The underlying questions must be: How and why is it that speakers come to accept external scales of value, to their own detriment? How and why do they resist this process?

Sociolinguists have put these questions aside for a long time, but it is a dangerous thing to do. We point out systematicity, but fail to explore the underlying motivations for shifts in power and solidarity which cause systematic systems to change. It is crucial, of course, to report our observations neutrally, but it is also crucial to explore below the surface, otherwise we take on the risk of seeming to condone the distributions that we observe.

The need for looking farther than the simple distributions is illustrated perhaps best by an essay written recently by a journalist who read Labov's New York study findings many years after the fact:

> No matter how many [linguistic] habits New Yorkers consciously unlearn, they will still unconsciously say some things differently from the rest of the country. They will still sound like New Yorkers, and they will still be ashamed. They will discover, despite all their efforts, the fundamental truth about the national hatred of the New York accent: America doesn't really hate us for the way we tawk. America hates us for who we are.
>
> (Tierney 1995: 16)

Language provides an unusual and unique opportunity to explore how people think about themselves as members of groups. Why they are willing to go along with being ashamed of themselves, why they will continue to try to change. This is where the real work begins.

9   The real trouble with Black English

It is not the Black child's language which is despised: It is his experience.

James Baldwin, "If Black English isn't a language, then tell me, what is?"

(1979)

The 1990 census reported that the US African American population grew about 10 percent between 1980 and 1990, for a count of 29,930,524, or about 12 percent of the country's total population. A portion of these almost 30 million persons speak the language which is sometimes called African American Vernacular English, for some part of the time.[1] Various authors have put the number of AAVE speakers between 80 and 90 percent of the black population (Smitherman 1977, Baugh 1983), although it seems that this estimate is based on the supposition that AAVE is the language of inner-city communities, specifically of the working class and the poor (Rickford (forthcoming) calls the 80-90 percent figure a *guestimate*). According to Rickford (ibid.) the last important work on comparative use of AAVE in a black community was done in Detroit in the 1960s, a study which indicated that there was some reason to use socioeconomic factors in the estimation of who is more likely to use this language.

It is hard to say with any assurance how many African Americans are native speakers or regular users of AAVE because the term AAVE itself is inexactly defined, as we will shortly see in detail. There are supra-regional phonological and grammatical features of AAVE, but there is also social and regional variation, as is to be expected of any spoken language. The language of African Americans living in the rural south is different than that of the Latino and European Americans who live alongside them, but it is also different than the AAVE spoken in urban centers in the south (Cukor-Avila 1995). Morgan and DeBerry (1995) provide insight into the way that African American youth integrated into urban Hip Hop culture must choose among grammatical, lexical, and phonological variables which identify them as aligned with either the west or the east coast. AAVE is, in short, a functional spoken language which depends on structured variation to layer social meaning into discourse.

Close study of it has shown the systematic effects of language-internal and language-external constraints (Baugh 1983, Rickford and Rickford 1995).

Smitherman points out that just as important as the phonological and grammatical components of AAVE are the cultural and stylistic ones, and she provides examples of how these elements work together:

> Think of black speech as having two dimensions: language and style. Though we will separate the two for purposes of analysis, they are often overlapping. This is an important point, frequently overlooked in discussions of Black English ... Reverend Jesse Jackson preach: "Africa would if Africa could. America could if America would. But Africa cain't and America ain't." Now here Reverend Jesse is using the language of Black Dialect when he says "ain't" and when he pronounced can't as "cain't." But the total expression, using black rhythmic speech, is the more powerful because the Reb has plugged into the style of Black Dialect. The statement thus depends for full communication on what black poet Eugene Redmond calls "songified" pattern and on an Afro-American cultural belief set.
>
> (1977: 3)[2]

Given this perspective, it is hard to claim that only poor or working-class African Americans are speakers of AAVE. Upper-middle-class blacks may seldom or never use grammatical features of AAVE, but such persons are often heard marking their language in a variety of ways to signal solidarity with the greater African American community. This may mean the use of AAVE intonation, tag questions, and address systems, or, more subtly, rhetorical features and discourse strategies. These strategies are what Smitherman calls the African American Verbal Tradition (AVT), and include signification, personalization, tonal semantics, and sermonic tone (1995).[3]

Smitherman provides an insightful analysis of the African American community's differing responses to Anita Hill and Clarence Thomas during the congressional confirmation hearings on Thomas's appointment to the Supreme Court. Smitherman's study found cultural differences in discourse style: Hill's rhetorical devices were distinctly white, while Thomas

> capitalized on and ruthlessly exploited the African American Verbal Tradition for all it was worth. He seized the rhetorical advantage, swaying Black opinion by use of the touchstones of the Oral Tradition and sociolinguistically constructing an image of himself as culturally Black and at one with the Folk.
>
> (1995: 238–239)

This analysis of culturally specific rhetorical styles makes one thing very clear: even when no grammatical, phonological, or lexical features of

AAVE are used, a person can, *in effect*, still be speaking AAVE by means of AVT rhetorical devices. Thus, while the core grammatical features of AAVE may be heard most consistently in poorer black communities where there are strong social and communication networks, AAVE phonology (particularly intonation) and black rhetorical style are heard, on occasion, from prominent and successful African Americans in public forums. These may be individuals who grew up in AAVE-speaking communities but who are bidialectal, or others who grew up with a different variety of English altogether, and still chose to try to acquire AAVE and use it on occasion (with differing degrees of success, as seen in Baugh 1992). African Americans who never draw at all on any grammatical or stylistic features of AAVE certainly do exist, although their number would be very hard to estimate. According to Smitherman, Anita Hill is one such African American, at least within the context of her testimony before the Senate confirmation hearings for Clarence Thomas.

For our purposes, it is enough to note that AAVE is a spoken language available in some degree to most if not all African Americans, and that there are grammatical and stylistic features of this language which are constant over space. These grammatical structures sometimes show strong contrast to parallel structures in other US Englishes, but they are consistent and logical within themselves. AAVE has been the focus of formal study for more than thirty years, and linguists have attained a good – but not complete – understanding of its workings.

Nevertheless, in spite of many years of empirical study which establish AAVE as a normally functioning spoken human language, its very existence is often doubted and denied, by African and European Americans alike. The real trouble with Black English is not the verbal aspect system which distinguishes it from other varieties of US English, or the rhetorical strategies which draw such a vivid contrast, it is simply this: AAVE is tangible and irrefutable evidence that there is a distinct, healthy, functioning African American culture which is not white, and which does not want to be white. This is a state of affairs which is unacceptable to many. James Baldwin, who wrote and spoke so eloquently of the issues at the heart of the racial divide in this country, put it quite simply: "the value [of] a black man is proven by one thing only – his devotion to white people" (1988: 5).

These statements will make many people unhappy and others mad. Our common culture tells us constantly that to fulfill our democratic ideals we must be *one nation, indivisible*. In the 1960s we put an official end to racial segregation in schooling, housing, public places, and the workplace. What does it mean then to say that there is an African American culture distinct enough from other American cultures to have its own variety of English, a variety that persists in the face of overt stigmatization? As we look at the way people talk about AAVE below, we will see that the problem is a complex one. European American reaction to AAVE runs the gamut from indifference to denial and denigration to anger and resentment.[4] For African Americans, the subject of AAVE seems to be particularly difficult because it forces individuals to choose between languages and cultures. For some, AAVE is not a vehicle of solidarity, but the focus of a painful debate on what it means to be black.

NON-BLACK ATTITUDES TOWARD AAVE

Pejorative attitudes toward AAVE by non-blacks are easy enough to document, and the socially constructed complaints about it are very similar to the complaints about other stigmatized social and regional varieties. These complaints tend to fall into two categories: targeted lexical items or grammatical features which cause immediate reaction, and general issues of language purity and authority.

European and African Americans have very different concerns about AAVE: whites seem to be most comfortable voicing overt criticism about phonological matters and sometimes about grammar, but black concerns focus almost exclusively on grammatical issues, as will be seen below.[5]

One of the most salient points of phonological variation which is strongly stigmatized from outside the black community might be called the great *ask–aks* controversy.

The verb *ask* is commonly defined as meaning to call for information, request a desired thing, or inquire. There are two pronunciations heard commonly in the US: [æsk] and [æks]. In rapid speech, a third pronunciation [æst] is often heard, derived from [æsk]. The *Oxford English Dictionary* establishes this variation between [æsk] and [æks] as very old, a result of the Old English metathesis *asc-*, *acs-*.[6] From this followed Middle English variation with many possible forms: *ox*, *ax*, *ex*, *ask*, *esk*, *ash*, *esh*, *ass*, *ess*. Finally, *ax* (aks) survived to almost 1600 as the regular literary form, when *ask* became the literary preference. Most people know nothing of the history of this form, and believe the *aks* variant to be an innovation of the AAVE community. In fact, it is found in Appalachian speech, in some urban dialects in the New York metropolitan area, and outside the US in some regional varieties of British English.

Non-AAVE speakers are eager and willing to point out this usage, which is characterized as the most horrendous of errors:

> On the last day that I met with my adopt-a-class last year, I told the students that they will have to learn to read, write, do math, and speak English properly if they are going to get a first-rate job and be a success. I told them there was one word that will mark them as uneducated. . . . A young girl raised her hand and said, "The word is ax." . . . I asked her if she could pronounce the word properly. She said, "Yes, it is ask." . . . I felt terrific. By simply raising that one word on an earlier occasion, I had focused their attention on something that I think is important,

and I am sure you do as well. . . . You were present at Martin Luther King, Jr. High School last week when the opening ceremony was conducted regarding the High School Institute for Law and Justice. A young girl in the class was asked to read her essay. The content of her essay was excellent, but at one point she pronounced the word "ask" as "ax." I believe that everyone in the room recognizing the mispronunciation was distressed and, regrettably, the substance of her essay was [thus made] less important.

(Edward I. Koch, Mayor of New York City, to the Chancellor of Education, *Harper's Magazine*, March 1989: 21–22)

I guess what I'd like to say is that what makes me feel that blacks tend to be ignorant is that they fail to see that the word is spelled A-S-K, not A-X. And when they say *aksed*, it gives the sentence an entirely different meaning. And that is what I feel holds blacks back.

(female call-in viewer, *Oprah Winfrey Show* 1987)

My husband came here from Germany and he learned how to say a-s-k, so why can't you?

(overheard)

All of these criticisms of the stigmatized *aks* variant assume that its use is the result of ignorance or stupidity following from lack of education. Why else, this reasoning goes, would someone hold on willfully to such an ugly, contemptuous usage? More disturbing is the simple acceptance of a single variable as a suitable basis for judging not only the content of the message, but also the character and intelligence of the messenger. Former New York Mayor Koch dismisses a presentation which he otherwise finds well done and convincing *on the basis of a single sociolinguistic variant*; *Harper's* prints his letter to the Chancellor of Education without comment.

The authority cited here is the written language: *aks* is wrong because we write *ask*. This kind of criticism is particularly illogical, given the large-scale lack of correspondence between sound and symbol in English. The call-in viewer, citing the authority of the written language, provided excellent proof of this. She spoke what is commonly considered MUSE, and like others who speak unstigmatized varieties of American English, she did not aspirate the *h* in *what*; she pronounced *spelled* [spelt], *different* [difərnt] and *sentence* [seʔəns].

Uninformed criticisms based on the written language are troublesome, but they are overshadowed by other more general condemnations of AAVE which extend to criticisms of African American culture and values. Such criticisms are often openly made, in particular by newspaper columnists, as in a sports column:

Ungrammatical street talk by black professional athletes, and other blacks in public professions such as the music industry, has come to be accepted. Indeed, "Moses, you is a baaad damn shootin' individual" comes a lot closer to proper English usage than many public sentences uttered by black athletes. . . . But there's a problem here. Black athletes – and black musicians and TV performers, etc., – are role models for young black children. We in the media have begun to pass on the street language of black "superstars" verbatim . . . and what this is doing is passing the message to a whole new generation of black children that it's OK to talk that way; more than OK, it's terrific to talk that way . . . the situation is compounded by leading black characters in several network television shows, who use street grammar to advance the feeling that they are young and cool.

The dilemma is that it doesn't make much difference for the black professional athletes, etc., who talk this way – they're wealthy men who are going to live well off their bodily skills no matter if they can talk at all, much less correctly . . . if a black child emulates one of the dumb-talking black athletes he sees being interviewed on TV, he is not going to be thought of as a superstar. He is going to be thought of as a stupid kid, and later, as a stupid adult. . . . They probably aren't talking that way because they think it's right; they're talking that way because it's a signal that they reject the white, middle-class world that they have started to live in the midst of.

(Bob Greene's Sports Column, *Chicago Tribune*, December 3, 1979)

While censure of AAVE is not hard to find, it is not often that such criticisms and the underlying assumptions are so openly and unapologetically voiced.

Greene identifies two professions which he associates with successful African Americans: sports and entertainment. What these people have in common, in his estimation, is the fact that they speak AAVE, that they are in the public eye, and that they have the power to lead the black youth of America astray. His point, and it is factually true, is that with the exception of these two groups, very few African Americans who achieve mainstream economic and social success are able to do it without the necessity of linguistic and, to some degree, cultural assimilation.

What seems to bother Greene so much is the fact that the gatekeeping mechanism is not perfect: it does not extend to all African Americans. Some have successfully evaded the language of what he freely identifies as that of the white middle class. It is irritating to him that these people have managed to become successful without *good language*, but there is something even more upsetting. As a sports journalist, he finds himself compelled to pass on the language he hears from athletes, thus becoming complicit in letting the secret out to black children: not all African Americans give in linguistically, and yet they still get to the top.

Greene makes a series of factually incorrect assumptions. Black children learn AAVE not from television actors and sports figures (as Greene surmises), but in their homes, as their first and native variety of US English. More importantly, Greene assumes that the only role models that African American children have are these sports and entertainment individuals, and further, that a good role model will not sound black. For him, the two are mutually exclusive. His message is clearly stated:

> If you're a black child, and you're not one of the 100 or so best slam-dunkers or wide receivers in the world, you can go ahead and emulate the way you hear your heroes talk. But the chances are that you'll wind up as the hippest dude passing out towels in the men's washroom.
>
> (ibid.)

The stereotypes that underlie Greene's assumptions are of course very disturbing, but there are other issues here which are more subtle and perhaps more damaging.

This is a good example of both explicit threat and unfounded promise in one statement. The threat is real enough: black children who don't learn white English will have limited choices; what he claims is demonstrably true. But the inverse of this situation, the implied promise, is not equally true: black children who learn MUSE will not be given automatic access to the rewards and possibilities of the white middle-class world. Greene actually touches upon the fallacy underlying this promise when he acknowledges (later in his column) that successful blacks who wear uniforms (airline pilots, army officers) are often taken for service personnel in public places.

Non-black discomfort with AAVE is often externalized in this paternalistic voice. It can be seen to work in a variety of forums, including popular fiction. The novel is one of the most interesting points of access to current language ideology, in that the way that characters in novels use language and talk about language can be revealing.[7] The following excerpt from a romance novel titled *Family Blessings* provides a typical social construction of an idealized relationship between a MUSE speaker and an AAVE speaker. Here the hero, a young white police officer, has taken on the job of setting an African American child straight:

> "Yo."
> "What you talkin' like a black boy for?"
> "What *you* talkin' like a black boy for?"
> "I be black."
> "You might be, but no sense talking like a dumb one if you ever want to get anywhere in this world . . ."
> . . . "I could turn you in for dat, you know. Teachers in school can't even make us change how we talk. It's the rules. We got our culture to preserve."
> "I'm not your teacher, and if you ask me, you're preserving the wrong side of your culture . . . listen to you, talking like a dummy! I told you,

if you want to get out someday and make something of yourself and have a truck like this and a job where you can wear decent clothes and people will respect you, you start by talking like a smart person, which you are. I could hack that oreo talk if it was real, but the first time I picked you up for doing the five-finger discount over at the SA station, you talked like every other kid in your neighborhood. . . ."

"I'm twelve years old. You not supposed to talk to me like dat."

"Tell you what – I'll make you a deal. I'll talk to you nicer if you'll talk to me nicer. And the first thing you do is stop using that F word. And the second thing you do is start pronouncing words the way your first-grade teacher taught you to. The word is *that*, not *dat*."

(Spencer 1995: 102–103)

Like Greene's sports column, the hero in this novel has both threats and promises for the African American child. The kind of authority cited is different: Greene draws on his own mastery of middle-class written English, as exemplified in his profession as a writer, whereas this fictional character has nothing more to underscore his pronouncements about language than his own observations and the trappings of his own success. *This is what you can have*, he says, *if you start sounding like me. If you do not, you do so out of stubborness and stupidity, and there is no hope for you.*

Occasionally there is a public outpouring of pure emotion, without any of the common-sense arguments, complex rationalizations, or threats and promises which are such an integral part of more organized institutionalized subordination tactics. Such outpourings are useful, because they get right to the heart of the matter.

I am sitting here just burning . . . the ones that want to speak or care to speak that way, they want to be different. I believe they put themselves that way to be separate.

(European American call-in viewer, *Oprah Winfrey Show* 1987)

For those who cannot overlook the fact that AAVE exists, it seems to symbolize black resistance to a cultural mainstreaming process which is seen as the logical and reasonable cost of equality – and following from that, success – in other realms. Alternately, AAVE evokes a kind of panic, a realization that desegregation has not done its job. The reasoning seems to be that the logical conclusion to a successful civil rights movement is the end of racism *not because we have come to accept difference, but because we have eliminated difference.* There will be no need for a distinct African American (or Mexican, or Vietnamese) culture (or language), because those people will have full access to, and control of, the superior European American one.

When a black woman tells a reporter about the solidifying function of AAVE in her community, his response first acknowledges that language as viable, but then he rejects her construction of the language as one with a positive function and recasts the language as a willful act of political resistance:

(BLACK WOMAN)   So we gotta have our survival mechanism within our community. And our language is it. It lets us know that we all in this thing together.
(REPORTER)   Black English is not Standard English spoken badly – Black English is revenge.

(CBS Evening News, December 5, 1985)

The *Oxford English Dictionary* defines revenge as "The act of doing hurt or harm to another in return for wrong or injury suffered; satisfaction obtained by repayment of injuries." Thus AAVE is not seen as first and foremost a positive feature of a vibrant black community. Instead it is a wilfull act of rebellion: destructive, hurtful, and primitive in its motivations. The reporter attempts to construct an objective picture and definition of AAVE, but then falls back on more traditional views, seeing it as an excluded and resentful outsider.

This kind of reasoning is seen even from linguists on occasion. The ongoing convergence–divergence controversy (is AAVE becoming more or less distinct? closer or farther away from MUSE?) might be understood as an uneasiness with the idea that the African American community has a healthy, thriving, naturally evolving culture of its own which resists mainstreaming. An example of this is found in Labov and Harris's study of language use in Philadelphia, which established (on the basis of vocalic and verbal system changes) that the city is "separating into two distinct speech communities: white and black" (1986: 20). But that study moves past this empirical finding to make a curious set of suggestions:

it should be possible to bring children closer to the systems used by other dialects without changing their personalities and their friendship patterns. From everything we have seen so far, this kind of deep-seated change can happen if white and black youth are in contact in the early years. The way will then be open for the group to shift as a whole, with the convergence that is the result of mutual influence. If the contact is a friendly one, and we achieve true integration in the schools, the two groups may actually exchange socially significant symbols, and black children will begin to use the local vernacular of the white community. But even without such a thorough integration, we can expect that the children will learn from each other, and the present trend towards separation may be reversed.

(21)

Here we have the idea that if black children only had enough friendly contact with the white community they would be more than happy to give up their home language; that is, that the loss of AAVE would be the result of successful and "thorough integration."[8] The possibility that speakers of the white vernacular might be influenced by AAVE language or adopt it is not considered. Housing segregation on the basis of race, an evil, is equated with the persistence and spread of AAVE.

Non-black attitudes toward AAVE are complex, because AAVE taps into the most difficult and contentious issues around race. AAVE makes us uncomfortable because it is persistent, and because it will not go away, no matter what we do to denigrate it and the people who speak it. Even when we acknowledge its existence, our offical policies around this (and other) stigmatized varieties of language are policies of patronage and tolerance rather than acceptance. The irony is that AAVE is the distinct language of a cultural community we don't want to acknowledge as separate; at the same time, the only way we know how to deal with our discomfort about AAVE is to set it apart.

AFRICAN AMERICAN ATTITUDES TOWARD AAVE

Within the African American community, discussions around AAVE seem to embody some of the most difficult and painful issues of identity and solidarity.

To begin with, it must be stated that it is hard to find any African American, regardless of profession, politics, or personal belief, who would deny the practical necessity of bidialectalism and selective assimilation to MUSE norms. The fact that black children with aspirations outside their own communities must learn a *language of wider communication* (Smitherman 1995) is acknowledged as a fact of life. Opinions on this range from sober utilitarianism and resignation to righteous anger:[9]

> Pragmatic reality forces the burden of adjustment on groups who are outside positions of influence and power. It does little good to claim that street speech is a valid dialect – which it is – when the social cost of linguistic and other differences can be so high.
>
> (John Baugh, linguist)

> our position is quite clear. We believe that for people to excel they must acquire and use to their advantage the language of power and the language of finance. Standard American English is that. I admit it is not fair, but I did not create those rules. We only assist people in working their way up through them.
>
> (Dr. Bernadette Anderson, accent-reduction therapist)

> The worst of all possible things that could happen would be to lose that language. There are certain things I cannot say without recourse to my language. It's terrible to think that a child with five different present tenses comes to school to be faced with those books that are less than his own language. And then to be told things about his

language, which is him, that are sometimes permanently damaging. ... This is a really cruel fallout of racism. I know the Standard English. I want to use it to help restore the other language, the lingua franca.

(Toni Morrison, author, poet, Nobel Prize winner)

Language is political. That's why you and me, my Brother and Sister, that's why we sposed to choke our natural self into the weird, lying, barbarous, unreal, white speech and writing habits that the schools lay down like holy law. Because, in other words, the powerful don't play; they mean to keep that power, and those who are the power-less (you and me) better shape up mimic/ape/suck-in the very image of the powerful, or the powerful will destroy you – you and our children.

(June Jordan, poet, writer, political activist)

Studies and interviews with African Americans indicate that while anger is rarely openly voiced, arguments for bidialectalism based on personal experience are quite common:

I have some associates that find it very difficult to work and maintain any kind of decent job, because of the fact that they cannot adequately speak, so to speak, the normal language.

(man on the street, CBS Evening News, December 5, 1985)

But my opinion always has been that you have to learn to survive in the real world, and if you speak black English there's no way you're going to survive. There's no way you're going to get a job that you really want. There's no way that you're going to make an income that's going to make you live right.

(female university staff, interviewed for Speicher and McMahon 1992: 399)

Clear and logical arguments for bidialectalism are made regularly, and still this issue does not lay its head. But this cannot be surprising. To make two statements: *I acknowledge that my home language is viable and adequate* and *I acknowledge that my home language will never be accepted* is to set up an unresolvable conflict.[10] Alice Walker, who in her novels about African Americans often uses language issues to illustrate the emotional cost of assimilation, has put it more succinctly: "It seems our fate to be incorrect," she said in a 1973 interview, "... And in our incor-rectness we stand" (O'Brien 1973: 207). The day-to-day pressure to give up the home language is something that most non-AAVE speakers cannot imagine, and it is here that novelists provide insight into a cultural phenomenon which is otherwise inaccessible.

Darlene tryin to teach me how to talk. She say US not so hot ... peoples think you dumb. What I care? I ast. I'm happy. But she say I feel more happier talkin like she talk. ... Every time I say something the way I say it, she correct me until I say it some other way. Pretty soon it feel like I can't think. My mind run up on a thought, git confuse, run back and sort of lay down. . . . Look like to me only a fool would want you to talk in a way that feel peculiar to your mind.

(Walker 1983)

"I done my homework. You already seen it," Shoni said.

"I did my homework. You already saw it," LaKeesha said.

"That too," Shoni said. Both sisters laughed. "Why you all the time be trying to get me to talk white?"

"It's not white; it's correct." She didn't feel as sure as Esther and Mrs. Clark were when they said it. Sometimes she was a little afraid that she was talking white, that she could lose herself in the land where enunciation was crisp and all verbs agreed. And at home, especially on weekends, it was hard to hold on to that language of success and power. . . . "When you go to work, you have to know the right way to speak," she added, looking in Shoni's eyes as if she was sure of what she was saying, even though she wasn't.

(Campbell 1995: 270)

Pressure to assimilate to MUSE norms originates from outside and from inside the African American community. In both of these excerpts, black women are being encouraged by other black women to acquire the white language, a language, they are told, which will bring them not only success and power, but happiness (*But she say I feel more happier talkin like she talk*). To accept this proposition in the face of direct personal evidence to the contrary, is the challenge that these characters, like other AAVE speakers, must somehow meet.

Evidence of real resistance to linguistic assimilation is hard to find. The most cited example is surely James Baldwin's moving editorial "If Black English isn't a language, then tell me, what is?" (*New York Times*, July 29, 1979). The writings of June Jordan call clearly for the recognition of the validity of AAVE, as in her essay on language, empowerment, and subordination, "Nobody mean more to me than you and the future life of Willie Jordan" (1985). Another rare instance is found in the highly autobiographical account of the Simpson murder trial by the African American prosecutor, Christopher Darden:

[It] isn't to say all black people sound alike; of course not. But who can deny that we have our own dialect and our own accent? . . . It seemed to me that by the time I got to college, we were given a choice. We could learn to speak more mainstream, to sound more white, or we could be proud of our heritage and acknowledge that culture extends to language as well as paintings and books. I was proficient in English. I could read it and write it expertly, and I knew the rules for speaking it. And so I felt no need to change the way I spoke, to ignore the heritage and the background that formed my diction, my speech patterns, and the phrases I used.

(1996: 77)

Most efforts to seek public validation of AAVE are less visible, and are met with a great deal of resistance. An African American journalist responds in an opinion piece to such a group organized in Madison, Wisconsin:

> In Madison, Wisc., for example, some blacks are trying to push the value of BEV, according to a recent report in the Wisconsin State Journal. They want to change the way professionals, teachers and the government view the lazy verbiage of the ghetto.
> The group argues that black English is merely different, not a disability.
> I disagree with that. I think it is dysfunctional to promote BEV – or even legitimate it with an acronym. And the dysfunction exists not so much among the students as with their ill-equipped African-American "leaders" and educators.

(Hamblin 1995)

We will see in the examples below that people rationalize linguistic subordination in a number of ways. Some successful African Americans (for example, John Baugh and Bernadette Anderson, above) acknowledge the schism between promises and threats, but are resigned to the fact that there is nothing practical to be done about it. Others choose to deny the issue completely by refusing to recognize the language at all: "There is no such thing as Black English. The concept of Black English is a myth. It is basically speaking English and violating the correct rules of grammar" (male audience member, *Oprah Winfrey Show* 1987).

We have seen in Part II of this book that AAVE is not accepted, and may never be accepted, as a socially viable language by the majority of US English speakers. Thus, one of the two statements (*I acknowledge that my home language is viable and adequate* and *I acknowledge that my home language will never be accepted*) cannot stand, and must be challenged or amended if the conflict is to be resolved. Extreme examples of this are available, even in print:

> Although we were surrounded in New York by a number of poorly spoken and frequently stereotypical black and poor Southern dialects, my siblings and I soon learned to hear it for what it was – the language of the street, the language of black trash. The language that went right along with Saturday-night knife fights to settle a grudge.

(Hamblin 1995)

Another strategy in resolving the conflict, and it is often used, is to challenge not the existence of AAVE, but its definition. Thus for Rachel

Jones, an African American woman writing an essay for *Newsweek* entitled "What's wrong with Black English" (1990), Malcolm X, Martin Luther King Jr., Toni Morrison, Alice Walker, James Baldwin, Andrew Young, Tom Bradley, and Barbara Jordan don't talk black or not black; they "talk right." This conclusion follows from her (not completely true) observation that none of these people employ or employed AAVE grammar or idiom in their public addresses. For Jones, the fact that most of these African Americans depend on AAVE intonation, phonology, and rhetorical features to mark their spoken language for solidarity with the black community is irrelevant. In this way, the definition of AAVE becomes very narrow: it encompasses only the grammar of the language in as far as syntactical and morphological rules are distinct from MUSE.

Many public statements about AAVE by African Americans combine a variety of approaches to neutralize the conflict inherent to the subordination process. Most of the time there is a great deal of complex rationalization, as well as a great deal of emotion, in these statements. And each of them relies to some extent on the well-established strategies in the language subordination process: appeal to written language norms, mystification of grammar, assumption of authority, and disinformation.

> What black children need is an end to this malarkey that tells them they can fail to learn grammar, fail to develop vocabularies, ignore syntax and embrace the mumbo-jumbo of ignorance – and dismiss it in the name of "black pride."
>
> (Rowan 1979: 36)

Here Rowan, a journalist, has stated his belief that AAVE speakers must be taught grammar because, apparently, they do not acquire any to start with; that they have insufficient lexicons, and that their language functions without syntax. These statements are misinformed, and lean primarily on that part of the mystification process which would have native speakers of a language hand over authority.

> I'm a Northwestern student presently, and I got to be a Northwestern student because of my grammar and because of the way I can speak. Black English may have had its place back in the times of slavery, back in the times when we had no way of educating ourselves ... now we do have a way of educating ourselves, and I think by speaking the way [an AAVE speaker] speaks, you are downgrading society. You are saying that you don't want to educate yourself. We have a different way to educate ourselves today.
>
> (female audience member, *Oprah Winfrey Show* 1987)

There is an interesting equation in this young woman's statement. She tells the audience that she was able to study at a prestigious university *because* of the variety of English which she speaks; that is, because she does not speak AAVE. From this we might conclude that any MUSE speaker can gain admittance to Northwestern on that basis alone, which is an obvious error. People are admitted to a university on the basis of grades, test scores, and essays, among other things; performance in school and on standardized tests follows in great part from a command of the written language, a skill not acquired equally well by all MUSE speakers. The audience member has moved from spoken language to written language without consideration, and she then moves on to the assumption that education, if effective, will negate language differences, which must equal poor language, which in turn "downgrad[es] society." It is worth noting that another young African American woman in the audience, an AAVE speaker, points out to this Northwestern student that there is a material difference between written and spoken languages, but her statement is ignored.

The association of AAVE with slavery is not an uncommon one, and it is perhaps the most difficult one to address. The exact origins of AAVE are unclear, and the source of great debate among linguists.[11] That the African American diaspora was crucial in the development of the language is undeniable, but it does not follow from this historical fact that the language is now dysfunctional or has no good purpose. Later in the Winfrey taping, Smitherman points out that the language developed as a vehicle of solidarity in a time of oppression.

The next quotation is a particularly interesting one in ideological terms:

> I do not approve of Black English. In the first place, I do not under-stand it; in the second place, I think the objective of education is to lead out. I think that in our society – though we ought to take advan-tage of the cultural differences that really make Americans American – we ought to eliminate those differences which are either the basis or result of divisiveness in our society.
>
> (Donald McHenry, former US Ambassador to the United Nations, in *Jet* 1980, 57(25): 40, as cited in Starks 1983: 99–100)

McHenry's statement is interesting in the way it is similar to the criticisms of non-blacks: it is the only time I have been able to document an African American citing communication difficulties as a reason to reject AAVE. Even those most vehemently negative about the language generally admit that it is comprehensible, or do not touch on this issue at all. McHenry also draws in arguments often heard in the debate around bilingualism and the English Only movement. These include questions about what it means to be an American citizen, and the often-voiced fear that the nation-state cannot survive willful refusal to assimilate to supra-regional norms. This is not a new complaint; in 1966 the superintendent of public instruction of California went on record with his prediction of complete breakdown of communication: "Correct English just has to be taught to the next generation unless we want a replay of the Tower of Babel bit around 1984" (cited in Drake 1977a: 91).

McHenry restates the common belief that the only way to achieve the ideal society is to become a homogenous one, and to this end we must eliminate not all differences, but those which are *divisive*. The conflict between the wants of peripheralized groups and the needs of the majority are raised here quite clearly. But there is a question which is not addressed: the connection between language and those basic human rights which are protected by law from the tyranny of majority rule.

There is no doubt that there is great internal conflict in the African American community centered around AAVE. Those who are bidialectal feel the need to justify their choice to be so; blacks who are not comfortable speaking AAVE are often defensive about their language, and protective of their status as members of the black community. The greater African American community seems to accept the inevitability of linguistic assimilation to MUSE in certain settings, but there is also evidence of mistrust of blacks who assimilate too well:

> Suspicion and skepticism are common Black reactions to Black users of LWC [the *language of wider communication*, or MUSE] rhetorical styles. These perceptions exist simultaneously with the belief that one needs to master LWC in order to "get ahead." I call it "linguistic push-pull"; Du Bois calls it "double consciousness." The farther removed one is from mainstream "success," the greater the degree of cynicism about this ethnolinguistic, cultural ambivalence. Jesse Jackson knows about this; so did Malcolm X and Martin Luther King; so does Louis Farrakhan. The oratory of each is LWC in its grammar but AVT in its rhetorical style.
>
> (Smitherman 1995: 238)

Rickford finds vocal rejection of mainstream language more often in adolescent blacks, as in the case of a teenager from Redwood City, California, who indicates how serious an offence it is to cross the line linguistically: "Over at my school, if they – first time they catch you talkin' white, they'll never let it go. Even if you just quit talking like that, they'll never let it go!" (Rickford 1992: 191). He also provides examples of how angry adolescents can be when pushed on this matter: "It pisses me off when the Oreos – they be tryin to correct your language, and I be like, 'Get away from me! Did I ask you to – correct me? No! No! No, I didn't! Nuh-uh!'" (ibid.).

On occasion, African Americans have gone on record with their own experiences as bidialectal speakers. Those experiences are seldom benign:

> Hearing the laughter ... and being the butt of "proper" and "oreo" jokes hurt me. Being criticized made me feel marginal – and verbally impotent in the sense that I had little ammunition to stop the frequent lunchtime attacks. So I did what was necessary to fit in, whether that

meant cursing excessively or signifying. Ultimately I somehow learned to be polylingual and to become sensitive linguistically in the way that animals are able to sense the danger of bad weather.

The need to defend myself led me to use language as a weapon to deflect jokes about the "whiteness" of my spoken English and to launch harsh verbal counter-attacks. Simultaneously language served as a mask to hide the hurt I often felt in the process. Though over time my ability to "talk that talk" – slang – gained me a new respect from my peers, I didn't want to go through life using slang to prove I am Black. So I decided "I yam what I yam," and to take pride in myself. I am my speaking self, but this doesn't mean that I'm turning my back on Black people. There are various shades of Blackness; I don't have to talk like Paul Laurence Dunbar's dialect poems to prove I'm Black. I don't appreciate anyone's trying to take away the range of person I can be.

(Aponte 1989)

It seems that African Americans who speak MUSE are not immune from a different kind of trouble: Aponte's experiences and reactions to those experiences are perhaps the best possible illustration of Smitherman's push-pull, and his story seems to be a common one. Blacks who speak primarily AAVE are subject to ongoing pressure to assimilate to MUSE norms in a number of settings outside their communities; in fact, they are threatened with exclusion if they do not. Blacks who do not speak AAVE may be treated with scepticism and distrust. Language ideology becomes a double-edged sword for those who are monodialectal – threats originate from inside and outside the home language community.

At this point it is necessary to consider that there are many persons of African descent resident in the US who immigrate from the Caribbean and from Africa, and who come to this country speaking another language. Within the indiginous African American community there is a complicated set of reactions to these immigrants which can be overtly negative, in ways which are not always visible to outsiders. Edwidge Danticat's 1994 novel, *Breath, Eyes, Memory*, brought these issues into the consciousness of the public. Her story of the Haitian experience in the US makes clear how important a role language plays in the negotiations between African Americans and immigrants of African descent.

My mother said it was important that I learn English quickly. Otherwise the American students would make fun of me or, even worse, beat me. A lot of other mothers from the nursing home where she worked had told her that their children were getting into fights in school because they were accused of having "HBO" – Haitian Body Odor. Many of the American kids even accused Haitians of having AIDS because they had heard on television that only the four H's got AIDS – heroin addicts, hemophiliacs, homosexuals and Haitians.

I wanted to tell my mother that I didn't want to go to school. Frankly, I was afraid.

(Hinojosa on National Public Radio, All Things Considered,
September 30, 1994)

Her experience (as well as documented experiences of other Haitian immigrants) indicates that there is a hierarchy among immigrants who come into the African American community, and the Haitians are very low in the pecking order. How AAVE fits into the complex issue of acquisition of English for native speakers of Haitian Creole and other Caribbean and African languages is something which has not yet been explored, but which deserves to be studied both as a linguistic issue and as a social one.

It would be useful, in this context, to look in depth at the way prominent African Americans deal with the conflict inherent to the choice between languages. Here I consider two examples: a set of statements by Oprah Winfrey during a 1987 taping of a talk show on "Standard and 'Black' English," and an episode related by Shelby Steele in his 1991 book *The Content of Our Characters*.[12]

In the case of Oprah Winfrey, it is important to remember that during this taping she is acting as a host to her invited guests, a facilitator to the audience discussion, and simultaneously as a participant with opinions of her own. The introductions she reads from cue cards are perhaps not entirely her own formulations; her statements may sometimes be made in a spirit of fostering discussion. But in general, it is clear that she is willing to give her opinion on the questions at hand: on occasion she claims the floor when audience members want to speak. Her comments are peppered with formulations such as *I know, to me, I think, I don't understand*. She also uses constructions like *if you don't know, you must know, don't you know*, in those instances where she puts her own opinions forth.

Winfrey's stance on AAVE is a complex and conflicted one. At first glance, it might seem that she stands firmly on the side of standardization and linguistic assimilation. As has been seen with other African Americans, she does not *directly* deny the existence of AAVE (which she consistently calls "so-called" Black English, perhaps because she is uncomfortable with the term rather than the language itself), but she challenges AAVE using many of the strategies seen above.

She first attempts to relegate AAVE to the realm of the secondary: "Are we talking about correct English or are we talking about dialect?" (3);[13] when audience members protest this, she regroups by defining for them the difference between Black English and Standard English, a difference which turns out to rest exclusively on subject–verb agreement:

To me standard English is having your verbs agree with your subject. That's what standard English is to me. I mean, is that what your definition of standard English is?

(3)

Does it mean that you are ashamed because you choose to speak correctly, you choose to have your verbs agree with your subject? Does that mean you're ashamed?

(5)

Like Rachel Jones, Winfrey seems to have a definition of Black English which focuses only on grammatical agreement and excludes phonology and rhetorical devices. She identifies Martin Luther King Jr., Whitney Young, Mary McCleod Bethune as speakers not of Black English, but of Standard English. Once again, Jesse Jackson is raised as an example of someone who speaks AAVE but knows how to shift in his public discourse to a style appropriate for the most formal settings (3). The fact that Jesse Jackson strongly marks his public discourse with AAVE rhetorical devices, and sometimes uses AAVE grammatical strategies *regardless of his audience*, does not come up. She quotes Jackson's famous statement that "excellence is the best deterrent to racism" (12) but fails to discuss her equation between *lack of excellence* and the native language of the African American community.

Winfrey focuses the discussion of Black English on the social repercussions this language brings with it in the world outside the African American community. She seems truly distraught and dismayed when young African Americans in the audience tell her that they want to use their own functional language and reject pressure to assimilate. Here, Winfrey's own status as a successful businesswoman and employer of many seems to push to the forefront. Given her own position, she does not understand young blacks who still voice their resistance to assimilation. In fact, she challenges a white panelist on this count: "Let me ask you, why would you want to tell black people or make black people believe that corporate America is going to change for them?" (12).

Winfrey justifies her rejection of AAVE on the basis of the documented history of its reception. However, when call-in viewers or audience members who agree with this basic premise move on to openly deride AAVE, she momentarily switches allegiance. In four cases there are comments from whites which cause her to pause and come to the defense of AAVE or AAVE speakers. She sometimes does this with humor (the first example below), but there is also tangible uneasiness when the discussion moves beyond grammar to statements which are at the very least intolerant, and in some cases move into the realm of racism.

1ST CALLER: I am sitting here just burning ... I believe they put themselves that way to be separate, just like the way they do with ... radio stations ... We don't have the White Music Experience, you know, Voice of the Whitey, you know. I mean, they are putting themselves in these categories.

WINFREY: What do you call Barry Manilow?

(4)

2ND CALLER: ... what makes me feel that blacks tend to be ignorant is that they fail to see that the word is spelled a-s-k ... that gives the word a different meaning ...

WINFREY: Why does it give it a different meaning if you know that's what they're saying?

(7–8)

8TH AUDIENCE MEMBER: ... I just think that anybody, Polish, Black, English, Hispanic, should learn to speak the proper English. And I believe if they can't speak the proper English, they should go back to their own country ... [crosstalk]

DR. SMITHERMAN: I would like to know what country do black people go back to. [crosstalk]

WINFREY: What did you say, Dr. [Smitherman]? What did you say?

DR. SMITHERMAN: I said I would like to know what country do black people go back to.

WINFREY: Okay, yes ma'am.

(8–9)

9TH AUDIENCE MEMBER: ... You could speak your own language, you could have your own way, but don't force someone else to have to suffer and listen to it.

WINFREY: ... Why is it causing you to *suffer*?

(9; original emphasis)

Overall, Winfrey's stance is complicated by her own participation in the corporate structures, whose gatekeeping mechanisms she subscribes to and openly propagates. For example, she asserts that employers (of which she is one) have the right to demand that employees represent employers as they wish to be represented (8–9), a right which she believes extends to language.

When audience and panel members point out to her fallacies in common-sense arguments, or present counter-arguments, Winfrey has one of three strategies:

1 She appeals to the authority of those panel or audience members who support her position:

What about what Dr. Anderson mentioned earlier, though – it's about representation.

(8)

PANEL MEMBER, A RADIO ANNOUNCER: In corporate America, if you want to put an extra burden, a yoke on your neck, then speak slang, speak incorrect English and grammar, because you're not going to get the job.

WINFREY: You're not. You are not.

(12)

2 She responds herself with more common-sense arguments:

> This is the point that needs to be made here, and for all you children who decide not to do your homework and that it's not important, that speaking correctly is an indication – just a slight indication – to the person who is going to hire you that perhaps maybe you can do the job. Speaking incorrectly is an indication to them that maybe you cannot. It doesn't mean that it's accurate.

(11)

3 Or she cuts away completely:

> 3RD AUDIENCE MEMBER: This is a fact. White America use black dialect on commercials every day. Be observant, people. Don't let nobody tell you that you are ignorant and that you don't speak right. Be observant. They started off Channel 7 Eyewitness news a few years ago with one word: whashappenin. So what's happening, America?
> WINFREY: We'll be right back.

(9–10)

Winfrey's discomfort with the underlying conflict reaches it peak when audience members attempt to use her and her language as an example of the necessity of assimilation and the rewards which follow. It is interesting that the African American guests who hold up Winfrey's language as a model never point out that Winfrey herself, like so many other blacks prominent in the public eye, is often heard to use AAVE intonation when speaking with black guests, and that she relies on AAVE rhetorical devices on many occasions.

The last substantive comment sums up the conflict as it exists for her: "I personally don't understand why if you go to school and you're taught English and you're taught to have the verbs agree with the subject, how that suppresses who you are. I've never understood that" (13). Winfrey would like the issue to be a simple one of grammatical relations, which would allow her to make decisions as an employer which would be free of racial implications. Ideally, she believes, education should neutralize language distinctions stemming from differences in race and class. She has the best interest of her community and people in mind, and a clear picture of the steps necessary for African Americans to achieve economic and social equality. She seems to see a role for herself here, in educating those who come after as a part of the process called *dropping knowledge* within the African American community. She has traveled this road herself, after all. She has made choices, some of which raise hard questions: "Does it mean that you are ashamed because you choose to speak correctly, you choose to have your verbs agree with your subject?" (5). When she is confronted with evidence that there is a connection between identity and language choice, that negative reactions against

AAVE have to do not with the message, but the messenger, her ability to rationalize her choices and the reality of linguistic assimilation is challenged.

Shelby Steele provides very different insight into the conflicts which face African Americans. Steele is one of a group of prominent scholars and writers who form the core of an African American conservative thinktank, who have been public in their criticism of the civil rights establishment. Some of the central ideas of this body of work include the supposition that human nature is more important than race, and that national interest is more important than ethnic affiliation. His *The Content of Our Character* is interesting here because he addresses, in a limited way, the issue of language. His discussion illustrates the way that rationalization works in the language subordination process. Steele's current position on AAVE, although never clearly stated, seems to be assimilationist. What he relates in his essay is the logic which allows him to make the transition from accepting his own language as viable and functional, to rejecting it.

As a teenager, Steele was a speaker of AAVE in public situations which included non-AAVE speakers. The story he tells here is probably a fairly typical experience for young blacks when they establish social contacts outside the African American community. Here, an older white woman continually and repeatedly corrects both AAVE grammatical and phonological features in his speech.

> When I was fourteen the mother of a white teammate on the YMCA swimming team would – in a nice but insistent way – correct my grammar when I lapsed into the black English I'd grown up speaking in the neighborhood. She would require that my verbs and pronouns agree, that I put the "g" on my "ings," and that I say "that" instead of "dat." She absolutely abhorred double negatives, and her face would screw up in pain at the sound of one. But her corrections also tapped my racial vulnerability. I felt racial shame at this white woman's fastidious concern with my language. It was as though she was saying that the black part of me was not good enough, would not do, and this is where my denial went to work.
>
> (58)

Steele's initial reaction is anger at the woman's rejection of "the black part of me [as] not good enough." This episode seems to have been his first direct experience with language-focused discrimination. Thus he confronts the conflict between the experience of being discriminated against and his experiences with AAVE as a viable and functional language. As a 14-year-old, then, Steele was not yet convinced that AAVE was an inappropriate or bad language. Corresponding to his anger toward the woman is a recognition of the link between it and his race ("the black part of me"). On this basis, his early conclusion is that the woman who has corrected him is racist.

Now, he does something perhaps unusual. He confronts the woman through her son, and she seeks him out angrily to have a conversation about her motives in correcting his language.

> A few days later she marched into the YMCA rec room, took me away from a Ping-Pong game, and sat me down in a corner. It was the late fifties, when certain women painted their faces as though they were canvases ... it was the distraction of this mask, my wonderment at it, that allowed me to keep my equilibrium.
>
> She told me about herself, that she had grown up poor, had never finished high school, and would never be more than a secretary. She said she didn't give a "good goddamn" about my race, but that if I wanted to do more than "sweat my life away in a steel mill," I better learn to speak correctly. As she continued to talk I was shocked to realize that my comment had genuinely hurt her and that her motive in correcting my English had been no more than simple human kindness. If she had been black, I might have seen this more easily. But she was white, and this fact alone set off a very specific response pattern in which vulnerability to a racial shame was the trigger, denial and recomposition the reaction, and a distorted view of the situation the result. This was the sequence by which I converted kindness into harassment and my racial shame into her racism.

(59)

First we must note that his original position has reversed on a number of levels:

Prior to confrontation	*After confrontation*
her racism	her simple human kindness
his anger, resentment	his racism
wrongdoing denied	acceptance of wrongdoing
acknowledges AAVE	rejects AAVE
draws a link between race and language	denies a link between race and language

This is an interesting example of how ideology functions to keep participants from becoming aware of the place of subordination or dominance they themselves occupy in the social structure. Steele is recounting the way in which he was made aware of his position as subordinated, and chose to change his allegiance to the dominant group. There is no doubt that he is sincere about the story that he tells, or that he truly believes the common-sense arguments he puts forth. But he uses a number of coercive strategies to manufacture consent from his audience, and they bear consideration. One is the way that Steele attempts to make his readers believe that there is a commonality of opinion regarding language. He knows, as they surely do, that AAVE is an inadequate language:

If she had been black, I might have seen [the truth] more easily. But she was white, and this fact alone set off a very specific response pattern in which vulnerability to a racial shame was the trigger, *denial and recomposition* the reaction, and a *distorted view of the situation* the result.

(emphasis added)

Steele assumes that his readers will share some basic beliefs:

- that there is a right and a wrong way to use English;
- that it is appropriate for more established and knowledgeable persons to direct younger ones to that better language;
- and that questions of right and wrong in language move beyond race.

He explains his inability to see these facts as a function of his immature view of the world and his unwillingness to accept personal responsibility (*If she had been black, I might have seen this more easily*). His youthful AAVE-speaking self relies on denial of the basic truth about language; his mature and reasonable self (the one who is like his readers) knows the truth of the matter. Thus, by linking the last logical proposition (questions of right and wrong move beyond race) to the first two (there is a good and a bad language, and it is appropriate to censure users of bad language), he coerces a certain degree of acceptance of his language ideology.

Steele relates this conversation with the mother of a friend as a kind of epiphany, in which he becomes aware of truths not just about himself, but about people in general. Thus we see how both Steele himself and this woman function as *imaginary formations*. Imaginary formations are understood as the way the subject (Steele), his interlocutor (the readers), and the object of their discourse (the woman who corrected him, and her motivations) are represented not as individuals, but as symbols of larger groups or types. In this analytical approach, people perceive and project themselves primarily as a representative of their specific place in the social structure. Thus, Steele represents himself as a successful African American who has moved beyond denial and racism to take responsibility for his own life.

More interesting, perhaps, is the imaginary formation of the white woman who leads him to accept the necessity of rejecting his home language. This woman is by her own account (and one he obviously does not disagree with) someone with little to recommend her: she has never finished high school and will never achieve a great deal of economic success; she even looks clownish. She has no conventionally accepted or recognized sources of authority or knowledge, beyond a history of personal difficulty and sacrifice. But because she is a MUSE speaker, she feels authorized to correct his language because if she does not do so, he is doomed to a life "in a steel mill." She tells him these things not because she has any investment in him (she denies such a motivation), but out of some greater urge to do good, an urge which is sufficient authority for Steele. This woman represents the hard-working, well-meaning Middle American MUSE speaker who knows best, and whose authority is not to be questioned. She was the mother of a friend, but she has transcended that role to become an imaginary formation.

We have seen various approaches to neutralizing Smitherman's "linguistic push-pull" and Du Bois's "double consciousness," but Steele's is a unique step which moves beyond denying or limiting AAVE. Whereas Winfrey was clearly unable to go along with criticisms of AAVE which devalued the messenger rather than the message, Steele accepts the criticism of the messenger as appropriate, along with rationalizations and safeguards which anticipate challenges. If you question or reject the common-sense arguments which underlie his position, you are practicing denial and recomposition. The rejection of arguments for linguistic assimilation is thus projected as racist.

What do Oprah Winfrey and Shelby Steele, along with all the other African Americans who have spoken out on the matter of the languages of the African American community have in common? Perhaps only two things can be pinpointed with any surety: the need to resolve the conflict, and the complexity of their responses. In every case opinions are formed by personal experiences outside the African American community which are often overtly negative. It cannot be denied that some of the most scornful and negative criticism of AAVE speakers comes from other African Americans.

One issue of great interest and importance is the differing perceptions of what actually constitutes AAVE. Some prominent and successful African Americans, in their criticism of the language and rejection of it, seem to be focusing exclusively on those grammatical features which distinguish it from other, non-black varieties of US English. Oprah Winfrey insists on MUSE verb paradigms, for example, but it seems that she would not insist on the abandonment of all AAVE rhetorical features, intonation or lexical choice, as she herself uses these on occasion and she points to other African Americans who do the same as good language models. MUSE speakers, on the other hand, in particular non-black MUSE speakers, have a much lower tolerance for non-grammatical features of AAVE than some seem to realize. This is an area which requires further study and research, because it isn't until speakers become aware of differences in perceptions that the underlying conflicts can be addressed.

AAVE is a source of controversy between the African American community and the rest of the country, and within the African American community itself, because it throws a bright light on issues we don't want to face. Equal rights and equal access are good and important goals, but we demand high payment. Perhaps it is too high; certainly, AAVE persists in spite of stigmatization of the most direct and caustic kind, and despite repercussions in the form of real disadvantage and discrimination. Clearly, AAVE speakers get something from their communities and from each other that is missing in the world which is held up to them as superior and better. But the conflict remains. "We're not wrong," says an exasperated AAVE speaker in response to criticism. "I'm tired of living in a country where we're always wrong" (*Oprah Winfrey Show* 1987: 7).

The real problem with black English is a general unwillingness to accept the speakers of that language and the social choices they have made as viable and functional. Instead we relegate their experiences and capabilities to spheres which are secondary and out of the public eye. We are ashamed of them, and because they are part of us, we are ashamed of ourselves.

10 Hillbillies, rednecks, and southern belles

The language rebels

One Virginian who went to Harvard in the early 1980s fantasized about putting a sign around his neck to foreclose some of the questions he repeatedly faced, or imagined he faced: "Yes, I am from the south. No, I do not know your uncle in Mobile. ... Both of my parents are, in fact, literate. ... No, I do not watch 'Hee Haw.' No, I do not own slaves. No, I do not want any."

Quoted by Edward Ayers, in "What we talk about when we talk about the South" (1996)

Northerners tend to think of the south as a homogenous and somewhat mysterious monolith, where English has an indiscriminate "twang" or a "drawl" and is peppered with funny, pan-regional idioms; nevertheless, when pressed northerners will divide the south into distinct parts. Geographers have noted a consistent identification of a "core" south or *Southern Trough*, which

cuts across Mississippi and Alabama, embracing parts of Arkansas, Louisiana, and Georgia at the edges. This trough appears to most Americans as the least desirable place in the United States to live. Other Southern states cannot take too much grim comfort from such disparagement of their Deep South neighbors, for the sides of the trough rise only gradually until they reach the usual boundaries of what Americans take to be the North, the Midwest, and the West. The whole South appears to be a vast saucer of unpleasant associations.

(Ayers 1996: 62–63)

The conceptualization of an undesirable south moves in concentric rings outward from this core *Deep South* or "Southern Trough," as seen in a composite "mental map" constructed from a study of environmental preferences voiced by students at the University of Minnesota (Gould and White 1974: 97) (Figure 10.1). These students found the most desirable areas of the country to be their own native Minnesota and California, with other high points in the Colorado High region. In contrast, they see the Southern Trough as the least desirable place to live.

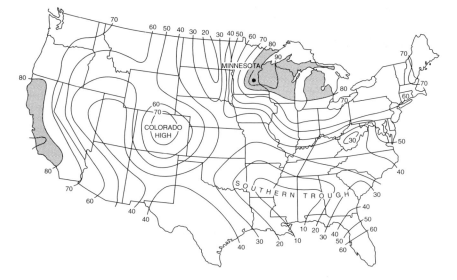

Figure 10.1 Negative evaluation of the "Southern Trough" as a place to live by University of Minnesota students

Source: Reproduced by permission of the authors from P. Gould and R. White (1974) *Mental Maps*. Baltimore, MD: Penguin, p. 98

The composite map of environmental preferences of Alabama students looks much like a mirror image of the Minnesota map, although these southerners, too, tend to see California as highly desirable (Figure 10.2).

In a range of studies focusing on *linguistic* perceptions, Preston (1986a, b, and c, 1989a and b, 1993, and elsewhere) found that northerners tend to draw rough distinctions between the Southern Trough and other southern states: Tennessee and Kentucky are the "outer south"; Texas is its own kind of south, whereas Florida is hardly south at all in the minds of most northerners. The "southwest" may include Texas, but may also exclude New Mexico and Arizona, which are often grouped with those states which are perceived as prototypically west. In spite of these perceived differentiations, northerners remain very unaware of what differentiates one southern variety of English from another, thus producing the one-size-fits-all accent when attempting to "sound southern."

The perceptions of students in Hawai'i about the distribution of main-land varieties makes very clear the schism between mental maps and linguistic evaluation (Figure 10.3). Here, Preston compares a traditional composite construction of *southern* (roughly the Trough) first to the Hawai'ian perceptual boundary of the south (which adds Texas, Kentucky, Tennessee, North Carolina, and the Virginias). The students were then asked to evaluate tape-recorded samples of speech from a much wider geographical range, resulting in the third boundary seen on the map.

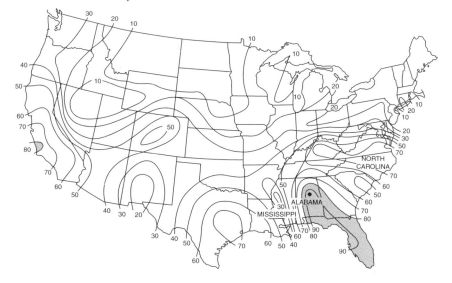

Figure 10.2 Positive evaluation of the "Southern Trough" as a place to live by University of Alabama students

Source: Reproduced by permission of the authors from P. Gould and R. White (1974) *Mental Maps*. Baltimore, MD: Penguin, p. 101

Clearly, what the Hawai'ians *hear* as a southern accent moves far beyond the boundary of what they identify as the south.

Thus, if we isolate those states which seem consistently to be marked as some kind of southern in cultural and linguistic terms (Table 10. 1), we are then talking about some 79 million people, or about 30 percent of the total population of the United States. This figure might be seen as too small, because it excludes those parts of Missouri, Illinois, Indiana, and the southwest where English is perceived as clearly southern in accent. On the other hand, the figure is clearly too large because it assumes that *all* 79 million people in the twelve named states are natives and speakers of the indiginous variety of English, which is clearly an assumption that cannot bear close examination. Finally, it does not take into account racial and ethnic diversity in the south which results in another dimension of language variation, particularly the presence of indiginous language communities where the core language may not be English at all (Spanish, Louisiana Creole, Native American languages), not to mention the large population of African Americans and the ways that southern AAVE differ from other geographical versions of AAVE. Thus it is only a very rough estimate to say that somewhere around 30 percent of the population speaks US English with an accent which is geographically marked "southern."

There seems to be a strong urge to synthesize the south into a single population united primarily in the fact that it is distinct from the north.

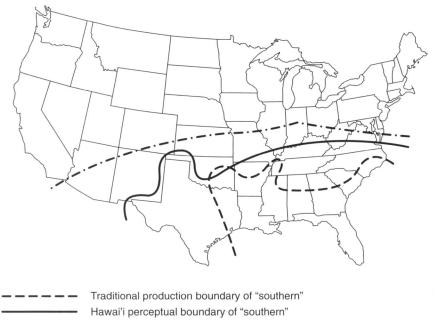

— — — — — — Traditional production boundary of "southern"
————————— Hawai'i perceptual boundary of "southern"
·—·—·—·—· Source of voices judged "southern"

Figure 10.3 Comparison of perceptual, production, and identification boundaries for the area "southern," from the point of view of Hawai'i respondents
Source: Preston 1989a: 129

This is a process southerners themselves both promote and reject, according to Ayers (and see Figure 10.4):

> The South plays a key role in the nation's self-image: the role of evil tendencies overcome, mistakes atoned for, progress yet to be made. Before it can play that role effectively, the South has to be set apart as a distinct place that has certain fundamental characteristics. As a result, Southern difference is continually being recreated and reinforced. Americans, black and white, somehow need to know that the South is different and so tend to look for differences to confirm that belief. This is not something that is only done to the South by malevolent, insensitive non-Southerners. The North and the South have conspired to create each other's identity as well as their own. The South eagerly defines itself against the North, advertising itself as more earthy, more devoted to family values, more spiritual, and then is furious to have things turned around, to hear itself called hick, phony, and superstitious. The South feeds the sense of difference and then resists the consequences.
>
> (1996: 66)

The American South is ...
dynamic, fastpaced and modern ...
oldtimey, charming and hospitable ...
... and a wonderful place to visit!

Figure 10.4 How the south sees itself
Source: http://www.webcom.com/~markplag/vs/

Table 10. 1 Population of the southern states in comparison to overall population figures for the US

State	Population
Alabama	4,040,587
Arkansas	2,350,725
Florida	12,937,926
Georgia	6,478,216
Kentucky	3,685,296
Louisiana	4,219,973
Mississippi	2,573,216
North Carolina	6,628,637
Oklahoma	3,145,585
South Carolina	3,486,703
Tennessee	4,877,185
Texas	16,986,510
Virginia	6,187,358
West Virginia	1,793,477
Southern states	79,391,394
Total US	248,709,873
Percent southern	31.92

Source: 1990 census figures

How the south evaluates its language is an important part of this self-perception. In a survey of 798 adult residents of Georgia, individuals answered questions about what it means to "have a southern accent", and were subsequently asked to evaluate their own language (the results presented as "heavy" southern or "no" accent as seen in Figure 10.5). In any such direct inquiry, some people will underreport their own usage

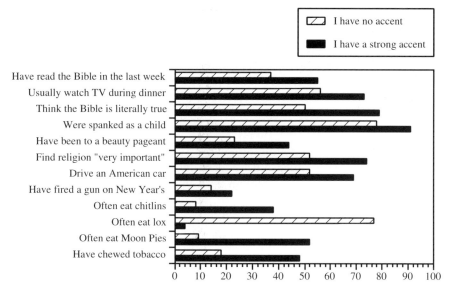

Figure 10.5 Responses of adults residing in Georgia to the yes/no question "Being southern means that you . . ."

Source: Survey conducted April 12–24, 1995 by the Applied Research Center, Georgia State University. Margin of error +/– 3.4 points

(claim to have no accent when in fact they do) and others will claim an accent when they are not local to an area and have not successfully acquired a new phonology. Thus this poll is not one which can tell us who actually has a southern accent, or how "heavy" accents really are, but it can tell us that people attach bundles of social differences to degrees of southern accent.

For that reason, the poll is useful in ways perhaps not anticipated by the persons who constructed it. In the selection of questions to be asked, the pollsters reveal much of the preconceived notions about connections between certain ways of life and language markers embodied in "accent." But do these questions constitute a set of sociocultural distinctions truly relevant to the construction of definitions of "north" and "south"? Between real southern and half-hearted southern?

In this questionnaire, most stereotypes about the south are represented one or more times. The pollster is looking for southern/non-southern distinctions based on religious and cultural practices and beliefs, so that real southerners – those who will admit to having "strong" accents – are the ones who eat chitlins and Moon Pies, and drive an American car to church on Sunday mornings while other, less southern types are at home eating lox.

The fact that a southern accent lies at the heart of much of anyone's construction of the south can be documented in a variety of ways. In an opinion piece for a small paper, the attempt is made to construct sample "State Questions" in the same way that states have official flowers and mottos, on the basis of legislation recently introduced in New Mexico.[1] In this column, which is meant to be lighthearted and humorous, every state included has a question which draws strongly on stereotype, but the southern states are distinct from the northern in a specific way, as seen in this excerpt:

Vermont: "Is it completely organic?"
Florida: "So, how much did he leave her?"
New York: "You got a problem with that, buddy?"
California: "You got a green card, buster?"
Montana: "You from the government?"
Texas: "Yuh shure ah cain't carry it concealed?"
Alabama: "Ain't that right, Jimmy Bob?"
South Carolina: "May ah see yo driver's license and registration?"
Mississippi: "Hunh?"

(Beckerman 1996)

It seems necessary to establish southern varieties of English on the basis of phonology and syntax as well as on local history, culture, fashions, or reputation. The effect of this is to underscore the social and linguistic differences, with an addition: the departure, from standard accepted *spellings* raises education issues in a subtle but important way. Northern ("unaccented") US English is projected as somehow closer to the written representation and therefore there is no need to use phonetic cues. The contrast in the presentation of two kinds of language – correctly spelled and "literary" northern and incorrectly spelled and "illiterate" southern is also an excellent example of Bourdieu's *strategies of condescension* (1991: 68–71). This is a tactic whereby an empowered individual – someone with social legitimacy in terms of employment and language and other kinds of authority – appropriates the subordinated language for a short period of time. In this case, the author of the opinion piece is in fact a professor of anthropology, which provides him not only with traditional authority as a highly educated academic and speaker of the mainstream language, but also as someone who has studied human culture, and therefore is expected to have an unusual degree of understanding of the way human beings interact. Thus this author has outer trappings which authorize him to choose between legitimate and subordinated language, and to publically appropriate the latter to make a point. Bourdieu points out that this strategy of condescension is in fact a part of a larger strategy of subversion (ibid.), or, within the framework set up for this study, part of the overall language subordination model.

Are there cultural, historical, linguistic differences between north and south? Of course, and sometimes popular consideration of these differ-

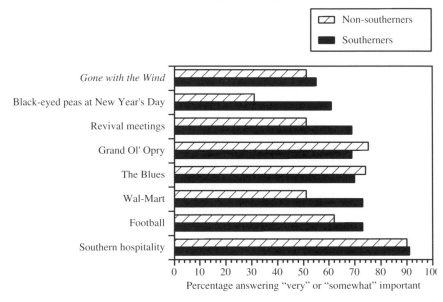

Figure 10.6 Results of a *Journal-Constitution Southern Life* poll in which 1,078 southerners and 507 non-southerners answered the question "How important are the following to your definition of today's South?"

Source: Poll conducted in February and March 1995 by the Institute for Research in Social Science, University of North Carolina at Chapel Hill. Margin of error +/– 3 points for southerners and 5 points for non-southerners

ences does come close to identifying some of them, independent of language issues (Figure 10.6). In this second poll, the distinctions between northern and southern center primarily in those areas which are not widely advertised: the tradition of eating black-eyed peas on New Year's Day, for example, is little known in the north. In contrast, perceptions differ very little in matters having to do with stereotype. One notes especially that about 50 percent of both groups find *Gone with the Wind* relevant to a definition of the south. This is a clear demonstration of the strength and durability of stereotypes in defining both self and other.

In real-life terms we see what instinctually and objectively we know to be true: there is a great deal of diversity in the south. Those southerners who are or have been most prominent in the public eye make this evident: Senators Strom Thurmon and Al Gore; writers William Styron and Dorothy Allison; journalists Dan Rather and Cokie Roberts; actors Julia Roberts and Burt Reynolds. But the southerners who seem to come most quickly to the minds of northerners are the fictional ones, and more than that, the stereotypical fictional ones: Andy Griffith and Gomer; Pa and Ellie Mae and the rest of the *Beverly Hillbillies*; the horrific backwoodsmen and the banjo player from the film *Deliverance*; Jonathan Winters' portrayal of the benighted southerner determined to go over Niagara Falls in his pickup truck instead of a barrel; Scarlett, and her Mammy.

One of the primary characteristics of the stereotypical southerner is ignorance, but it is a specific kind of ignorance – one disassociated from education and literacy:

> [William Natcher, a member of the House of Representatives from Kentucky] mumbled in a Mississippi drawl nobody understands.
> (National Public Radio, March 23, 1994. Reporter: Cokie Roberts)

> I got an interview with an extremely elite undergraduate college in the northeast. They conducted the first substantial part of the interview in [another language] and it went well. When they switched to a question in English, my first answer completely interrupted the interview ... they broke out laughing for quite a while. I asked what was wrong and they said they "never would have expected" me to have such an accent. They made a big deal about me having a [prestigious accent in the second language] and such a strong Southern accent. Of course, I had been aiming for bland standard English. After that, I got a number of questions about whether I'd "be comfortable" at their institution. Subtle, but to me it was not ambiguous.
> (university foreign-language professor, native of the south)

> For 37 years, Charles Kuralt has shown us what network news can be – calm, thoughtful, perceptive. Beneath that deceptive North Carolina drawl, there's a crisp intelligence.
> ("Daily Guide," *Lansing State Journal*, April 3, 1994: 1)

Together, these comments on the relationship between language, intelligence, and communication demonstrate the ways in which language barriers are built and rationalized. In the first case, the reporter (notably herself from New Orleans, the child of lifelong politicians and a featured speaker at an annual conference "Southern Women in Public Service") projects to her listeners an unwillingness to understand the southern accent in question. Although she is clearly in a position to ascertain Representative Natcher's place of origin, she is content to misrepresent this, lumping all drawling and incomprehensible southerners together into a group of non-conformers who deserve to be pointed out and ridiculed.

While the first example demonstrates an irritability which is at odds with journalistic objectivity, the second – this one anecdotal – demonstrates northern discomfort when a link is drawn between intellectual authority and the south. What is so interesting about this exchange is the fact that a person may be taken seriously *only as long as he uses a socially prestigious language*, even though it is not English. Once this person begins to speak his own language, working hard to accommodate to the linguistic expectations of his audience, he is rejected. He remains the same person, expressing the same range and quality of ideas, but his currency is devalued by a language which links him to the anti-intellectual south. While the reporter in the first instance was irritable about the accent which she found out of place and inappropriate (and hence worthy of rejection); the search committee members in the second example have nothing to do with their discomfort but to externalize it as humor. This they find socially acceptable, regardless of the way it affected the job candidate.

In the third example, the author does not deny that a southerner has used language in a clear and perceptive way. Instead, she specifically draws attention to the way that Kuralt's language *confounds expectations*. Humor, which can be loosely defined in just this way – the reaction when reality confounds expectation – often focuses on the juxtaposition of a certain kind of intelligence with southern language:

> Gov. Clinton, you attended Oxford University in England and Yale Law School in the Ivy League, two of the finest institutions of learning in the world. So how come you still talk like a hillbilly?
> (Mike Royko, "Opinion," *Chicago Tribune*, October 11, 1992)

> Federal law requires commercial airliners to carry infants trained to squall at altitudes above two hundred feet. This keeps the passengers calm, because they're all thinking, "I wish somebody would stuff a towel into that infant's mouth," which prevents them from thinking, "I am thirty-five thousand feet up in the air riding in an extremely sophisticated and complex piece of machinery controlled by a person with a southern accent."
> (*The Dave Barry 1995 Calendar*, Tuesday, April 4, 1995)

In contrast to the northern construction of intelligence which is closely linked to a high level of education, there is a stereotypical southern intelligence which follows from common sense and life experience. Typified by the character of Sheriff Andy Taylor in the popular television series *Mayberry RFD* and *The Andy Griffith Show*, this is the southerner whose intelligence is native rather than acquired. Many plots and comic situations in *Mayberry* depended on the construction of southern mother-wit and its contrast to the less instinctual, acquired northern intelligence.

As was the case with Disney animated stories, in this situation comedy southern accents are restricted to those who fit the stereotype: while Andy has a North Carolina accent, his son, aunt, and cousins do not. Nor do the philosophizing barber or the mild-mannered town accountant, or the teacher (a serious love interest of the main character, and – in line with the patterns noted earlier in the Disney films – a speaker of mainstream English), or the pharmacist. The only southern accents in this southern town are the deceptively clever Andy, the dimwitted but good-hearted car mechanics (Gomer and Goober), and the occasional rural characters who come into town to make music or straighten out legal problems resulting from clan feuds, illegal stills, or excessive violence (e.g. Ernest T. Bass).

There are no regularly appearing African American characters in this particular corner of the south.[2]

It is primarily on the basis of intellect linked to education that northerners try hardest to convince southerners that their language is deficient. In ideological terms, this is the process by which some sixty million people are supposed to accept the fact that the language they speak is naturally subordinate to its neighbors. The fact that the stereotypes which underlie this reasoning are imaginary formations is irrelevant; their power is still real, and they are effective. The process is successful when the targets of these efforts become complicit in the subordination process.

Of course, this process is not limited to the south. However, what is so particularly interesting about subordination tactics in this case is that the object of subordination is a whole nation of people, united in terms of history and culture rather than in terms of race or ethnicity – more usually the case when language is systematically attacked as a tool in mainstreaming tactics. It is fairly easy to conceive of the strategies and processes by which African Americans – 12 percent of the population living in communities through the country – are rendered susceptible to language subordination, and come to embrace and propagate a language ideology which works to their own disadvantage. But the process is a bigger challenge when the targeted group is as large and as internally diverse as the southern US. Many persons born and raised in the south have no desire to live anywhere else, and thus it would seem that threats of exclusion and gatekeeping would be less effective. To someone living in the heart of Georgia or South Carolina or Tennessee, the idea that they need to acquire an "accentless" variety of midwestern English to succeed might seem ludicrous. Nevertheless, personal anecdotes indicate that northern bias and standard language ideology have an increasingly long reach:

> "It's ironic," says [Judith] Ivey [actor], who is from the Lone Star State, "that probably the one project that will give me the most exposure [a movie set in the south] . . . is one that requires my Texas accent. Particularly since I was told that if I didn't get rid of it, I would have a very limited career.
>
> (Liebman 1993)

> School official [X] said the [accent reduction] course began when she heard people complain that their accents interfered with business. "Instead of listening to what you're saying, they're passing the phone around the office saying, 'Listen to this little honey from South Carolina.' It's self-defeating. It's annoying. It's humiliating."
>
> (Riddle 1993)

> Soon after Atlanta was awarded the 1996 Olympics a year ago, a column appeared in the Atlanta Business Chronicle exhorting people to "get the South out of our mouth" to impress all the expected visitors. The

author, [X], a communications consultant from New Jersey, wrote: "By cleaning up our speech, maybe we can finally convince the world that we're not just a bunch of cow-tipping morons down here."

(Pearl 1991)

[X], a human resources worker at Southern Bell, is trying her best not to sound like a Southern belle ... she is up for a promotion, and she is worried the decision will be made by Northerners. ... She is also taking night speech classes at Kennesaw State College. Unless she can drop the accent, she fears, the promotion committee "might not think I'm so sharp."

(ibid.)

In all of these cases, southerners exhibit insecurity about their language and a willingness to accept responsibility for poor communication or bad language, but they do so *only when in contact with the direct criticism of the northerner*. In the third case above, the person voicing the criticism and calling for acceptance of responsibility and change toward northern norms is in fact, from New Jersey. But she still claims the right to speak for all the people in that region where she lives and works: she wants the world to see her as something other than a "cow-tipping moron" in spite of the fact that she lives in the south. It is unclear whether she rejects the "cow tipping moron" stereotype as unfair and untrue, or subscribes to it and wishes not to be included in that group. In either case, she believes that the way to accomplish such a goal is to convince the rest of the south to talk as she does. But here she takes on a Herculean task, for the south provides, more than any single ethnic, racial, or national origin group, strong resistance to language subordination.

The news media has been shown to be particularly enamored of stories having to do with accent reduction, and those reports always include a discussion of such efforts in the south. "Hush mah mouth! Some in South try to lose the drawl!" (Pearl 1991) is not an unusual headline or introductory comment in these kinds of reports. They often contain some small commentary from dissenting southerners: "Somebody was going to judge me on the way I spoke, then I would judge him as being close-minded" (ABC Evening News, December 15, 1991).

The news media does not often report on southern resistance to the language-mainstreaming process. In doing so, however, journalists still manage to put a decidedly ideological spin on the rejection of subordination. In a newspaper report on the death of an accent-reduction course in South Carolina owing to lack of interest, the reporter summarizes:

So why did interest die out? With tongue firmly in cheek, [the instructor] offered three possible reasons: Everybody's cured. Everybody thinks the rest of the world talks funny. Or, in a country that now has a Southern President and vice president, maybe nobody much cares anymore.

(Riddle 1993)

Clearly it is difficult for northerners and mainstream language speakers to take seriously the idea that the south could be content with itself in terms of language. It is equally difficult to imagine, in spite of professed wishes to this effect, that southerners would somehow magically lose their accents, and could be "cured" of this disability which is so uniquely their own.

The author's final thought touches on some complex underlying issues of power and its distribution. In a new and unusual situation (both president and vice president from the south), in which the south has political dominance (at least in symbolic terms), can the illusion of northern linguistic superiority survive? The wish or compulsion to assimilate linguistically to a more dominant language necessarily presupposes a recognition of the social dominance of that language. If there is a shift in the traditional distribution of power, the traditionally subordinated may no longer be content to be complicit in a process which disadvantages them. Riddle raises this complex issue, but does not seem to be aware that she has done so, for she then dismisses it with an appeal to boredom or laziness.

Another reporter writes of a "Pro-Drawl Movement" in which the resistance is trivialized, and once again the strategy of condescension extends to the representation of southern US English in quasi-phonetic terms:

Ludlow Porch's radio talk show is at the center of Atlanta's Southern resistance. Mr. Porch, whose voice is as slow and sweet as molasses in January, gets a steady stream of female callers who call him "sweet thang" and male callers who call him "mah friend." When complimented, Mr. Porch is apt to say, "Well, ah'm tickled" or "Bless your heart."

But even Mr. Porch concedes that things are changing. He lives in a suburb where he goes for weeks without hearing a Southern accent. And he admits that, sometimes, he even catches himself "doin' silly things –– like pronouncin' mah 'g's."

(Pearl 1991)

Resistance filtered through the reporter's standard language ideology and condescension is resistance stripped of much of its power. Here Mr. Porch's language, and his concern about the fate of his culture and language, are made into humorous objects. He is then made to testify against himself, in that he admits that language changes, even as he watches. The journalist's only conclusion can be that language is changing *away* from southern norms, and *toward* northern ones. Thus once again, resistance is demonstrated to be useless.

When southern voices are heard uncensored, it almost always appears within southern boundaries, as in this column from the *Dallas Morning News*:

The [Southern League] encourages Southerners in the exercise of their indefeasible right to be Southern, never mind Northern reproaches and sneers.

To this praiseworthy end, a certain James E. Kibler, Jr., of Whitmire, S.C., exhorts Southerners to speak like Southerners rather than, well, non-Southerners. He'd rather we not just blend in but stand out. . . . Brother Kibler's linguistic preferences fly in the face of drastic changes in Southern society since World War II. . . . The language of the older South is the language of the small towns in which most Southerners grew up. Gone with the wind! The culture of the towns, and sometimes the towns themselves, have disappeared.

But Brother Kibler is right: The old way of speaking has charm and value. Language is a part of being. To talk one way is to be something that people who talk differently are not. This means the lords of language sometimes meet with defiance when they mandate change. Brought up saying "ice box" rather than "refrigerator," I would not now dream of speaking otherwise. I am frozen in solidarity with the past, on this question anyway.

Particular customs also can command defiant affirmation. A well-educated Texas woman I know relates how in the old days her equally well-educated mother, whenever a black cat crossed her path, would spit and say "damn."

It's a good custom, the woman still insists – not for any theological purpose it serves but rather as a tiny, feeble thread linking generations. The more such threads we break heedlessly, the more isolated we become in a society seemingly bent on annihilating memory itself. We're not supposed to love the past, we're supposed to hate it. Modernity drums this message into us relentlessly.

(Murchison 1996)

There is no doubt that in the delineation of the nation, we use accent as a cultural shorthand to talk about bundles of properties which we would rather not mention directly. When a northerner appropriates a pan-southern accent to make a joke or a point, he or she is drawing on a strategy of condescension and trivialization that cues into those stereotypes so carefully structured and nurtured: southerners who do not assimilate to northern norms are backward but friendly, racist but polite, obsessed with the past and unenamored of the finer points of higher education. If they are women, they are sweet, pretty and not very bright.[3]

Focusing on language difference allows us to package the south this way, and to escape criticism for what would otherwise be seen as narrow-mindedness. Without accent, it would not be possible to draw the nation's attention to the south's need for redemption without specifically raising those topics which make us nervous. If white southerners are not distinguishable by other ethnic markers, by characteristic physical features, or religion, language is one simple and effective way of distinguishing between self and other. Because in this case differences are historical and cultural, there is less footing for an ideology which subordinates and trivializes the language and the cultures attached to it.

Nevertheless, the process continues. Accent-reduction courses taught by northerners spring up, find some uneasy response in communities or individuals with strong northern ties, and then die away. Movies are made in which the lazy and narrow minded twang and drawl. Southern students who come north are taken aside and told that their native language phonology will be an impediment to true success. Job applicants are laughed at, and on the floor of Congress, reporters smirk and report not on the Representative's position, but on his or her language.

The south has resources to call on, ways to deflect subordination tactics, but only so long as it keeps itself intact and separate. Thus the institutions which are most responsible for the subordination process coax and wheedle toward the ultimate goal of cultural and linguistic assimilation, and are met with suspicion and defiance.

11 The stranger within the gates

"It was all my fault, your Majesty," said Jack, looking rather foolish. "I thought we must surely speak different languages, since we came from different countries."

"This should be a warning to you never to think," returned the Scarecrow severely.

Frank L. Baum, *The Land of Oz* (1904)

The 1990 census established that the United States is a nation of some 248 million persons, of whom 2,015,143 are Native American and 205,501 Hawai'ian. Thus it is an obvious and inescapable truth that the majority of people residing in the US are immigrants, or the descendents of immigrants, the greatest portion of whom came of their own will, while others came in chains. We are a nation of immigrants, but having made the transition and established ourselves, we have a strong urge to be protective of what is here; we talk at great length about closing the door behind us. At times, we have acted on this impulse:

- In the 1840s during a depression, mobs hostile to immigrant Irish Catholics burned down a convent in Boston.
- Congress passed the Chinese Exclusion Act in 1882, one of our first immigration laws, to exclude all people of Chinese origin.
- In 1942, 120,000 Americans of Japanese descent had their homes and other property confiscated, and were interned in camps until the end of the Second World War. At the same time, many Jews fleeing Nazi Germany during that war were excluded under regulations enacted in the 1920s.

(American Civil Liberties Union 1996)

Language often becomes the focus of debate when these complex issues of nationality, responsibility, and privilege are raised. English, held up as the symbol of the successfully assimilated immigrant, is promoted as the one and only possible language of a unified and healthy nation. Using rhetoric which is uncomfortably reminiscent of discussions of race in fascist regimes, a California Assemblyman notes the multilingual commerce in his home town with considerable trepidation: "you can go down and apply for a driver's license test entirely in Chinese. You can apply for welfare today entirely in Spanish. The supremacy of the English language is under attack" (report on pending English Only legislation in California, CBS Evening News, October 1986).

In considering the history of multilingualism and public fears around it, Ferguson and Heath noted that "whenever speakers [of other languages] have been viewed as politically, socially, or economically threatening, their language has become a focus for arguments in favor of both restrictions of their use and imposition of Standard English" (1981: 10). This is illustrated by the history of German use in the US, a language (and people) which particularly irritated Benjamin Franklin, who expressed his fears in a letter dated 1753.

> Those [Germans] who come hither are generally the most ignorant Stupid Sort of their own Nation, and as Ignorance is often attended with Credulity when Knavery would mislead it, and with Suspicion when Honesty would set it right; and as few of the English understand the German Language, and so cannot address them either from the Press or Pulpit, 'tis almost impossible to remove any prejudices they once entertain. . . . Not being used to Liberty, they know not how to make modest use of it. . . . Advertisements, intended to be general are now printed in Dutch [German] and English, the Signs in our Streets have inscriptions in both languages, and in some places only German: They begin of late to make all their Bonds and other legal Writings in their own Language, which (though I think it ought not to be) are allowed good in our Courts, where the German Business so increases that there is continued need of Interpreters . . . they will soon outnumber us, that all the advantages we have will not, in My Opinion, be able to preserve our language, and even our government will become precarious.
>
> (cited in Crawford 1992: 18–19)

If this kind of commentary is reminiscent of current-day fears focused on Asian and Latino populations, then the reasons for the shift are seen in part in numbers, as illustrated in Figure 11.1.

The relationship between shifting powerbases and the public consciousness of language use often focuses on legislation of one type or another, as in this news report on a vote to repeal an English Only law in Florida:

> In reality, Miami has been a bilingual city for a long time. The Miami Herald is printed every day in both English and Spanish. Automatic teller machines here offer both languages. And whether you're at the airport . . . or on the streets, you constantly hear English and Spanish. But after the Mariel boatlift of 1980 brought thousands of Cubans here,

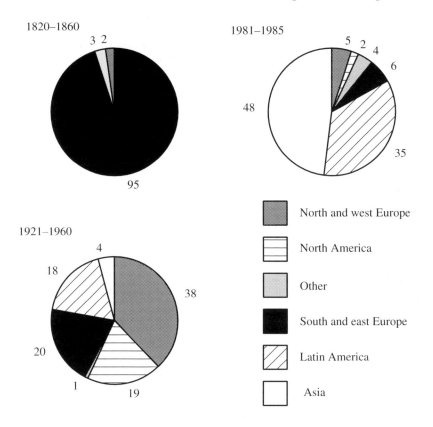

Figure 11.1 Legal immigrants (percentage) coming into the US in three time periods, by stated region of last residence

Source: US Government (1996) "Immigration to the US: the unfinished story." *Population Bulletin.* Washington DC: Population Reference Bureau, vol. 41.4, p. 16

voters overwhelmingly passed a law prohibiting the use of any language in official county business except English. For example, if you want to testify at a commission hearing, question your water bill, or make a formal complaint, it must be in English.

(ABC Evening News, May 14, 1993)

While most of the public debate around languages has to do with a deceptively simple question of *Which language?* here I want to look more carefully beyond that issue to the underlying one. When immigrants become bilingual (as happened, for example, in the case of the majority of the German immigrant population), the question is no longer which language, but *Which English?* or more specifically in this chapter *Which Accent?*

Table 11.1   Language spoken at home by persons 5 years or older

Language	No. of people
English only	198,600,798
Spanish or Spanish Creole	17,345,064
French or French Creole	1,930,404
German	1,547,987
Chinese	1,319,462
Italian	1,308,648
Other and unspecified languages	1,023,614
Tagalog	843,251
Polish	723,483
Korean	626,478
Other Indo-European language	578,076
Indic	555,126
Vietnamese	507,069
Portuguese or Portuguese Creole	430,610
Japanese	427,657
Greek	388,260
Arabic	355,150
Native North American languages	331,758
Other Slavic language	270,863
Russian	241,798
Other West Germanic language	232,461
Yiddish	213,064
Scandinavian	198,904
South Slavic	170,449
Hungarian	147,902
Hmong-Khmer	127,441

Source: 1990 US census data. Database: C90STF3C1

WHO HAS A FOREIGN ACCENT?

The census bureau estimates that 22,568,000 persons or 8.7 percent of the population of the United States was foreign-born in 1994, a figure which is nearly double the number of foreign-born in 1970 (4.8 percent).[1] A total of 31,844,979 persons – many of these not foreign-born – reported that they spoke a language other than English in the home, as is seen in Table 11.1. We note that this list does not specify a single language from the continent of Africa beyond the Arabic languages of the north. It must be assumed that as immigration from the mid- and southern African nations is limited, speakers of languages such as Swahili and Zulu are subsumed under the category "Other and unspecified languages."

If the purpose is to come to an approximation of who speaks English with a foreign accent, it is useful to have some accounting of proficiency in English. The census bureau attempts to access this information by simply asking the question. The published results are conflated into four groups: native English speakers who have no other language in the home

Table 11.2 (Non-English) language spoken at home and ability to speak English, by age

Age	Language spoken	Evaluation of English-language skills: census count		
		"Very well"	*"Well"*	*"Not well" or "Not well at all"*
5–17	Spanish	2,530,779	993,417	643,457
	Asian or Pacific Island	455,339	224,821	135,430
	Other	948,573	262,442	128,676
18–64	Spanish	6,105,722	2,589,195	3,425,937
	Asian or Pacific Island	1,496,466	1,048,835	755,324
	Other	4,312,500	1,315,685	658,210
65+	Spanish	398,568	223,350	434,639
	Asian or Pacific Island	99,461	82,351	173,594
	Other	1,515,069	570,205	316,934

Source: 1990 US census data. Database: C90STF3C1

(this would include, for example, people who have limited second-language ability through schooling);[2] and then three universes, as seen in Table 11.2: speakers of Spanish, speakers of Asian and Pacific Rim languages, and speakers of other languages which do not fall into any of the previous groups. This last group must include a great variety of languages, from those spoken in Africa to Scandinavia and middle and eastern European.

A graphic representation of the 18–65-year-old group from this table is given in Figure 11.2. Here we see that there is in fact a differential in the individual's assessment of ability to speak English according to national-origin subgrouping. In all three groups, the majority of non-native English speakers claim a very good command of their second language. The differential between "very good" and "not well at all" is smallest for the Asian-languages group, which is in turn the smallest of the three groups overall.

We note especially that there are four million people in the "Other language" category who call their own English "very good" and another million or so of this same group who find their English not very good at all. This mysterious "Other language" group is in fact larger than the Asian-languages group. While this profusion of numbers still does not provide an exact count of how many people speak English with a foreign accent, it does raise two crucial points.

First, millions of people resident in the US are not native speakers of English, and use a language other than English in their homes and personal lives. As established in Chapter 2, any individual who takes on the task of learning a second or third language in adulthood will have some degree of L2 accent, a degree which is not readily predictable and

Millions

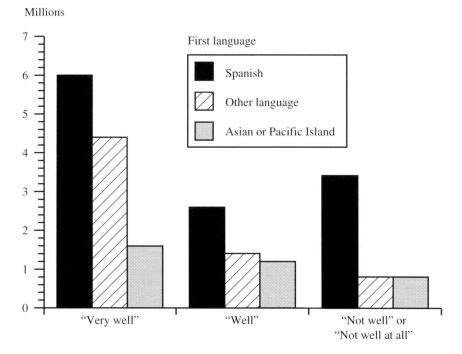

Figure 11.2 Persons between 18 and 65 years who claim a first language other than English, and their evaluation of their English-language skills
Source: 1990 census

will not correlate, overall, to education, intelligence, or motivation. Thus there is a large population of US residents who speak with an L2 accent.

Second, there are preconceived notions about non-native speakers of English which have repercussions even in the way we count their numbers and talk about them. The US Census Bureau distinguishes between Spanish, Asian, and other languages. It is from this departure point that we look at the way foreign-language groups and the language stereotypes associated with those groups are used to classify – and often to dismiss – individual needs and rights.

FROM BALI HAI TO NEW DELHI: WHAT IT MEANS TO BE ASIAN

We have seen that the non-south US tends to conceptualize all 25 million southerners as a linguistically and culturally homogenous monolith, in spite of the proximity between the north and south, and in spite of a great deal of common ground in historical and cultural terms. Thus it will

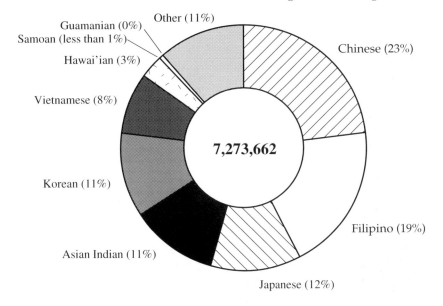

Figure 11.3 Breakdown of "Asian or Pacific Islander" category in the 1990 US census, by national origin

not be surprising that the urge to lean on stereotype is magnified when immigrant groups come into consideration.

The Census Bureau lists a figure of almost 7.3 million Asians in the US population. Figure 11.3 breaks down this figure, according to census data, into more specific national origins. In examining this chart, it immediately becomes apparent that even in its more specific form, the subgrouping 'Asian' is internally immensely complex and diverse. It might be argued that generalizations are necessary when dealing with this kind of data, for as seen in Table 11.3, the nations of Asia and the Pacific are numerous. In linguistic terms, even this breakdown is deceiving.[3]

We take for example India, a nation of 844 million persons which recognizes fifteen official national languages each with a large number of dialects. India is linguistically complex, especially when viewed in comparison to the US, but it is not the exception to the rule. It is not even extreme in the larger global view. We consider China (population 1.1 billion), with fifty-five official minority nationalities and eight major languages in addition to literally hundreds of other languages from Mongolian to Hmong; or Fiji with a mere 740,000 residents spread out over 7,000 square miles of islands on which fifteen languages (in addition to Fijian) are spoken.

While it would be an unreasonable burden on the Census Bureau to make note of each and every world language spoken in the US, the great

Table 11.3 Nations of Asia and the Pacific

Asian nations	Pacific nations
Afghanistan	American Samoa
Bangladesh	Australia
Bhutan	Belau
Brunei	Cook Islands
Cambodia	Easter Island
China	Fiji
Hong Kong	French Polynesia
India	Guam
Indonesia	Hawi'ian Islands
Japan	Kiribati
Kazakhstan	Marshall Islands
North Korea	Micronesia
South Korea	Midway Islands
Kyrghyzstan	Nauru
Laos	New Caledonia
Macau	New Zealand
Malaysia	Niue
Maldives	Norfolk Island
Mongolia	Northern Mariana Islands
Myanmar	Papua New Guinea
Nepal	Pitcairn
Pakistan	Samoa
Philippines	Solomon Islands
Russia-Asian	Tokelau
Singapore	Tonga
Sri Lanka	Tuvalu
Taiwan	Vanuatu
Tajikistan	Wake Island
Thailand	Wallis and Futuna
Turkmenistan	
Uzbekistan	
Vietnam	

disparity between *how* we make official note – what we see when we look outward at the majority of the world's population – and the *reality* of those nations, bears some consideration. What are the repercussions of the fact that we group together persons as different as the native people of Hawai'i – US citizens with a history which should be very familiar to us – with Cambodians who sought political asylum in the US and middle-class exchange students from New Delhi? How can policies which do not distinguish between the immigration patterns and educational and language backgrounds of such disparate peoples be functional?

And why do we do this? Is expediency the single most viable answer? Or is it simply that when it comes to language, we hear a single "Asian" accent?

An obvious but disturbing answer is that we feel justified to group so many distinct nations and peoples and languages together because they all look alike to "real" Americans, to European Americans. *Asian* evokes an association not to national origin, but to race. In Chapter 5, we looked briefly at one example of how Asian stereotypes are used in entertainment film as a kind of shorthand, in the 1993 film *Falling Down*:

> *The proprietor, a middle-aged ASIAN, reads a Korean newspaper . . .*
> *the Asian has a heavy accent . . .*

DE-FENS: . . . You give me seventy "fie" cents back for the phone . . .
What is a fie? There's a "V" in the word. Fie-vuh. Don't they have
"v's" in China?
ASIAN: Not Chinese, I am Korean.
D-FENS: Whatever. What difference does that make? You come over
here and take my money and you don't even have the grace to learn
to speak my language . . .

(Smith 1992: 7–8)

Here, the script uses the generic term "Asian" in a way that echoes the exchange between fictional characters. Neither the script writers nor D-Fens, the white-collar worker on the edge of his sanity, make a distinction between Chinese and Korean (although it is interesting that the shopowner is *reading*, and reading Korean rather than "Asian" or, perhaps more significantly, English).

The Korean has committed three sins in the eyes of the customer: he has "come over here" and, having immigrated, he "takes my money" by establishing himself in a social position in which he has economic capital and goods to dispense. These sins are compounded by the fact that the shopowner "doesn't have the grace to learn to speak my language."

Of course, the evidence is just the opposite of what the customer is claiming: *the shopowner does speak English.* He speaks English well enough to get into a rousing argument with the customer, to assert his rights as owner of the shop, and to ask the customer to leave. But, crucially, he does not speak English to the customer's satisfaction, because he speaks English with an *Asian* accent. Here we are reminded of Heath's characterization of situations in which non-native speakers of English gain social or economic currency: "their language has become a focus for arguments in favor of both restrictions of their use and imposition of Standard English" (1981: 10).

Non-native English-speaking Asian Americans, as a large and diverse group, experience something in common, regardless of their economic status, education, or national origin: there is a special stigma attached to their presence which is externalized in reactions to the way they speak English. So conditioned are we to expect a different world view, a different accent, that we hear one where none is present. This was demonstrated in the Florida study of university student comprehension of lecture material (see Chapter 6). Individuals experience this regularly, as shown in the following examples.

A young woman of Asian Indian family, but a native and monolingual speaker of English, relates a story in which a middle-aged man in a music store is unable to help her when she asks for a recently released Depeche Mode tape (Kapoor 1993). "You'll have to speak slower because I didn't understand you because of your accent," he tells her. She is understandably hurt and outraged: "I have no discernible accent. I do, however, have long dark hair and pleasantly colored brown skin. I suppose this outward appearance of mine constitutes enough evidence to conclude I had, indeed, just jumped off the boat and into the store." The pain of this experience is real whether or not a foreign accent is present. In this case, the harm was real, but without repercussions which affected the young woman in a material way. Others are more unlucky.

In February of 1992, at the Department of the Treasury building on Main Street in San Francisco, a Treasury official called down to the lobby with a question. Irritated by the quality of response that he or she received, this official made a formal complaint of "communication difficulties" based on Filipino accent. He or she did not provide the name of the security guard responsible for the poor service. Subsequent to this report, the General Services Authority directed the subcontractor who supplied the security guards to remove *all five Filipino agents* who had been on duty that evening, because of "language barriers."[4] The men removed from their positions were not given regular employment at another site, but were used as fill-ins on a variety of assignments, which caused them significant financial and other problems.

While we saw in Chapter 8 that this kind of treatment is not unusual, the reaction of the men in question was quite remarkable. As a group, they sued their employer under Title VII, "to restore our honor and dignity." For Filipino Americans, the charge of insufficient or inadequate English is especially stinging, as English is one of the primary languages of education in their homeland, where in the 1975 census more than fifteen thousand claimed it as a first language and in 1980 almost half a million listed it as a second language (Grimes 1992). The five men in question had lived in the US for most of their lives, and their public comments on the case left no doubt that the harm was as much emotional as economic: "It was a slap to my face," "It deeply hurt my feelings."

In fact, the attorneys for the security guards established to the court's satisfaction that they were qualified and experienced workers, with between three and nine years on the job without any complaints about their language abilities. The court found for the security guards, but a question was never raised: how was it that an anonymous official could bring about the removal of five men with solid work histories, solely on the basis of an unsubstantiated claim of an irritating and distracting accent? If the guards in question had been Italian or Norwegian speakers, would the same progression of events be imaginable?

The issue is not so much accent as "otherness," as illustrated in a series of court cases involving Asian American English:

> Managerial level employee [LS] told Xieng he was not being promoted because he could not speak "American."
>
> (*Xieng* 1991: Appeal Court Opinion: 5)

> the complainant's supervisor had removed her because of concern about the effect of her accent on the "image" of the IRS, not any lack in either communication or technical abilities.
>
> (*Park*: EEOC press release, June 8, 1988)

Our relationship to the Far East and Pacific is shaped to a great degree by the facts of nineteenth-century colonialism, in which the US, young in comparative terms, followed the European model in the way that smaller nations were overcome and dominated politically, economically, and socially. We have a history of dealing with the Asian world as a warehouse of persons and goods available to suit our own purpose and fill our own needs, a practice justified by the supposition that those people are inherently weaker. Because they are also cast as manipulative and wont to use natural wiles and treacherous means to achieve their own ends, we are able to rationalize aggressions toward them. Thus the primary male Asian stereotype is of an intelligent, clever, but crafty and unreliable person. A secondary stereotype grows out of the mystification of Asia, the mysterious "Orient" where hardworking but simple people ply their crafts and study arcane philosophies, attaining wisdom and a spirituality specific to their race. We are uncomfortable with Asians unless they correspond to the stereotypes we have created for them.

There is a great deal of affection for Charlie Chan, the wiser Chinese detective employed by the Honolulu Police Department (played first by the Swedish-born Warner Oland and then by Sidney Toler, both in "yellow face"), who dispensed calm fortune-cookie wisdom and always solved the crime. His sons, played by Keye Luke and Victor Sen Yung (both native Chinese), provided the comic foil. As Americanized second-generation types, they played the gap between expectation and reality for all it is worth. While the actors portraying Charlie Chan contrived Chinese accents, the sons (both of whom came to the US as very small children) spoke English as a primary language and with a markedly urban discourse style ("Pop!"). In a similar way, the 1937 film of Pearl S. Buck's *The Good Earth* also used white actors to play the leads, to the satisfaction of reviewers who found that the main character met (stereotypical) expectations: "Physically, Muni becomes satisfactorily celestial, imbued with racial characteristics" (*Variety*, January 29, 1937: 3).

Female Asian stereotypes focus on submissiveness, beauty, a need for strong male direction, and a talent for tragedy (the opera *Madam Butterfly* and the popular musical *Flower Drum Song* provide good examples of these stereotypes). While Asian stereotypes have evolved in this century for males (overachieving in education and business, whether the business be a green grocery or computer-chip research and development), female images seem to be more resilient.

In Chang-Rae Lee's critically acclaimed 1995 novel, *Native Speaker*, a Korean American narrator called Henry Park first tells the story of how he came to fall in love with his wife, an American who is of interest to him not just as a woman, but because as a speech pathologist she works with children who are non-native speakers of English, helping them to acquire that difficult language. "People like me are always thinking about still having an accent," he tells her in their first discussion. What he does not say, but which is clear from real-life experiences of people like Ms. Kapoor, is that people "like" Henry Park must always be thinking about having an accent, because that is what is expected of them: to be different, and to externalize that difference with language.

Caught between his own and public expectations, Henry Park can please no one. When his wife leaves to travel without him, and perhaps forever, her note of explanation is a simple list of descriptors for him, which include

> *illegal alien*
> *emotional alien*
> *Yellow peril: neo-American.*

Later he finds another scrap of paper with a definition of himself on it that she could not quite include on the final list: *False speaker of language.*

Like African Americans, Asian Americans have more and more difficult hurdles to leap before they can transcend stereotype and be accepted as individuals. Accent, when it acts in part as a marker of race, takes on special power and significance. For many in the African American community there is little resistance to the language subordination process, in part because the implied promises of linguistic assimilation – while obviously overstated – are nevertheless seductive, *precisely because the threats are very real*. The seduction of perfect English, of belonging absolutely to the mainstream culture of choice, is one that is hard to resist for Asian Americans as well.

It is easy to establish that language variation is linked to race, and more specifically that foreign-language accent is linked to national origin. But once accomplished, what is to be done with such a collection of facts? Perhaps the only realistic thing is to ask harder questions of ourselves. Discrimination against Asian Americans which centers on language, but which has more in actual terms to do with race, is an established practice. How is it that in a nation so proud of its civil rights legislation and democratic ideals, people can so easily use *accent* to exclude, to limit discourse,

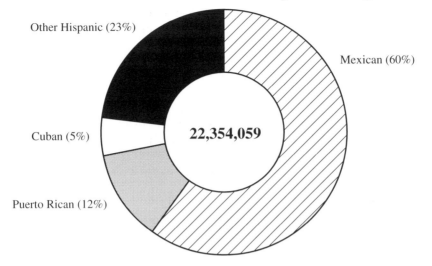

Other Hispanic (23%)

Mexican (60%)

22,354,059

Cuban (5%)

Puerto Rican (12%)

Figure 11.4 Hispanics counted in the 1990 US census

and to discredit other – very specific – voices, because they simply do not sound white enough?

It is necessary and important at this point to look at another large group, composed in large part of non-native speakers of English. The Spanish-speaking people of this country comprise nations within the nation. As speakers of languages other than English, they are also subject to the process of homogenization which has been seen for other groups.

CHIQUITAFICATION

The group of peoples which the Census Bureau calls "Hispanic" included some 22 million US residents in the 1990 census.[5] As was the case for the Asian population, this overarching term hides a great deal of ethnic variety, in this case compounded the racial diversity, as seen in Figure 11.4 and Table 11.4

As might be predicted, Mexican Americans account for most of the Latino population, with a much smaller Puerto Rican population and a Cuban population of just over one million, or about 5 percent of the whole. Almost a quarter of *Latino* is made up of "Other," in this case comprising primarily Central and South Americans (just over a million residents each) and half a million Spaniards. About half a million persons could or would not be specific in identifying their national origins.

It is important to note that the racial classifications do not include *mestizo*, and thus persons of mixed European and Native American ancestry – a large portion of the population of Mexico and Central

Table 11.4 Hispanic origin by race

Race	Non-Hispanic	%	Hispanic	%
White	188,424,773	83.1	11,402,291	52.1
Black	29,284,596	12.9	645,928	2.9
American Indian, Eskimo, or Aleut	1,866,807	0.8	148,336	0.7
Asian or Pacific Islander	6,994,302	3.1	232,684	1.1
Other race	239,306	0.1	9,470,850	43.2
Total	226,809,784	100	21,900,089	100

Source: 1990 US census data. Database: C90STF3C1

America – must choose between allegiances (a fact which probably accounts for the large number of persons who identified themselves as "other race"). This oversight is compounded by the assumption of an over-arching Spanish monolingualism which spans more than ten countries in three continents. The Mexican population of more than 88 million includes more than 5 million speakers of indigenous Indian languages (about 8 percent of Mexico's total population), of whom almost half a million are monolingual and speak no Spanish at all (Grimes 1992). Guatemala's population of 9.3 million is approximately 55 percent Indian and 44 percent mestizo. The Indian population includes some 20,000 speakers of Kanjobal, 5,000 of whom are reported to be in Los Angeles (ibid.).

In addition to racial and ethnic diversity, "Latino" subsumes persons from all economic groups, political and religious backgrounds, and does not recognize a residency status differential. It overlooks the fact that many ethnically Spanish-speaking persons live here on land their families have owned for many generations, and predate European settlement. In addition to this group, which cannot logically be called "immigrant," there are populations of more recent arrivals, short-term residents, cyclical immigrants made up primarily of farmworkers, and individuals who seek asylum in the US to escape political persecution, in addition to undocumented workers.

The use of language as a preliminary qualifier in the construction of ethnicity is an established custom, but it is nevertheless a troublesome one, as the scope and depth of "Hispanic" has made clear. Zentella (1996) speaks and writes of what it was like for her as a child to have had a singing and dancing Chiquita Banana as a solitary Latina figure in the public eye. Thus she uses the term *chiquitafication* to speak of public policies and practices which homogenize Latino cultures and languages into a tidy and digestible package for the rest of the nation. Three areas which concern her greatly are

- the construction of a homogenous "Hispanic community" that refuses to learn English;

- the belittling of non-Castilian varieties of Spanish;
- and the labeling of second-generation bilinguals as semi- or a-linguals.

(1996: 1)

The second of these concerns points to an issue which has not been raised much in this discussion, and that is that language ideologies are not restricted to the English-speaking world. Discourse around "good" and "lesser" language, "appropriate" and "inappropriate" varieties can be found wherever people care to look. For each nation, there is a supra-cultural awareness of which are the "right" varieties, although there will also be competing constructions of social acceptability – for without those who find the "right" language unacceptable in social terms, stigmatized language would not flourish as it does. Table 11.5 presents the simplest answers one would be likely to get in asking an average person on the street "Where is the best [language] spoken?" and "Where is the worst [language] spoken?"[6]

For Spanish, with a much greater geographic coverage than any of the other European languages with the exception of English, standard language ideology has established Castilian Spanish and, following there-from, Castilian literature and culture as inherently superior and more worthy of study than New World language or language artifacts, as Zentella notes. Within Central and South American nations, there are similarly constructed ideologies, so that in Mexico there is a conception of three *normas* or levels of speaking: *la norma culta*, which Valdés (1988: 119) calls "educated standard," *la norma popular* ("a less elaborate and cultivated style"), and *la norma rural* ("This style of speaking generally sounds rustic to city people and is normally associated with rural lifestyles and backgrounds") (ibid.), as well as a conception of good and bad varieties over space, so that the Spanish spoken in the Yucatan is stig-matized. Overarching the national constructions of "good" and "bad"

Table 11.5 Popular constructions of "good" and "bad" language for other countries

Country	"Good" "Proper" "Cultured" "High"	"Low" "Bad" "Inappropriate"
Italy	Florence	Sicily Calabria
Spain	Burgos Valladolid	Huelva
England	Oxford Cambridge	Liverpool Birmingham
Turkey	Istanbul	Black Sea Southeast Anatolia
Northern India (Hindi)	Delhi	Bombay Calcutta
Pakistan (Urdu)	Lucknow	Hyderabad

language, however, is a very persistent idea that *Castilian* is the only real, original language. This functions much in the same way as it does in the US, when popular belief may point to Ohio as "Standard US English" but then defer to that mythical beast "the King's English," or a British norm.

As interesting as it would be to compare the way language subordination tactics function across language and cultural boundaries, here I would like to concentrate instead on the first and third of Zentella's concerns. Together they summarize some conflicts about the process of language subordination which are instructive and important.

Zentella states that there is a troublesome, contrary-to-fact "construction of a homogeneous 'Hispanic community' that refuses to learn English" in the US, and she goes on to demonstrate how dangerous such homogenization can be. This is a willful policy which

> encourages wholesale demonizing of the type reflected in a memo written by John Tanton when he was Chair of US English, the group that has been lobbying to make English the official language of the United States since 1981. Tanton portrayed Hispanic Catholicism as a national threat to the separation of church and state, and declared that a Latin American tradition of bribery imperiled US democracy. His most outrageous insult was a vulgar reference to "the Hispanic birthrate," charging that "perhaps this is the first instance in which those with their pants up are going to get caught with their pants down."
>
> (Zentella 1996: 9)

Zentella's analysis of US English and other English Only movements as xenophobic, hostile, and threatening to more than just language rights is clear and convincing (see also Crawford, ed., 1992 for a lengthy discussion). When she sets out to counter their arguments with hard data, she does so carefully:

> Despite the continued influx of monolingual immigrants, Veltman (1983) found that Hispanics are undergoing language loss similar to, and even exceeding that of other groups in US history. Language shift is most advanced among the US born, who constituted the majority (64%) of the US Latino population in 1990; immigrants shift to English within 15 years ...
>
> (1996: 10)

But somewhere an issue has gone missing.

Tanton and his colleagues construct not only a *homogenous* "Hispanic" community, but a *resistant* one. Zentella attacks both premises: it is not true, she asserts, that Hispanic immigrants are resistant to, and reject, the importance of English or the necessity of learning it. She claims that this is not true because the numbers show us that they do indeed learn it. But does the result preclude resistance to the process, or resentment of the necessity? Further, if this kind of resistance does exist, is it necessarily bad? Would the existence of a Spanish-speaking community in Florida or Texas or New Mexico which does not use and manages to function without English render Tanton's claims credible? Would asserting the right not to be bilingual (a right which would bring along with it many great difficulties) be tantamount to an attack on American democracy? It is clear that Zentella does not mean to make this claim, and that she is constructing "resistance" in a purposefully narrow way.

However, the third concern (*the labeling of second-generation bilinguals as semi- or a-linguals*) does demand a wider conception of resistance. This question moves beyond the issue of whether or not bilingualism is necessary and reasonable (something she, and most others, take for granted) to the issue of *Which English?*

Some immigrants live in communities of monolingual English speakers, where a Spanish accent stands out. Others live in communities where multiple varieties of English coexist in relative harmony, in which Spanish, English, and Chicano or another variety of Latino English each have a sphere. Chicano English, Puerto Rican English and Cuban English in Los Angeles, New York, and Miami are individual varieties of English, distinct in certain syntactical, morphological, and discourse markers from one another and from other varieties of English (Penfield and Ornstein-Galicia 1985; Zentella 1988; Valdés 1988; García and Otheguy 1988). There is a recognized Chicano American and Latino American literature which is taken as a serious object of study.

When Zentella protests the labeling of second-generation Spanish-language immigrants as semilingual or a-lingual, she is discussing a related phenomenon, that of code switching. Code switching is the orderly (rule-based) alternation between two or more languages, a subject of great interest to linguists and one which is widely studied. This complicates the picture of the Spanish-speaking universe considerably. We have distinct languages, each with its own stylistic repertoires: Spanish and English. To these we add more recently developed but distinct varieties of English, for example Chicano English as it is spoken in Texas. Now we have also the phenomenon of living and working with three languages, and switching among them as determined by language-internal (syntactical and morphological) rules as well as social and stylistic ones. The criticism Zentella discusses is aimed at switching, which may seem to an unsympathetic outsider nothing more than a language hodge-podge, and is often labeled *Spanglish*.

In fact, I would argue that whether the object of subordination is the act of style switching, or pressure to use a specific language, the ultimate goal of language subordination remains the same: to devalue and suppress *everything Spanish*.

To call code-switching *Spanglish* in a dismissive way is just another subordination method with a long history: to deny a language and its people a distinct name is to refuse to acknowledge them. There is a shorthand at work here, and that is, there is only one acceptable choice: it is not enough for Spanish speakers to become bilingual; they must learn the *right* English – and following from that, the right US culture, into which they must assimilate completely.

On rare occasion, there will be public commentary which makes clear that the offer we make to immigrants is contingent on a *certain kind of English*, as in this radio essay which begins with images of confusion and bloodshed in a multiethnic urban setting:

> Los Angeles has cosmopolitan eyes and ears. We know a Korean bill-board from a Chinese one even though we may not read either language. Those bloody names that spill out of the television every night – Gorazde, San Cristobal. They don't sound so foreign here as they might in the Dakotas. So, why are we frustrated at the sound of own voices?
>
> (Morrison 1994, broadcast)

Note the clever tactic of a straightforward demand for cooperation: *We* are frustrated by *ourselves*, by the multilingualism of Los Angeles. By coercing participation in this way, the commentator makes *his* frustration *everyone's* frustration. Thus, a great deal of latitude can be assumed in matters where he might not otherwise feel entitled to impose his opinion:

> It's because over the counters in our banks, over the tables in our restaurants, and over the phones in our offices, in job interviews and in meeting rooms, Los Angeles speaks not just with dozens of foreign languages, but with dozens of variations of English, not to mention our own native accent, from Ice-T to Beverly Hills 90210. It's all English, we're all speaking the same language, but that doesn't mean we're communicating. How do you bring up something that's more personal than bad breath and more embarrassing than an unzipped fly? How do you tell people who are speaking English that it's a kind of English we can't understand? Mostly we don't even try. We say "thank you," and then we hang up the phone and call back a few minutes later, hoping that someone else will answer.
>
> (ibid.)

Having assumed that all immigrants want to be bilingual, and work toward that goal in order to have a common vehicle of communication, the switch is made: the total lack of English is unimaginable, but the wrong English, accented English (and specifically elsewhere in this essay Spanish-accented and Asian-accented English) literally *stinks of unwashed humanity*. There are no excuses made for rejecting the communicative burden; it is acceptable just to "hang up the phone." Presumably it is this mindset which was at work when an anonymous Treasury department worker, irritated by a Filipino accent, hung up only to make another call, one which cost five men their jobs.

The commentator moves on to make some concessions: accent is immutable, past a certain age, even when people would like to acquire a perfect English.

> The newcomers want to learn English. . . . The cruelest thing about this is that learning the words is the easy part; learning the accent may never happen. An expert in these things says that after puberty, muscles that have formed one language for years just can't change very easily to a new one.
>
> The friction of all these accents bumping into one another has created a new enterprise – accent reduction classes, although accent acquisition is the preferred neutral term. All accents are considered equal, and reducing an accent implies superiority, and that isn't politically correct, even though everyone knows an English accent gets you invited to lunch, but a Spanish accent gets you dirty looks.
>
> (ibid.)

Finally, we come to the heart of the matter. Certain accents are frustrating and disturbing, and worthy of *reduction*, as he has admitted that elimination is an impossibility. *We* want to reduce these accents, but there's a complication: in so doing we are making a negative statement about the social identities to which they are attached. In order to soften this blow and render accent reduction more palatable, another tactic is employed: the concern with fairness is labeled "politically correct," a neat and very quick way to render the idea behind it petty and worthy of rejection. *I know that this is wrong on some level*, the commentator is saying, *but it is done so much – why fight it?*

The negative impact of a Spanish accent in some parts of the country is considerable, as we see here, and elsewhere. Not only are these accents stigmatized, but there is no hesitation to act on prejudice associated with language, as in this anecdote recounted by a doctoral student conducting research on attitudes toward Spanish in San Diego's business community:

> I was on an early morning flight where most of the passengers were gentlemen in business suits. The passenger in the seat next to mine asked about [the recording equipment], and I explained briefly about my research. He was very curious and wanted to know what results I expected. I told him that I didn't know what I might find, and he offered his personal opinion. He told me that he worked in sales for a large company in San Diego, and that it was his job to hire salesmen. He told me quite frankly that he would never hire anyone with a strong foreign accent, and especially not a Mexican accent. I asked him why. His only response was, "That's smart business. I have to think of the customers. I wouldn't buy anything from a guy with a Mexican accent."
>
> (Spicher 1992: 3–4)

Whether or not it is actually smart business to willfully ignore the needs and wants of a population of more than 20 million consumers is doubtful, but it is a question which can't be explored here in detail. Nevertheless, this anecdote is more useful than any number of statistics, because it makes some things painfully clear: the degree of accent is irrelevant when the focus is not on content, but on form. The businessman cannot conceive of a middle-class Spanish-speaking population with money to spend, and therefore the entire Mexican American population is worthy of rejection.

Stereotypes around Chicano and Latino Americans are almost exclusively negative, in all forms of popular culture. Penfield and Ornstein-Galicia identify the exception to this, the Californian *Don* or the New Mexican *Rico* who as "symbols of the aristocratic class ... were both linked more to Spain than Mexico" (1985: 78). These characters in film (*The Mark of Zorro*) or popular fiction speak an English which is accented, but elegant and archaic. Both men and women speak this kind of "noble Spaniard" English:

> "Come out," she said.
> "Ay! They have me fast. But when they do let me out, *niña*, I will take thee in my arms; and whosoever tries to tear thee away again will have a dagger in his heart. *Dios de mi vida!*" ...
> "But thou lovest me, Carlos?"
>
>> (Gertrude Atherton (1901) *The Doomswoman: An historical romance of old California*, as cited in Simmen 1971: 40)

More usually the stereotypes for Mexican Americans depart from the *greaser*, a classification subdivided into three types: "a Mexican *paisano* – poor rural inhabitant; as a *mojado* – 'wetback' or illegal alien; and as a *bandido* – a robber wearing 'huge sombreros ... tobacco-stained fingers and teeth, and grotesque dialect and curses'" (Penfield and Ornstein-Galicia 1985: 78). These characters are portrayed as speaking English with extreme dialect features; the more stereotypical the role, the more extreme the features:

> Billee the Keed. Ah, you have heard of heem? He was one gran' boy, senor. All Mexican pepul his friend. You nevair hear a Mexican say one word against Billee the Keed ... so kind-hearted, so generaous, so brave. And so 'andsome. Nombre de Dios! Every leetle senorita was crazy about heem ...
>
>> (Walter Noble Burns, *The Saga of Billy the Kid*, as cited in Pettit 1980: 162)

Recent stereotypes in film and television, note Penfield and Ornstein-Galicia, have one thing in common: Mexican Americans are almost always portrayed as violent; they are drug-pushers, gang-members, pimps. A particularly extreme example of a trivialized character was Frito Bandito, a 1980s counterpart and mirror image of the wholesome Chiquita Banana. In the 1980s, however, the Latino community was vocal and persuasive enough to convince the Frito-Lay company to drop that negative character (1985: 84).

The Spanish-speaking population of the US is very large, and has more resources and expertise with US law and the legal system than other groups. Latino resistance to all kinds of discriminatory practices is well organized, and extends to language matters, especially when education is at issue. Unlike a smaller and more fragmented Asian population, many Spanish speakers are ready and willing to speak out on these issues. Unfortunately, they continue to have to battle, because as the San Diego businessman makes clear, equal opportunity and equal standing are not always forthcoming.

SUMMARY

Foreign accent is a sharp dissecting tool, and it is one that we are willing to use liberally and without concern for the harm it does. The degree of accentedness is not necessarily relevant; we have seen that where no accent exists, stereotype and discrimination can sometimes manufacture one in the mind of the listener.

A high degree of education does not necessarily bring with it any protection from discrimination based on foreign accent, as was seen in the case of *Fragante v. City and County of Honolulu*, and *Hou v. Pennsylvania Department of Education*. In fact, some people are willing to reject foreign accent in a public way when expectations about social prominence are affronted and stereotypes confounded. This was the case in a 1987–1988 search for a president at the University of Michigan, when a Regent allegedly told student reporters that his institution "would never hire a president with a foreign accent" (Wainess 1994) in explanation of that Regent's opposition to a particular candidate, a native speaker of Greek. The Regent was voicing an illegal intent, but this statement – made public six years after the search with the rest of the documentation – still passed without public commentary.

A person who is a non-native speaker of English may want nothing more than to assimilate to the language and culture of the mainstream, but because sincerity and application are not enough to replace one accent with another, hard work toward a non-stigmatized variety of US English will not necessarily protect anyone from discrimination. This is a lesson hard learned:

> One student in the [accent reduction] class ... a 22-year-old from Columbia, feels that the course is critical to his future. "To tell you the truth," he said during a break, "this class is my last hope. If it doesn't work out, I'm going back to my country."

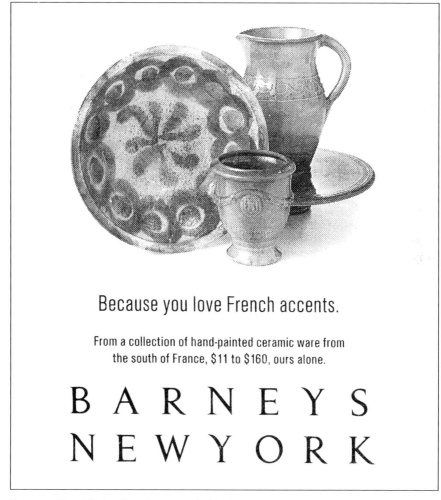

Because you love French accents.

From a collection of hand-painted ceramic ware from
the south of France, $11 to $160, ours alone.

B A R N E Y S
N E W Y O R K

Barneys New York advertisement. © 1995 Barneys New York

The problem, he said, is that he feels that his accent sets him apart
from others, even though he has lived in this country for nine years.
He graduated from Newton High School in Queens and is now a junior
at Queens College.

"I was practically raised in this country," he said, speaking in a soft
lilting accent. "But I have this accent. Does that mean I'm not an
American? I don't know."

(Hernandez 1993)

It is crucial to remember that it is not *all* foreign accents, but only accent
linked to skin that isn't white, or which signals a third-world homeland,

that evokes such negative reactions. There are no documented cases of native speakers of Swedish or Dutch or Gaelic being turned away from jobs because of communicative difficulties, although these adult speakers face the same challenge as native speakers of Spanish, Rumanian, and Urdu.

Immigrants from the British Isles who speak varieties of English which cause significant communication problems are not stigmatized: the differences are noted with great interest, and sometimes with laughter. A student asks to speak to a professor after class. "Fine," says the native of Scotland, a long-time resident of Ireland and England. "You can call tomorrow afternoon." The student is perplexed: having asked to *see* this professor, she is told to *telephone*. When the confusion is cleared up (in the professor's variety of English "to call" means "to stop by") they laugh about it. Another professor, a native of India and a bilingual, life-long speaker of English, is met with a colder reception when similar difficulties arise.

"Because you love French accents," proclaims a large advertisement for pottery by an upscale New York department store. "Better get rid of your accent," sings an angry Puerto Rican youth in response to more hopeful dreams of a better life outside the imaginary barrio of *West Side Story*.

There are many people who must cope, day by day, with the fact of stigmatized foreign accent. Some of them have other currencies – political and economic power, social preeminence, artistic excellence, other public achievements – with which to offset the disadvantages an accent brings with it and to disarm the prejudiced listener. In face-to-face conversation, most listeners, no matter how overtly negative and hostile, would be hard-pressed to turn away and ignore Cesar Chavez or Derek Wolcott, Butros Butros Ghali or Liu Xiaobo, Benazir Bhutto, or Corazon Aquino.[7]

But most do not have these resources. People have always come to the United States because in the mind of the world it is a place of real opportunity. The hidden costs of democracy, of assimilation, are not spelled out in the papers they must file to live here, but in the stories of people like Henry Park. The narrator of *Native Speaker* draws a vivid picture of himself and all immigrants: "They speak ... not simply in new accents or notes but in the ancient untold music of a newcomer's heart, sonorous with longing and hope" (Lee 1995).

What the newcomer must learn for him or herself is the grim reality of limitations imposed by a standard language ideology.

Conclusions
Civil (dis)obedience and the shadow of language

The language which we are speaking is his before it is mine. How different are the words *home, Christ, ale, master*, on his lips and on mine! I cannot speak or write these words without unrest of spirit. His language, so familiar and so foreign, will always be for me an acquired speech. I have not made or accepted his words. My voice holds them at bay. My soul frets in the shadow of his language.

James Joyce, A Portrait of the Artist as a Young Man (1916)

No one can make you feel inferior without your consent.

Eleanor Roosevelt, This is My Story (1939)

The process of language subordination targets not all variation, not all language varieties, but only those which are emblematic of differences in race, ethnicity, homeland, or other social allegiances which have been found to be less than good enough. Dedicated practitioners of language subordination do not complain about most of the variation which is active in US English. There has never been an outcry about Chicagoans' inability to distinguish between *merry, Mary*, and *marry*. Nor are there essays in local papers on the stupidity and unworthiness of people who say *cawfee* rather than *cahfee* or *cuu-offee*. People do not lose jobs because they wait *on line* rather than *in line*. There may be an occasional ruffled feather about the use of *hopefully* or *healthy*, about split infinitives and dangling participles, or *who* versus *whom*, but such debates – while often loud and sometimes acrimonious – eventually fade, because these are points of language variation leading to change which are largely completed, and solidly entrenched in the language of the middle class.

But people do lose jobs and schoolchildren are belittled because their native language makes it difficult for them to differentiate between *l* and *r* sounds; because their sentence intonations are Latino; because they say *y'all* rather than *all of you*, *aks* rather than *ask*.

The demand that the disempowered assimilate linguistically and culturally to please the empowered is – purely in linguistic terms – an impossibility. In the first part of this book I have presented a great deal of empirical evidence to support this point. A person's accent (the bundle of distinctive intonation and phonological features) is fixed or hard-wired in the mind, and once past a certain age it can only be very laboriously changed, to a very limited degree, regardless of commitment, intelligence, and resources. Thus the constant public debate on good English, on the one right English, is as fruitless an exercise as the hypothetical congressional debate on the ideal height and weight for all adults. We cannot purge language of variation linked to social difference, but more important than that undeniable fact: *it should not matter*. If as a nation we are agreed that it is not acceptable or good to discriminate on the grounds of skin color or ethnicity, gender or age, then by logical extension it is equally unacceptable to discriminate against language traits which are intimately linked to an individual's identity and expression of self.

But people *are* judged on the basis of language form rather than language content, every day. Without hesitation or contemplation, workers are turned away, children are corrected, people are made to feel small and unimportant in public settings. The process of language subordination is so deeply rooted, so well established, that we do not see it for what it is. We make no excuses for preferences which exclude on the basis of immutable language traits.

Having established that this process works, and having looked hard at how it works for both the powered and the disempowered, a logical question has not yet been raised: What now?

When I discuss this question with my students – a racially and ethnically mixed group of bright young people of both sexes, well educated, thoughtful – this is where the deadlock will occur. Some, enraged by the practices they have studied and observed (and perhaps experienced), will demand that we stop all pretenses in the school to teach "standard" English. They contemplate passive resistance and large-scale civil disobedience, and a United States in which the equation between national unity and linguistic homogeneity has been examined and discarded as untenable and unfair. Others point out that because children are still in the language acquisition stage, they should theoretically be able to acquire mainstream language as a second variety of English – and should do so. Idealism does not put food on the table, this argument goes.

It is a strong argument. Economic rationalizations are the most often raised, most loudly voiced, and the most classic of all common-sense arguments used to coerce the few into the ways of the many: Assimilation is the *cost of success*.

The question is, can this unbroken circle of intimidation truly not be broken, or do we like things the way they are? Language serves as a convenient excuse to turn away. Are we unwilling to consider a nation in which the cost of success is *achievement* measured by other, fairer, means?

It has been demonstrated time and again, and not just in this volume, that ideology is most effective when its workings are least visible, and standard language ideology in the US functions like a silent but efficient machine. Its practitioners are terribly skillful at coercing consent and participation from those people and groups who suffer the most under the weight of language ideology. Thus the most factual stand – every language is in fact completely viable and functional, therefore we do not need and should not attempt standardization – is doomed, at the present time. A realistic goal must be a much smaller one: to make people aware of the process of language subordination. To draw their attention to the misinformation, to expose false reasoning and empty promises to hard questions.

If in the face of clarity and truth about standardization, the way it works, and its social connections and meanings, peripheralized language speakers and communities choose to try to assimilate to the linguistic (and cultural) norms of another group, then that is a choice freely made that must be respected. But at this time, there is little or no truth in advertising in the process of language standardization. Right now, people attempt to conform and to assimilate because they are inundated with promises and threats if they do not. The threats are real: the evidence is at hand in the experiences of the people whose stories are told here. The promises, however, are not so real. Because discrimination on the basis of language has not to do with the language itself, but with the social circumstances and identities attached to that language, discrimination will not go away when the next generation has assimilated. Mainstream US English is a flimsy cover to hide behind in the face of serious intent to exclude on the basis of race or ethnicity.

Eleanor Roosevelt's statement on the connection between inferiority and cooperation is one that I have thought about for a long time, in the writing of this book. It captures two basic elements of the language subordination process: First, one person or group must want to make another person or group believe that their language – and hence their social allegiances and priorities – are inferior. Second, that targeted person or group must become complicit in the process.

But it also raises the important issue of language system and language content, or linguistic and social grammaticality addressed in the first chapter. I raise this topic here because I anticipate that a common response to the arguments set forth in this book will be that I am – as I have been called in the past – a language anarchist. One of those lax, liberal types, for whom anything goes. Who has no respect for language or the traditions of the past, and no interest in teaching those traditions to children. No interest in aesthetics, and an unwillingness to talk of *quality* in spoken language, for fear that somebody will be marginalized.

In fact, I will state very clearly that in my opinion, it is not a sin against humankind to have standards and preferences about the spoken language. As a product of the institutions that I have written about in this book,

I have been exposed to stereotypes for my whole life. I hope that I have learned to look beyond them to see and to hear the person behind the cultural expectations, but even then, I have preferences. I can, and I do, choose among storytellers. I can decide that Jane tells a joke better than Joan. That political candidate Park is better than candidate Goldstein in off-the-cuff debate. One song lyric may delight me while another falls flat.

As a speaker of a variety of US English which is not stigmatized, on occasion I feel inferior about my own language. I can recall times when I failed to make a point because I could not articulate my thoughts clearly. I have used too many words when a few would have sufficed. Most of all, I have felt inferior on those occasions when I have been moved by spoken language which is clear, precise, vivid, and following from this, effective for me personally. But because I belong to the social (and hence, to the language) mainstream which isolates me from the process of subordination, any feelings of inferiority *are of my own making*. Other value systems are not forced on me; I am allowed the consolation of my mother tongue. I am free of the shadow of language, and subject only to the standards that I accept for myself.

Language subordination is not about relative standards and preferences in the way language is used. Language subordination does not say that Joan can't tell a joke, but rather that *Joan is not worth listening to*, because her English makes it clear that she was born on the Bayou, or in Harlem, Puerto Rico, Hong Kong, or on the Pine Ridge Reservation. Whether Joan is the best or the worst teller of jokes ever born, some people will never know because they will not listen to what she has to say: how she says it is enough to know that it is unworthy of their consideration.

Language subordination is about taking away a basic human right: to speak freely in the mother tongue without intimidation, without standing in the shadow of other languages and peoples. To resist the process, passively or actively, is to ask for recognition, and acknowledgement. It is a demand for the simple right to be heard.

Notes

1 THE LINGUISTIC FACTS OF LIFE

1 While the more general language issues discussed here will be applicable to all English spoken on the Continent, the exploration of specific authority and prescription issues focuses on the US and does not draw on material from other English-speaking countries.

2 Bolinger defines *language shaman* as follows:

> In language there are no licensed practitioners, but the woods are full of midwives, herbalists, colonic irrigationists, bonesetters, and general-purpose witch doctors, some abysmally ignorant, others with a rich fund of practical knowledge – whom we shall lump together and call SHAMANS. . . . sometimes their advice is sound. Sometimes it is worthless, but still it is sought because no one knows where else to turn.
>
> (1980:1)

3 For example, Cameron considers at some length why linguists have been resistant to acknowledge the relevance of prescriptivist approaches to language. Milroy and Milroy consider this stance as well, and come to the same conclusion that Cameron does:

> the reservation about prescription that is commonly expressed has, in practice, led to a general tendency to study language *as if* prescriptive phenomena play no part in language . . . when we view language as fundamentally a social phenomenon, we cannot then ignore prescription and its consequences. The study of linguistic authoritarianism is an important part of linguistics, and as linguists we feel an obligation to attempt to close the gap between specialist and non-specialist views on the nature and use of language.
>
> (Milroy and Milroy 1991: 5, 11)

Dennis Preston, who has produced a large body of literature on the way attitudes toward language are relevant to variation and change, is even more to the point on this issue of participant-oriented rather than analyst-oriented approaches to the study of language:

> What linguists believe about standards matters very little; what non-linguists believe constitutes precisely that cognitive reality which needs to be described in a responsible sociolinguistics – one which takes speech-community attitudes and perception (as well as performance) into account.
>
> (1993: 26)

4 Any language which is no longer acquired as a first language, and is no longer used in day-to-day communication by a community of persons, is considered

to be dead, whether or not it survives in a literary form. Many languages have died and left no record behind. In addition, there is one known and documented case of a language which was once dead but which has been rejuvenated. Hebrew, which for a long period was preserved as a written and ritualistic language of the Jewish people, and was dead by the technical definition, is now spoken as a first language by a good proportion of the population of Israel.

5 For a modern-day example of this process at its extreme, see Skutnabb-Kangas and Phillipson (1994), particularly on the systematic and violent repression of Kurdish language and culture in Turkey.

6 Examples of US English provided here and in other parts of this study come from a variety of sources. If they are borrowed from other studies, those studies will be cited. Often the examples come from my own collection of spoken English gathered informally, in which fragments of conversations overheard in public places are later written down.

7 I use the standard linguistic convention of preceeding a *linguistically* ungrammatical sentence with *.

8 Milroy and Milroy draw a contrast between what they call Type 1 and Type 2 complaints about language. If the opposition expressed is to language change itself, they term this Type 1; Type 2 complaints are concerned with "careful and effective written usage" (1991: 41). I do not adopt their Type 1 and Type 2 distinction because I find it important to distinguish between two sets of issues:

1 the confusion between written and spoken language
2 the judgments of linguistic and socially constructed grammaticality.

9 "Copula" is a term for the verb "to be" when it joins subject to predicate, as in *Maria is a physicist* (Maria = physicist) or *The movie was terrible* (movie = terrible).

AAVE forbids copula deletion where other US Englishes would forbid contraction.

*She not home, but Danny
*She's not home, but Danny's
(She's not home, but Danny is)

For a detailed consideration of the role of the copula in AAVE grammar and the history of the study of this feature, see Rickford *et al.* (1991).

10 Among speakers of AAVE, the use of habitual *be* shows variation over space and by age of the speaker.

11 The 1992 edition of the *American Heritage Dictionary of the English Language* points out that the word *rhetoric* has undergone a shift in usage:

The word rhetoric was once primarily the name of an important branch of philosophy and an art deserving of serious study. In recent years the word has come to be used chiefly in a pejorative sense to refer to inflated language and pomposity. Deprecation of the term may result from a modern linguistic puritanism, which holds that language used in legitimate persuasion should be plain and free of artifice – itself a tendentious rhetorical doctrine, though not often recognized as such. But many writers still prefer to bear in mind the traditional meanings of the word. Thus, according to the newer use of the term, the phrase empty rhetoric, as in *The politicians talk about solutions, but they usually offer only empty rhetoric*, might be construed as redundant. But in fact only 35 percent of the Usage Panel judged this example to be redundant. Presumably, it can be maintained that rhetoric can be other than empty.

This is a curious note to find in a dictionary: *linguistic puritanism* is not defined, and there is even a bit of a tone which might be taken to mean that the editors are torn: they are surprised (and perhaps not quite satisfied) with the decision of their usage panel, but they also point out the fact that rhetorical rules are not objective: they are *doctrines*.

12 Natural Morphology (a functionalist approach in the study of linguistics which sees the primary purpose of language as communication) seeks in part to understand rules governing language structure as arising from neurobiological and sociocommunicative constraints. So that within a theory of Natural Morphology, a universal preference for shorter word strings would derive from limits on the mind's ability to store and retrieve information, and would enhance the function of the language. An extreme functionalist approach would thus argue that some elements of the form of the message (its length, for example) are relevant to the effectiveness of the message, and thus to the evaluation of message content.

13 All major and most minor papers carried reports of Quayle's visit to a school, during which he encouraged a student competing in a spelling competition to misspell *potato*. ("Mr. Quayle's 'e' for effort" *New York Times*, June 17, 1992).

14 This is, of course, a fairly modern development. Early writing systems of western European languages were not consistent at all: all alphabetic written language begins as simple transcripts of spoken speech.

15 I am grateful to Robert Beddor, who allowed me to read his school journals and extract the examples used here.

16 Functionalist and formalist approaches to the study of language provide one of the major bones of contention among linguists. In its most extreme form, functionalists start with the belief that all naturally occurring human language exists and is structured exclusively as a vehicle of communication. A less radical approach would claim more simply that communication is the function that motivates language, but some formalists would take issue with this as well:

> Communication is *a* function of language, not *the* function. [He mentions thought, play, dreaming, deception, etc. as others.] . . . even if [language] did arise primarily for that function, it would not therefore follow that its structural development would have progressed in lockstep with its functional development.
>
> (Newmeyer 1983: 100–101).

I am thankful to Joe Salmons for discussions on these issues.

17 In this discussion I have taken a short cut which some will find questionable, in that I have not considered in any depth what is meant by literacy, a term which has been widely used and which stands at the center of much scholarly and educational debate. Here I use *literate* both in its narrowest way, as a reference to the skill needed to read and write, and in some of its broader connotations, as a measurement of cultural knowledge. The history of thought about literacy is one which I don't have time to explore here, but it is obviously an interesting and important one. In particular, it would be useful to understand the point in our history in which our perceptions of the relationship of the written and spoken language began to change, as it seems that the subordination of spoken to written language may be a fairly new cultural phenomenon. I am very thankful to Deborah Keller-Cohen for valuable discussions of this topic.

18 In a convincing essay on the advantages of multiculturalism, Charles Taylor discusses examples of the kind of reasoning which ranks literate cultures as inherently more valuable than oral ones (1994: 42).

19 Earlier it was established that all living languages change; it can also be stated unequivocally that all change is preceded by variation. However, it *cannot* be claimed that all variation is followed by change.

20 I follow standard linguistic conventions in using /r/ brackets to indicate a phoneme (a class of phonetically similar sounds occurring in complementary distribution in a given language); [r] brackets for a phone, or actual occurrence of a specific sound; and (r) to talk about a sociolinguistic variable (a sound with specific social markings) under investigation.

21 Although no sociolinguistic study of this variable has come to my attention, the social significance of this variable in the New York City area is quite salient.

2 THE MYTH OF NON-ACCENT

1 The *Oxford English Dictionary* divides the use of *myth* into three domains: (1) purely fictitious narratives which serve to illustrate and explain natural or social phenomena (The Legend of Hercules; Noah and the Ark); (2) fictional or imaginary persons, objects or places (Big Foot, Santa Claus, Shangri-La); and (3) untruths, or rumors.

2 The standardization process targets as an end product an idealized, homogenous *spoken* standard (which will never be fully realized) and a literary, or *written* standard, which is much more prone to norms, rules, and the restriction of variation. The idealized spoken standard is distinct from *supra-regional vernaculars*, which are spoken languages that promote convergence, but with norms which are less subject to covert and overt legislation (Milroy 1992: 1–2).

3 There is a large body of work on the structure, function, and history of AAVE. There is a smaller body of work on what is called here Jewish English. There is almost no work on Native American English which deals directly with *supra-regional* phonological features. Work on Native American English has focused primarily on syntactical and morphological features, and the controversial issue of the origin of this variety of English (Craig 1991 provides an excellent overview of the literature). There is also a good body of work on Indian English as it is specific to each tribe (see Leap 1992 and Chapter 6 of this book). Nevertheless, linguists who work with Native Americans, Native Americans themselves, and non-Native Americans who live in contact with them provide a wealth of anecdotal information which points to the existence of such a pan-regional accent (one which transcends tribal boundaries), which is overtly stigmatized. The 1991 edition of *The New Mexico Indian Tribal Court Handbook* directly addresses this issue in its prologue:

> An American in a French court would have as many difficulties as if he or she were in an Indian Court, but we tend to forgive the French because we know of their history and we give them credit that they have accomplished the merit badge of high culture. Yet, the French will not struggle to conduct their Court in English, although Indian Courts will. And when we hear the broken English and the accent of an Indian Judge or advocate, we assume that he or she is unintelligent, although we would never do that to Henry Kissinger.

I would like to thank Bill Piatt for bringing the *Handbook* to my attention.

4 Dialect is a term which linguists use primarily to talk about language differences over geographic space. It is, however, a fairly prickly term. Laypersons often associate the word dialect as something less developed, capable, or worthy, and hence always subordinate to a language. This is an unfortunate

and miscast use of the term. Thus I avoid *dialect* more generally and use, as many linguists do, the term *variety*.

5 A pidgin is a contact language which arises when three or more cultures establish regular contact, usually for commercial reasons, for example in a shipping port. A pidgin has no native speakers, and is reduced, with simplified morphological and syntactical features taken from the contributing languages. Pidgins can exist over long periods of time. A creole is something very different. When pidgin speakers settle down in closer proximity to each other and when children are born into a setting where pidgin is spoken, they take the raw data of the pidgin and in the process of language acquisition they expand it into a fully functioning language. Hawai'ian Creole English was once a pidgin, but has been a creole for many generations.

6 Here I have touched an issue which cannot be called, by any stretch of the imagination, a point on which linguists agree. There is great controversy around what has been called the "critical period." Some linguists dismiss it entirely (Aitchinson 1991), while others are still committed to it, though in forms different from the original theory put forth by Lennenberg (1967). In his chapter "Baby Born Talking – Describes Heaven" Pinker (1995) nicely summarizes the current state of our understanding:

> In sum, acquisition of a normal language is guaranteed for children up to the age of six, is steadily compromised from then until shortly after puberty, and is rare thereafter. Maturational changes in the brain, such as the decline in metabolic rate and number of neurons during the early school-age years, and the bottoming out of the number of synapses and metabolic rate around puberty, are plausible causes. We do know that the language-learning circuitry of the brain is more plastic in childhood; children learn or recover language when the left hemisphere of the brain is damaged or even surgically removed (though not quite at normal levels), but comparable damage in an adult usually leads to permanent aphasia.
>
> (293)

7 This is not a perfect analogy; it has no room for the acquisition of syntax and morphology, for the use or production of language. A house cannot produce anything. But it remains a useful analogy, in as much as this limitation is recognized.

8 I avoid an in-depth discussion of communicative competence here, because it raises the issue of cultural and stylistic appropropriacy, which will be addressed later.

9 There is work being done in phonetics which suggests that the more alike two languages are, the more difficult it is for language learners to successfully target the new sounds (Flege 1994, Flege and Bohn 1989, 1990). Further support for this is seen in preliminary studies of the way adult African Americans who are native speakers of Standard US English varieties make mistakes when trying to acquire AAVE (Baugh 1992).

3 THE STANDARD LANGUAGE MYTH

1 These definitions were answers to queries posted to various CompuServe discussion forums in summer 1995, requesting personal definitions of "Standard English." Answers came from adults in all parts of the country, who provided them in the knowledge that they would be used here in whole or part.

2 The on-line MLA bibliography lists fifty-six articles written between 1966 and 1994 which use the standard/*sub*standard distinction. This usage is seldom seen

in writings about British or US English and is restricted almost entirely to studies of variation in German. The standard/non-standard contrast seems to be the one most often used in the current literature for English. James Milroy points out to me that a *substandard* object must necessarily be defective, while *non-standard* could be used simply as the opposite of standard.

3 Smitherman has used the term the Language of Wider Communication (LWC) or "a language that facilitates communication beyond one's own speech community, i.e. in this country, European American 'standard English'" (1995: 228). Smitherman's definition is useful in her analysis of rhetorical styles and conflicts, but for the purposes of this study it is too general in its division between specific language communities and a monolithic European American Standard US English.

4 LANGUAGE IDEOLOGY AND THE LANGUAGE SUBORDINATION MODEL

1 Eagleton (1991) provides a range of definitions for ideology, from the narrow to the more broadly defined, along with arguments for and against them. The definition used here falls at level four of five possible levels of inclusiveness in an approach to ideology. The danger of such a broad approach is, as Eagleton points out, that it puts perhaps unacceptable limitations on ideology as something solely limited to the dominant bloc.

2 The term *standard language ideology* was coined by James and Lesley Milroy. Their work in this area was the first impetus for much of my own thinking on this issue, which has been further influenced in particular by the work of Fairclough, Silverstein, Eagleton, Bourdieu, and Foucault. The definition I provide here has evolved from those provided in earlier publications.

3 Labov has called this *linguistic insecurity* (1966: 332 ff.), and points to the process of hypercorrection toward a perceived standard as one of its correlates. We will return to this topic in a later chapter.

4 The more common use of *hegemony* is in the sense of dominance or domination, but here I use the Gramscian definition. Gramsci provides an interesting example of an attempt to bend linguistic facts to a greater social end. In his writings he argues strongly for teaching the lower and working classes a standardized Italian, and equates this process with passing on literacy, a necessary tool to fight oppression:

> it is rational to collaborate practically and willingly to welcome everything that may serve to create a common national language, the non-existence of which causes friction particularly in the popular masses among whom local particularisms and the phenomena of a narrow and provincial mentality are more tenacious than is believed. In other words, it is a question of stepping up the struggle against illiteracy.
>
> (1985: 182)

Gramsci's confusion of symptom with cause (he sees friction following from the fact of language heterogeneity) and his rejection of rural values would seem to be at odds with his goals more generally. He was apparently able to deal with language as if it were a commodity to be willfully manipulated and cleansed of regional and social variation on command. This is particularly strange as he very early recognized the relationship between the rise of public discourse around language and accelerated shifting in the established power structures and hegemony (ibid.).

5 See Gitlin's model for analysis of the media's representation of the Vietnam War (1980, and elsewhere).
6 Of course, the internal criticism has its genesis outside the community; it must be imported.
7 These examples are taken from (1) *Anthony Dercach v. Indiana Department of Highways* (in paraphrase); (2) student questionnaires on language attitudes collected from my own classes; (3) my interviews with employers in the Chicago area; (4) the *Oprah Winfrey Show* of November 19, 1987.

5 TEACHING CHILDREN HOW TO DISCRIMINATE

1 "Ethnic stereotypes were, of course, not uncommon in films of the early Thirties, and were usually essayed in a free-wheeling spirit of fun, with no malice intended. By the time the film was reissued in 1948 . . . social attitudes had changed considerably" (1988: 43). Kaufman's construction of the original caricature (Jews as wily and untrustworthy business people) as harmless is one which it is hard to take on good faith, given the general climate of anti-Semitism prevalent in Europe and the US in the 1930s.
2 In 1930, the Motion Picture Producers and Distributors of America (MPPDA) created a self-regulatory code of ethics. The office charged with this duty was put under the direction of Will H. Hays, and went into effect on July 1, 1934. The Hays Office outlined general standards of good taste and specifically forbade certain elements in film. The code specified that "no picture shall be produced which will lower the standards of those who see it. Hence the sympathy of the audience should never be thrown to the side of crime, wrong-doing, evil or sin." The specific regulations included "Revenge in modern times shall not be justified"; "Methods of crime shall not be explicitly presented"; "The sanctity of the institution of marriage and the home shall be upheld"; "Miscegenation (interracial sexual relationships) is forbidden." The Code specifically addressed the inadvisability of caricaturing national-origin groups or portraying them in offensive ways.
   In 1968 a rating system was put into effect, and the Code was no longer used.
3 Other interviews with AAADC representatives were further reported in the same paper:

> Although they are Arabs, Aladdin and Princess Jasmine, the heroes, talk like Americans. Merchants, soldiers and other ordinary Arabs have thick foreign accents. "This teaches a horrible lesson," says [the representative]. "Maybe they can't redub it now, but we asked them to please be sure there is no accent discrimination in the foreign-language versions."
>
> (Precker 1993b)

4 Sometimes a cast is a combination of those who must contrive the accent and those who are native speakers of the language in question, and bring that L2 accent to their performance, as was the case with *Gigi*.
5 It might be argued that many aspects of animated films are actually aimed at the adults who watch films with children, and that the children themselves are less likely to comprehend the stereotypes. The small body of studies in this area indicates that while children's attitudes toward particular language varieties are not fully developed until adolescence, they do begin forming as early as age 5 (Rosenthal 1974, Day 1980). Giles *et al.* (1983) found that significant changes occurred between the ages of 7 and 10 in children's attitudes toward different language varieties.

6 The first round of analysis was conducted as a graduate-level seminar project in social dialectology. The students who contributed to the analysis at that stage were Carlson Arnett, Jennifer Dailey-O'Cain, Rita Simpson, and Matthew Varley. The results of that project were presented as a poster at the 1994 "New Ways of Analyzing Variation" conference at Stanford University. The data presented here represents a second viewing of all films originally studied as well as the addition of three films not included in the original study: *The Lion King*, *The Aristocats*, and *Snow White*.

7 In the pilot study, each participant watched at least four films, although most had seen more than these initial four. To aid in the consistency of language characterization as well as coding for other variables, three films were viewed and coded as a group. Subsequently, I reviewed all films and checked the original coding.

8 Standard tests of correlation of the relationship of a character's nationality to his or her motivation (positive, negative, mixed) were shown to be highly significant at levels better than .001.

9 Characters of an age to pursue a partner who do *not* do so in the story line are usually portrayed as awkward, fat, or ugly (examples include the step-sisters in *Cinderella*, the witch-like Cruella de Ville in *101 Dalmations*, LaFou in *Beauty and the Beast*).

10 Other cases were also ambiguous. Whether Colonel Hardy and his wife Winifred, the military elephants in *The Jungle Book*, are logically speakers of an Indian language or of English could be debated. The same problem applies to this determination for the Indian Chief in *Peter Pan*.

6 THE EDUCATIONAL SYSTEM

1 There are, of course, widely divergent opinions on the more specific goals of public education. Conservative thought sees the school as a place where children learn the skills they need to become productive citizens who will contribute to the national economy (Sykes 1995), whereas more liberal approaches to education refuse to cast it as an issue of economics, but one of knowledge for the sake of knowledge, and humanist goals in the more classical sense (Berliner and Biddle 1995).

2 Linguists bear some of the responsibility for the prevalence of appropriacy arguments, in that they rarely have spoken up in protest at the misappropriation of the concept of communicative competence. That term, which was first coined by Hymes in an effort to capture the reality of the stylistic multiplexity of any speaker's repertoire, was neatly expanded to include the concept of social acceptability. If communicative competence is taken as a speaker's ability to use language appropriately in a social context, and we do not challenge the construction of "appropriacy," then we have opened a back door to exclusion on the basis of another kind of "correctness" logic. Cameron (1995: 234–235) explores this unfortunate turn in linguistic argument at length.

3 I am thankful to Jim Milroy for a discussion of this material.

4 I am grateful to Mary Jean Habermann, Director of the Bilingual Multicultural Education Unit of the New Mexico Department of Education, for her helpful discussion on these policies and for the materials she provided.

5 Sato (1989, 1991) looks at this issue in depth.

6 Headlines of a series of articles which appeared in the *Honolulu Advertiser* in September, 1987, by D. Reyes, as cited in Sato (1991).

7 This is the only aboriginal language to be thus recognized in the US. In 1990 the federal government recognized the right of Hawai'i to preserve, use, and

support its indigenous language. The movement to support and nurture the language is growing and seems to be successful. Grimes (1992) reports that there are 2,000 mother-tongue speakers out of 200,000 to 220,000 ethnic Hawai'ians (20 percent of the population), including 8,000 pure Hawai'ians and 81,000 at least half Hawai'ian.

8   There is significant tension in Hawai'i around language issues, and around HCE in particular. Chapter 8 provides an overview of two court cases which took place there involving language-focused discrimination in employment.

9   Some of the notes and correspondence on this issue and the debate it caused within the Department of Education were made available to me for the purposes of this study. While the proposed standards for testing pronunciation and accent were not adopted, the issue was divisive and difficult enough that I was allowed these materials with the understanding that they would be cited anonymously.

10   Quotes in this chapter originate from a series of telephone interviews conducted with school administrators in four states: two in the northeast, one in the midwest, one in the southwest. I also interviewed a key employee in a large company which develops and administers the testing and evaluation procedure for an entire state. Most parties agreed to be interviewed and quoted only if they remained anonymous. I have notes from these interviews as well as partial transcripts on file. Questions were posed about the way teachers were evaluated in matters of language, and the hiring process more generally.

11   The sources and citations in this recounting of the Westfield school case are taken from a discussion on the LINGUIST list, an on-line forum for linguists at <linguist@tamsun.tamu.edu>. The discussion is summarized under 3.563: Accents in Classroom, dated July 14, 1992. Contributors to the discussion included Victor Raskin (who provided the summary), Barbara Partee, Michael Covington, Catherine Doughty, and Susan Ervin-Tripp.

7   THE INFORMATION INDUSTRY

1   There are two types of data to be considered: general asides made about matters of language such as derisive or condescending commentary on the accents of political candidates, which is hard to document systematically, and news reports which are language focused.The broadcast news data cited here originates from the Television News Archives at Vanderbilt University. The archive has tape of ABC, NBC, and CBS *National News* broadcasts for every day since the mid-1960s; all of these are indexed. It also has MacNeil-Lehrer and CNN *Headline News* reports since those services began, but those broadcasts are not indexed. All of the reports I was able to find were from the big three networks, which have been supplemented with other reports from my own daily viewing.

2   Other studies have addressed this process over time, for example, Bailey (1991), Crowley (1989), Finegan (1980), among others.

3   Letter from Inlingua, "Your full service language center," dated June 7, 1994.

4   Grimes (1992) reports that Gullah, known otherwise as *Sea Islands Creole English* (or Geechee) is an English-based creole found in the coastal region from Jacksonville, North Carolina to Jacksonville, Florida and most particularly on the Sea Islands off the Georgia coast. There are some seven to ten thousand monolingual speakers of this language and another quarter million who speak some form of it. Grimes also notes that Gullah exists in limited contact with English and that it is closest to Bahamas Creole and Afro-Seminole, with which it has 90 percent lexical similarity (it shows influence from the African

languages of Fula, Mende, the upper Guinea coast, the Gambia River area). The language community is strong; there is government-supported bilingual education.

5 See especially Santa Ana (1996) on the use of metaphor in newspaper reporting.

6 The discussion here is based on the official ABC News Tape Library transcript, but with corrections to errors in that transcript. ABC denied permission to reproduce their official transcript for this analysis.

7 This tactic is often seen in the media's construction of those who oppose war. Gitlin (1980) demonstrates how during the Vietnam era, protest was disparaged in part by undercounting those who were part of the anti-war movement, and focusing on only certain peripheral types.

8 LANGUAGE IDEOLOGY IN THE WORKPLACE AND THE JUDICIAL SYSTEM

1 An earlier version of this chapter appears as "Accent, standard language ideology and discriminatory pretext in the courts" (Lippi-Green 1994).

2 I conducted two phone interviews with Ms. Mandhare in 1994.

3 Court-case citations are abbreviated as follows: *Sulochana Mandhare v. W. S. Lafargue Elementary School, the Lafourche Parish School Board, Parish of Lafourche* will appear in the text as *Mandhare*. This material originates from opinions, briefs, *Findings of Fact*, and other legal documents associated with each case. In the case of *Mandhare*, interviews with the Plaintiff are also cited. The references include a complete table of all court cases cited.

4 Later in this chapter I will explore in greater detail the reasoning of the courts, and their interpretation of matters regarding language use and prescription in *Mandhare*.

5 Title VII is specific to employment issues, and the legislation and court cases here cannot be applied to any other arena, for example education.

6 Companies employing fewer than fifteen workers are not bound by these statutes.

7 Discrimination is a matter of law:

> the effect of a statute or established practice which confers particular privileges on a class arbitrarily selected from a large number of persons, all of whom stand in the same relation to the privileges granted and between whom and those not favored no reasonable distinction can be found.
>
> (*Black's Law Dictionary* 1991: 323)

8 Under §703(e) of Title VII, an employer may defend his or her actions on the basis of national origin (1) "by demonstrating the 'business necessity' of the disputed employment practice – i.e., by showing the practice 'to be necessary to safe and efficient job performance" (Cutler 1985: 1168, fn. 20; citations omitted); or (2) by establishing a *bona fide* occupational qualification (BFOQ) (ibid.). The BFOQ is the more difficult case for the employer. The path taken depends on which of two different theories of liability is used: *disparate treatment*, in which proof of discriminatory intent is crucial, requires a BFOQ defense; for *disparate impact*, in which such proof is not required, the employer must establish only business necessity:

> The Plaintiff makes out a prima facie case by showing that the employer's selection device has a substantially adverse impact on his protected group ... it remains open to the plaintiff to show that "other ... selection devices, without a similarly undesirable ... effect, would also serve the employer's legitimate interest[s]."
>
> (1169; citations omitted)

9 Of course, the problems of associating specific regional or social dialects with specific foreign origins would be tremendous. Joe Salmons (personal communication) has brought to my attention work by Dillard (1992) which outlines the considerable difficulties of even identifying any salient features specific to Appalachian English (but see also Wolfram and Christian (1976) and Christian (1988), which provide evidence that these difficulties can be overcome).

10 The EEOC reviews complaints, and if it finds that a violation has taken place, it may take on the case and file suit for the employee against the employer. Raj Gupta, formerly of the EEOC estimates that the EEOC prosecutes 70 percent of such cases; in the other 30 percent, it may or may not grant a Notice of Right to Sue. Lack of such notice does not prohibit the employee from proceeding; the right to pursue such matters in the courts is sacrosanct. Thus the Notice of Right to Sue is primarily an indication to the employee of the strength of the case. For employees of federal government agencies, the EEOC conducts the hearing, which is empowered by Title VII to hear discrimination cases; if it finds the plaintiff, it can order remedies. The federal agencies can appeal only to the EEOC.

11 Tracking down and documenting these cases was a matter of many hours in the University of Michigan law library. Certainly, cases have been excluded by oversight: there are no summary statistics kept by the EEOC and no central logging system for these cases; many cases are not summarized for publication. Thus no guarantee can be made of thoroughness of representation. The search for cases included in this chapter was concluded in 1994.

12 This study was conducted in response to a series of inquiries from Congress on the effect of the 1986 immigration laws. Not all the GAO's findings were clear or interpretable, especially in the matter of specifically accent-based discrimination. The report in question outlines a number of reasons for this having to do with sampling and design questions.

13 Matsuda (1991) provides a thorough overview of the Fragante and Kahakua cases.

14 Jackie Macaulay, an attorney in private practice who deals with civil rights cases, has pointed out to me that the courts seems to be functioning on the basis of some "phantom legislature" which has mandated that a certain form of English is "Standard" and "unaccented" (personal communication).

15 It seems that three distinct kinds of expert witnesses testify in these trials: linguists (for example, Charlene Sato of the University of Hawai'i testified in *Kahakua*); speech pathologists; and "speech consultants." As discussed in a previous chapter, this last class is often composed of those who teach "accent reduction" classes, or otherwise have a vested interest in the official commendation of a "standard English." Some judges, especially the judge who heard *Kahakua*, are very receptive to arguments of this kind.

16 Ms. Mandhare tells a very different story. In interview, she alleged that her first year at the K-2 school was also the principal's first year, and that he openly admitted that he had promised her job as librarian to someone else. She reports that he asked her to request a transfer, which she did not wish to do. After this episode, he told her in a one-to-one meeting that she had a "very heavy accent."

17

> In many circumstances, as in literary forms, lectures, and radio broadcasts, writers and speakers are distant from their addressees in place, time, or both. They might be assumed to adhere to a weakened version of mutual responsibility . . . speakers still monitor what they say. . . . It is just that they do all this without feedback from listeners.
>
> (Clark and Wilkes-Gibbs 1986: 35–36)

The radio broadcasters, of course, are *reading* from prepared texts and so the distribution of communicative burden does not apply in the way it does in discourse.

18 Shuy (1993) and Miron (1990) provide an overview of this type of "forensic linguistics" in the courtroom; see also Levi (1994) for a comprehensive guide to publications on language and the law.

INTRODUCTION TO PART III

1 Labov summarizes:

> In the 17th and 18th centuries, many rising members of the English middle class found themselves in social situations where their native speech patterns were not appropriate. It was this aspect of social mobility which created a need for a doctrine of correctness, and led to the elevation of the school-master and the dictionary as authorities for speech both in England and America (Read.1939).
>
> (1966: 332–333)

I would argue that the chronology of events is not correct here: there must be a doctrine of correctness in the minds of speakers *before* there can be appropriacy-based criticisms for them to assimilate and react to. But it does seem that the overt codificaton of such norms and the elevation of school and educators in the guardianship role for language did accelerate during this period. Labov has touched here on the history of development of language ideology, which he then puts aside while he explores the phenomenon of hyper-correction.

2 Baugh (1992) examines the opposite phenomenon: what happens when MUSE speakers attempt to assimilate to norms of stigmatized varieties, particularly when African Americans who are not native speakers of AAVE attempt to acquire it. He finds that mistakes are made in both directions (hyper- and hypocorrection).

9 THE REAL TROUBLE WITH BLACK ENGLISH

1 See the section "Words about words" in Chapter 3 for a discussion of terms for the languages of the African American community.

2 Smitherman (1977) is written in part in AAVE and thus represents one of the few academic studies of AAVE in which that language is used in alternation with mainstream written language norms. Otherwise, written AAVE is limited primarily to fiction, as in the work of Langston Hughes, Zora Neale Hurston, and Toni Cade Bambara, among many others.

3 For a more detailed study of African American discourse styles, see Kochman's excellent 1981 study.

4 There is a complicated relationship between AAVE and non-black varieties of US English, only some aspects of which can be explored here. One important and divisive issue is the selective appropriation of AAVE lexical items into other varieties of English. Appropriation and its counterpart, supportive assimilation, are subjects which need to be explored systematically and objectively.

5 The two grammatical features of AAVE which seem to be most salient and which are most likely to engender poor reactions from non-blacks have to do with the verb "to be" (copula deletion, and singular -*s* marking) and with double negatives.

6 Metathesis is the process by which letters, sounds, or symbols are transposed, as in the change of Old English *brid* to modern English *bird*.

7 Eagleton has argued that literature has a singular relationship to the ideological process. He finds it to be

> the most revealing mode of experiential access to ideology that we possess. It is in literature, above all, that we observe in a peculiarly complex, coherent, intensive and immediate fashion the working of ideology in the textures of lived experience of class-societies.
>
> (1976: 101)

8 Labov's claims about divergence of black and white language in Philadelphia have been explored in depth elsewhere, particularly in Fasold (1987), a special issue of *American Speech* following from a conference panel dealing specifically with the divergence controversy. Some of the linguists participating in the discussion were critical of Labov's methodology and conclusions, but see particularly Vaughn-Cooke's contribution for a close discussion of Labov's conclusions about social policies and AAVE.

9 Baugh (1983: 122); *Oprah Winfrey Show* (1987: 2); LeClair (1994: 123–124); Jordan (1981: 62–63).

10 Jim Milroy points out to me, and quite rightly, that this conflict is one which must be common to many speakers of stigmatized language all over the world.

11 For a thorough representation of the positions of various linguists on these issues, see Mufwene (1993).

12 I am indebted to John Baugh for directing my attention to Shelby Steele's writings, which he also analyzed in part in his 1994 New Ways of Analyzing Variation (NWAVE) presentation at Stanford.

13 References to the Winfrey taping refer to page numbers in the original official transcript.

10 HILLBILLIES, REDNECKS, AND SOUTHERN BELLES

1 The question proposed for New Mexico in that legislature was "Red or green?" – a reference to the fresh chilies served with most meals. I am grateful to Richard Page for bringing this column to my attention.

2 The use of language to draw stereotype in entertainment was explored in a more general way in Chapter 5 in regard to a specific set of films. A quick overview of the way southern accent is used in adult film (*Cat on a Hot Tin Roof*, *In the Heat of the Night*, *Jezebel*, *Spencer's Mountain*, *A Streetcar Named Desire*, *Gone with the Wind*, *North and South*), indicates that this practice is very widespread.

3 Stereotypes of African American southerners are very different, but there seems to be little popular awareness – or discussion – of these differences.

11 THE STRANGER WITHIN THE GATES

1 Much greater proportions of the US population were foreign-born during the early part of this century. From a high of 14.7 percent in 1910, the percentage foreign-born declined to a low of 4.8 in 1970. Since 1970 the percentage has steadily increased.

2 Native speakers of English are not asked how well they speak their mother tongue. This is unfortunate, as it is almost certain that many would claim not to speak it well, having been drawn into the language subordination process.

3 Facts about demographics, language distribution, and speakers in various countries of the world are taken from Grimes (1992).

4 The facts of this case were taken from a series of newspaper reports and discussions with Ed Chen, an attorney for the ACLU, who also kindly provided much of the material. Newspaper reports include Gonzales (1993), Doyle (1993), McCormick (1993), Yang (1993).

5 Zentella discusses the various terms used for the larger ethnic classification of Spanish-speaking persons, and notes that while Latino activists do not like the government's use of "Hispanic," and prefer "Latino," "both terms have a long and respected history" (1996: 3).

6 Preston has demonstrated that Americans are willing to draw maps which make their opinions clear, and Dailey-O'Cain has replicated this experience in Germany (Dailey-O'Cain 1996). This kind of attitude has been documented for Garo, a language spoken in rural India and Bangladesh, as documented by Burling (in progress) and Carey (1919). The willingness of individuals to make such judgements is well documented, even if studies have not been done of every language or nation.

7 Cesar Chavez (Mexican activist for farm worker rights; deceased), Derek Wolcott (West Indian poet, awarded 1992 Nobel Prize for literature), Butros Butros Ghali (Egyptian former Secretary-General of the United Nations), Liu Xiaobo (Chinese student activist and dissenter, jailed after Tianamen), Benazir Bhutto (Pakistani activist, former prime minister), Corazón Aquino (president of the Philippines).

Bibliography

CITED RADIO AND TELEVISION BROADCASTS

Radio broadcasts

Drummond, W. (1990) "Hawai'ian language." *All Things Considered*. September 12. National Public Radio.

Hinojosa, M. (1994) "Haitian immigrants experience prejudice from blacks." *All Things Considered*. September 30. National Public Radio.

Morrison, P. (1994) Commentary: "Americans speak English – But we don't understand." *Morning Edition*. May 23. National Public Radio. Transcript 940016680.

National Public Radio News. March 23, 1994.

National Public Radio News. September 4, 1994.

Television broadcasts

"Accent Reduction." CBS Evening News. October 10, 1984.

"Black English." ABC Evening News. October 17, 1979.

"Black English." CBS Evening News. December 5, 1985.

"Dr. Grammar." NBC Evening News. April 26, 1993.

"English Only." CBS Evening News. October 21, 1986.

"Eye on America: Immigration." CBS Evening News. August 7, 1992.

"Final thoughts: Assimilation." NBC Evening News. December 19, 1992.

"Grammar hotline." ABC Evening News. February 16, 1986.

"Hawai'ian Pidgin." ABC Evening News. July 3, 1983.

"Headline News." CNN. March 12, 1993.

"Immigration." ABC Evening News. January 9, 1992.

"Immigration." CBS Evening News. May 19, 1992.

"Pronunciation." CBS Evening News. February 18, 1977.

"Southern Accents." ABC Evening News. December 15, 1991.

Other television broadcasts

McCrum, R. and R. MacNeil (1986) "Black on White." *The Story of English*. BBC.

Oprah Winfrey Show (1987) No. W309. "'Standard' and 'Black' English." November 19. Produced by D. DiMaio. Directed by J. McPharlin.

COURT CASES CITED WITH SOURCES

Andrews   1992: *George W. Andrews v. Cartex Corporation.* Civil Action No. 91-7109. 1992 US District Court.
Source: LEXIS 11468.

Ang   1991: *Ignatius G. Ang v. The Proctor & Gamble Company.*
Source: Federal Reporter (2d) 932: 540; LEXIS 8993; Fair Employment Practices Cases (BNA) 55: 1666; Employment Practices Decisions (CCH) 56: 40732.

Bell   1984: *Bell v. Home Life Insurance Company.*
Source: Federal Supplement 596: 1549.

Berke   1980: *Rozalia Berke v. Ohio Department of Public Welfare.*
Source: Federal Reporter (2d) 628: 980–81.

Carino   1981: *Donaciano Carino v. Regents of the University of Oklahoma.*
Source: Federal Reporter (2d) 750: 815; Fair Employment Practices Cases (BNA) 25: 1332–1338.

Carroll   1989: *Doritt Carroll v. Elliott Personnel Services.*
Source: Fair Employment Practices Cases (BNA) 51: 1173; Employment Practice Decisions (CCH) 52: 39508.

Casas   1983: *Casas v. First American Bank.*
Source: Fair Employment Practices Cases (BNA) 31: 1479.

Dabor   1991: *E.G. Dabor v. Dayton Power & Light Company.*
Source: LEXIS 2402.

Dercach   1987: *Anthony Dercach v. Indiana Department of Highways.*
Source: Fair Employment Practice Cases (BNA) 45: 899; LEXIS 13413.

Duddey   1989: *John Duddey v. David S. Ruder, Chairman Securities and Exchange Commission*, EEOC No. 05890115.
Source: EEOC materials and press releases.

Edwards   1978: *Violet B. Edwards v. Gladewater Independent School District.*
Source: Federal Reporter (2d) 572: 496; Fair Employment Practices Cases (BNA) 21: 1374; Employment Practices Decisions (CCH) 16: 8288.

Fragante   1987: *Fragante v. City and County of Honolulu.*
Source: Federal Supplement 699: 1429–1432.
1989: *Fragante v. City and County of Honolulu.*
Source: Federal Reporter (2d) 888: 591, 594–599; Matsuda 1991.

Garcia (a)   1978: *Christobal Garcia et al. v. Victoria Independent School District et al.*
Source: Employment Practices Decisions (CCH) vol. 17: para. 8.544. S.D. Texas.

Garcia (b)   1980: *Hector Garcia v. Alton V.W. Gloor, et al.*
Source: Federal Reporter (2d) 618: 264, Fair Employment Practices (BNA) 22: 1403.

Hou   1983: *Hou v. Pennsylvania Department of Education.*
Source: Federal Supplement 573: 1539–1550.

Ipina   1988: *Jorge M. Ipina v. State of Michigan Department of Management and Budget.*
Source: Federal Supplement 699: 132; LEXIS 15381.

Kahakua   1987a: *Kahakua v. Friday.*
Source: Federal Reporter (2d) 876: 896.
1987b: *Kahakua v. Hallgren*, No. 86-0434. District Hawai'i.
Source: Matsuda 1991 (no published opinion or summaries).

King   1978: *The Martin Luther King Junior Elementary School Children v.*
              The Michigan Board of Education, the Michigan Superintendent of
              Public Instruction and the Ann Arbor School District Board, Civil
              Action No. 77-71861 US District Court Eastern District of Michigan
              Southern Division.
              Source: Memorandum Opinion and Order of Charles W. Joiner
              (reproduced in Chambers 1983).
Kpodo   Pending: *EEOC v. Madison Hotel Corporation*, Civil Action No. 92-
              718 A. Eastern District Virginia, Alexandria Division.
              Source: EEOC materials.
Lubitz   1992: *John R. Lubitz v. H. Lawrence Garrett, III, Secretary of the*
              Department of the Navy.
              Source: Federal Reporter (2d) 962: 7; LEXIS 17272.
Mandhare   1985: *Sulochana Mandhare v. W. S. LaFargue Elementary School, the*
              Lafourche Parish School Board, Parish of Lafourche.
              Source: Federal Supplement 605: 238–243; Fair Employment Prac-
              tices Cases (BNA) 37: 1611, Federal Reporter (2d) 788: 1563;
              Fair Employment Practices Cases (BNA) 41: 64; Fair Employment
              Practices Cases (BNA) 42: 1014; LEXIS; interview with S. Mandhare
              March 29, 1993.
              1986: *Sulochana Mandhare v. W. S. LaFargue Elementary School, the*
              Lafourche Parish School Board, Parish of Lafourche.
              Source: Unpublished opinion of Chief Judge Clark, US Court of
              Appeals, Fifth Circuit, No. 85-3212.
Meijia   1978: *Meijia v. New York Sheraton Hotel.*
              Source: Federal Supplement 459: 375–377.
Park   1988: *Kee Y. Park v. James A. Baker III, Secretary of the Treasury*,
              EEOC No. 05870646.
              Source: EEOC materials.
Patel   1992: *US Equal Employment Commission v. Eiki International, Inc.*
              US District Court for the Central District of California.
              Source: EEOC materials, telephone interview with R. Gupta, EEOC,
              newspaper reports.
Rodriguez   1989: *Bernardino Rodriguez v. City of Hialeah.*
              Source: Federal Supplement 716: 1425; LEXIS 4616.
Sparks   1972: *Sparks v. Griffin.*
              Source: Federal Reporter (2d) 460: 433–443.
Staruch   1992: *Staruch v. US Bureau of Information.*
              Source: EEOC Opinion.
Stephen   1989: *Stephen v. PGA Sheraton Resort, Ltd.*
              Source: Federal Reporter (2d) 873: 276, 280–281.
Tran   1983: *Tran v. City of Houston.*
              Source: Fair Employment Practices Cases (BNA) 35: 471–473.
Vartivarian   1991: *Angel K. Vartivarian v. Golden Rule Insurance Company.*
              United States District Court for the Northern District of Illinois,
              Eastern Division. No. 88 C 1269.
              Source: LEXIS 6558.
Xieng   1991: *Phanna K. Xieng, et al. v. Peoples National Bank of Washington.*
              Source: Federal Reporter (2d) 821: 520; Washington State Appeals
              Court Opinion and *Findings of Fact* WL 269877.
              1992: *Phanna K. Xieng and Bathou Xieng, husband and wife v.*
              Peoples National Bank of Washington.
              Source: Washington State Supreme Court opinion dated January 21
              1993 (No. 59064-8).

REFERENCES AND OTHER WORKS CONSULTED

Addison, E. (1993) "Saving other women from other men: Disney's *Aladdin*." *Camera Obscura* 31: 4–25.

Aitchison, J. (1991) *Language Change: Progress or decay?* Cambridge: Cambridge University Press.

Alford, R. L. and J. B. Strother (1990) "Attitudes of native and nonnative speakers toward selected regional accents of U.S. English." *TESOL Quarterly* 24(3): 479–495.

Allen, H. B., ed. (1971) *Readings in American Dialectology*. New York: Appleton-Century-Crofts.

— and M. D. Linn, eds (1986) *Dialect and Language Variation*. Orlando, FL: Academic Press.

American Civil Liberties Union (1996) Briefing paper. http://www.aclu.org/library/pbp20.html.

Anisfeld, M., N. Bogo, and W. E. Lambert (1962) "Evaluational reactions to accented English speech." *Journal of Abnormal and Social Psychology* 65: 223–231.

Aponte, W. L. (1989) "Talkin' white." *Essence* 19: 11.

Arias, M. B. (1982) "Educational television: impact on the socialization of the Hispanic child." *Television and the Socialization of the Minority Child*. G. L. Berry and C. Mitchell-Kernan, eds. New York: Academic Press: 203–214.

Arnett, C., J. Dailey-O'Cain, R. Lippi-Green, and R. Simpson (1994) "Teaching children how to discriminate: standard language ideology and the perpetuation of linguistic stereotypes through Disney's animated films." Poster presentation, New Ways of Analyzing Variation (NWAVE) 1994, Stanford University.

Asante, M. K. (1982) "Television and the language socialization of black children." *Television and the Socialization of the Minority Child*. G. L. Berry and C. Mitchell-Kernan, eds. New York: Academic Press: 135–150.

Associated Press (1992) "Debate over teachers with accents." *New York Times*. July 5. Westfield, MA: section 1, p. 12.

Atkin, C. K., B. S. Greenberg, and S. McDermott (1983) "Television and race role socialization." *Journalism Quarterly* 60: 407–414.

Atkins, E. (1994) "Is black English legit? It's cool in hood, dissin' to some." *Detroit News*. May 2. Detroit, MI: 1b and 4b.

Atkins, J. D. C. (1887) *Annual Report* (of the Federal Commissioner of Indian Affairs). Washington DC: US Government Printing Office: xx–xxiv.

Atkinson, P. (1991) Extended review: "Decoding Bernstein." *Sociological Review*. 39: 647–654.

Ayers, E. L. (1996) "What we talk about when we talk about the South." *All Over the Map: Rethinking American regions*. E. Ayers, P. N. Limerick, S. Nissenbaum, *et al.*, eds. Baltimore, MD: Johns Hopkins Press, 62–82.

Babington, C. (1994) "Md. house passes language bill." *Washington Post*. March 29. Annapolis, MD: C5.

Bailey, G., T. Wikle, and T. Tillery, *et al.* (1993) "Some patterns of linguistic diffusion." *Language Variation and Change* 5(3): 359–390.

Bailey, R. (1991) *Images of English: A cultural history of the language*. Ann Arbor: University of Michigan Press.

Baird, S. J. (1969) "Employment interview speech: a social dialect study in Austin, Texas." Ph.D. thesis. Austin: University of Texas.

Baldwin, J. (1979) "If Black English isn't a language, then tell me, what is?" *New York Times*. July 29. New York: Op-Ed (Opinion Editorial).

— (1988) "A talk to teachers." *The Graywolf Annual Fire: Multicultural literacy*. R. Simonson and S. Walker, eds. St. Paul: Graywolf: 3–12.

Ball-Rokeach, S. J., M. Rokeach, and J. W. Grube (1984) *The Great American Values Test: Influencing behavior and belief through television.* New York: Free Press.

Bandura, A. (1969) "Social-learning theory of identificatory processes." *Handbook of Socialization Theory and Research.* D. A. Goslin, ed. Chicago, IL: Rand McNally: 213–262.

Baron, D. (1990) *The English-Only Question: An official language for Americans?* New Haven, CT: Yale University Press.

Bates, S. (1993) "English teachers offer lifeline to immigrants." *Washington Post.* December 13: A1.

Baugh, J. (1983) *Black Street Speech: Its history, structure, and survival.* Austin: University of Texas Press.

—— (1992) "Hypocorrection: mistakes in production of vernacular African American English as a second dialect." *Language and Communication* 12(3/4): 317–326.

Beckerman, S. (1996) "Questions probe states of mind." *Centre Daily Times.* April 24. State College, PA: 4A.

Behlmer, R. (1993) *Memo from Darryl F. Zanuck.* New York: Grove Press.

Behnke, K. E. (1930) *Speech and Movement on the Stage.* London: Oxford University Press.

Bell, C. and H. Newby (1971) *Community Studies. An introduction to the sociology of the local community.* London: George Allen & Unwin.

Bender, J. F. (1943) *NBC Handbook of Pronunciation.* New York: Thomas Y. Crowell.

Bennett, W. J. (1988) *Our Children and our Country: Improving America's schools and affirming the common culture.* New York: Simon & Schuster.

Berliner, D. C. and B. J. Biddle (1995) *The Manufactured Crisis: Myths, fraud, and the attack on America's public schools.* Reading, MA: Addison-Wesley.

Berry, G. L. and C. Mitchell-Kernan, eds. (1982) *Television and the Socialization of the Minority Child.* New York: Academic Press.

Blommaert, J. and J. Verschueren (1992) "The role of language in European nationalist ideologies." *Pragmatics* 2(3): 355–376.

Bolinger, D. (1980) *Language – The Loaded Weapon: The use and abuse of language today.* London and New York: Longman.

Bott, R., B. Bott, and B. Fennell (n.d.) "Titas, blalahs, and haoles: linguistic marks of in-group/out-group status in Hawaiian ethnic humor." Unpublished.

Boulet Jr., J. (1991) "Say no to bilingualism, yes to English." *Atlanta Journal/Atlanta Constitution.* June 5. Springfield, VA: A15.

—— (1993) "Florida's woes prove 'official English' bill needed." *Port Arthur News.* June 14. Springfield, VA: 7A.

Bourdieu, P. (1991) *Language and Symbolic Power.* Edited and introduced by J. B. Thompson. Translated by G. Raymond and M. Adamson. Cambridge, MA: Harvard University Press.

Brennan, E. M., M. A. Carranza, and E. B. Ryan (1980) "Language attitudes of Mexican-American adolescents in two midwestern cities." *Languages in Conflict.* P. Schach, ed. Lincoln: University of Nebraska Press: 148–156.

Burling, R. (1973) *English in Black and White.* New York: Holt, Rinehart & Winston.

—— (in progress) "The impinging world." Manuscript.

Burton, J. (1992) "Don (Juanito) duck and the imperial-patriarchal unconscious: Disney studios, the good neighbor policy, and the packaging of Latin America." *Nationalisms and Sexualities.* A. Parker, M. Russo, D. Sommer, *et al.*, eds. New York: Routledge: 21–41.

Buxton, F. and B. Owen (1972) *The Big Broadcast 1920–1950.* New York: Viking Press.

California Style Collective (1993) *Variation and Personal/Group Style.* New Ways of Analyzing Variation (NWAVE) 22, Stanford University.

Cameron, D. (1995) *Verbal Hygiene.* London and New York: Routledge.

Campbell, B. M. (1995) *Brothers and Sisters.* New York: Berkeley Books.

Carey, W. (1919) *The Garo Jungle Book.* Tura, Garo Hills, Assam: Tura Book Room.

Carranza, M. A. and E. B. Ryan (1975) "Evaluative reactions of adolescents toward speakers of standard English and Mexican American accented English." *International Journal of the Sociology of Language* 8: 3–102.

Caudill, E. (1989) *The Roots of Bias: An empiricist press and coverage of the Scopes Trial.* Columbia, SC: Association for Education in Journalism and Mass Communication.

Chambers, J. K. (1995) *Sociolinguistic Theory: Linguistic variation and its social significance.* Oxford and Cambridge, MA: Basil Blackwell.

Chambers, J. W., Jr., ed. (1983) *Black English: Educational equity and the law.* Ann Arbor, MI: Karoma Publishers.

Chana, U. and S. Romaine (1984) "Evaluative reactions to Panjabi/English code-switching." *Journal of Multilingual and Multicultural Development* 5(6): 447–473.

Christian, D. (1988) *Variation and Change in Geographically Isolated Communities: Appalachian English and Ozark English.* Tuscaloosa: University of Alabama Press.

Clark, H. H. and E. F. Schaefer (1989) "Contributing to discourse." *Cognitive Science* 13: 259–294.

Clark, H. H. and D. Wilkes-Gibbs (1986) "Referring as a collaborative process." *Cognition* 22: 1–39.

Coffey, S. (1994) "Why newspapers watch their language" (letter to the editor). *New York Times.* April 8. Los Angeles: A26(L).

Collins, J. (1992) "Our ideologies and theirs." *Pragmatics* 2(3): 405–416.

Comrie, B., ed. (1987) *The World's Major Languages.* London: Croom Helm.

Cooper, R. L. (1989) *Language Planning and Social Change.* New York: Cambridge University Press.

Cormack, M. (1993) "Problems of minority language broadcasting: Gaelic in Scotland." *European Journal of Communication* 8: 101–117.

Correll, C. J. and F. F. Gosden (1931) *Here they are – Amos 'n' Andy.* New York: Ray Long & Richard R. Smith.

Craig, B. (1991) "American Indian English." *English World-Wide* 12(1): 25–61.

Crawford, J. (1992) *Hold Your Tongue: Bilingualism and the politics of English Only.* Reading, MA: Addison-Wesley.

—— ed. (1992) *Language Loyalties: A source book on the official English controversy.* Chicago, IL: University of Chicago Press.

Crowley, T. (1989) *Standard English and the Politics of Language.* Urbana and Chicago: University of Illinois Press.

Cukor-Avila, P. (1995) "The evolution of AAVE in a rural Texas community: an ethnolinguistic study." Doctoral thesis. Ann Arbor: University of Michigan.

Cutler, S. (1985) "A trait-based approach to national origin discrimination." *Yale Law Journal* 94: 1164–1181.

Dailey-O'Cain, J. (1996) " 'That terrible Saxon dialect': standard language ideology in post-unification Germany." *SALSA III.* R. Ide, R. Park, and Y. Sunaoski, eds. Proceedings of the Third Annual Symposium about Language and Society. Austin: University of Texas: TLF 36, 315–334.

Danticat, E. (1994) *Breath, Eyes, Memory.* New York: Soho.

Darden, C. (1996) *In Contempt.* Written with J. Walter. New York: Regan Books (HarperCollins).

Darnton, J. (1993) "The English are talking funny again." *New York Times.* December 21. London: A13(L).

Davis, L. J. (1993) "Hear ye? The prisoners of silence." *Nation*. October 4: 354–356.
Day, R. (1980) "The development of linguistic attitudes and preferences." *TESOL Quarterly* 14: 27–37.
Debo, A. (1970) *A History of the Indians of the United States*. Norman: University of Oklahoma Press.
Dillard, J. L. (1972) *Black English: Its history and usage in the United States*. New York: Random House.
—— (1975) *All-American English*. New York: Random House.
—— (1992) *History of American English*. London: Longman.
Dooley, R. (1981) *From Scarface to Scarlett: American films in the 1930s*. New York: Harcourt Brace Jovanovich.
Doyle, J. (1993) "Filipino guards' claim upheld." *San Francisco Chronicle*. April 15: A13.
Drake, G. F. (1977a) "Black English and the American dream." *The Role of Prescriptivism in American Linguistics 1820–1970*. G. F. Drake, ed. Amsterdam: John Benjamins: 78–106.
—— (1977b) *The Role of Prescriptivism in American Linguistics 1820–1970*. Amsterdam: John Benjamins.
Drummond, W. J. (1990) "About face from alliance to alienation: Blacks and the news media." *American Enterprise* 1(July/August): 22–29.
Dunning, J. (1976) "Tune in yesterday." *The Ultimate Encyclopedia of Old-Time Radio 1925–1976*. Englewood Cliffs, NJ: Prentice-Hall: 31–36.
Eagleton, T. (1976) *Criticism and Ideology*. London: Verso.
—— (1991) *Ideology: An introduction*. London and New York: Verso.
Edelman, L. B., H. S. Erlanger, and J. Lande (1993) "Internal dispute resolution: the transformation of civil rights in the workplace." *Law and Society Review* 27(3): 497–534.
Edwards, J. (1989) *Language and Disadvantage*. Newcastle upon Tyne, England: Whurr Publishers.
Ehrenreich, B. (1990) "Language barrier." *The Worst Years of Our Lives: Irreverent notes from a decade of greed*. New York: Pantheon Books: 45–48.
Ehrlich, E., ed. (1951) *NBC Handbook of Pronunciation*. New York: Harper & Row.
—— and R. Hand, eds (1984) *NBC Handbook of Pronunciation*. New York: Harper & Row.
Eisenstein, M. (1983) "Native reactions to non-native speech: a review of empirical research." *Studies in Second Language Acquisition* 52: 160–176.
—— and G. Verdi (1985) "The intelligibility of social dialects for working class adult learners of English." *Language Learning* 35(2): 287–298.
Emery, M. and E. Emery (1992) *The Press and America: An interpretive history of the mass media*. Englewood Cliffs, NJ: Prentice-Hall.
Eppinger, J. (1990) "Hawai'i's new Japanese accent." *Adweek's Marketing Week* 31(38): 30(2).
Eschholz, P., A. Rosa and V. Clark eds (1990) *Language Awareness*. New York: St. Martin's Press.
Etlin, M. (1992) "Working with immigrant kids: 'incredibly satisfying'." *NEA Today* 11(2): 6–7.
Faber, M. (1992) "The joy of teaching 'biliteracy'." *NEA Today* 11(5): 6.
Fairclough, N. (1989) *Language and Power*. London and New York: Longman.
—— (1992a) "The appropriacy of 'appropriateness'." *Critical Language Awareness*. N. Fairclough, ed. London and New York: Longman: 35–56.
—— (1992b) *Discourse and Social Change*. Cambridge: Polity Press: 33–55.
—— ed. (1992c) *Critical Language Awareness*. London and New York: Longman.

Fanon, F. (1967) *Black Skin, White Masks*. New York: Grove Press.

Farr, M. (1991) "Dialects, culture, and teaching the English languages arts." *Handbook of Research on Teaching the English Language Arts*. J. Flood, ed. New York: Macmillan: 365–371.

Fasold, R. W. (1987) *Are Black and White Vernacular Diverging? Papers from the New Ways of Analyzing Variation (NWAVE) XIV panel discussion*. Special issue of *American Speech* 62(1) (Spring).

Faust, D. and J. Ziskin (1988) "The expert witness in psychology and psychiatry." *Science* 241: 31–35.

Feagin, C. (1979) *Variation and Change in Alabama English: A sociolinguistic study of the white community*. Washington DC: Georgetown University Press.

Ferguson, C. A. and S. B. Heath, eds (1981) *Language in the USA*. Edited with the assistance of D. Hwang. Cambridge and New York: Cambridge University Press.

Finegan, E. (1980) *Attitudes toward English Usage*. New York and London: Teachers College Press.

Fishman, J. A., ed. (1986) *Language Rights and the English Language Amendment. International Journal of the Sociology of Language* 60 (monograph).

Flege, J. E. (1994) "Second-language speech learning: theory, findings, and problems" (prepublication version). *Speech Perception and Linguistic Experience: Theoretical and methodological issues*. W. Strange, ed. Timonium, MD: York Press.

—— and O.-S. Bohn (1989) "An instrumental study of vowel reduction and stress placement in Spanish-accented English." *Studies in Second Language Acquisition* 11: 35–62.

—— and O.-S. Bohn (1990) "Interlingual identification and the role of foreign language experience in L2 vowel perception." *Applied Psycholinguistics* 11(3): 303–328.

Foucault, M. (1984) "The order of discourse." *Language and Politics*. M. Shapiro, ed. New York: New York University Press: 108–138.

Fraser, F. (1993) "Wrong color, right skills." *Toronto Star*. March 4. Toronto: A23.

Friedrich, P. (1989) "Language, ideology, and political economy." *American Anthropologist* 91(2): 295–312.

Froiland, P. (1994) "Quality in a box: learning English on company time." *Training* 64 (February): 62–66.

Gal, S. (1988) "The political economy of code switching." *Codeswitching: Anthropological and sociolinguistic perspectives*. M. Heller, ed. Berlin: Mouton de Gruyter: 245–264.

—— (1992) "Multiplicity and contention among ideologies: a commentary." *Pragmatics* 2(3): 445–450.

Gallois, C. and V. J. Callan (1981) "Personality impressions edited by accented English speech." *Journal of Cross-Cultural Psychology* 12(3): 347–359.

García, O. and R. Otheguy (1988) "The language situation of Cuban Americans." *Language Diversity: Problem or Resource? A social and educational perspective on language minorities in the United States*. S. L. McKay and S.-l. C. Wong, eds. Boston, MA: Heinle & Heinle: 166–192.

Gee, J. P. (1990) *Social linguistics and literacies: Ideology in discourse*. London and New York: Falmer Press.

Giles, H. (1971) "Ethnocentrism and the evaluation of accented speech." *British Journal of Social and Clinical Psychology* 10: 187–188.

—— (1984) *The Dynamics of Speech Accommodation*. Berlin: Mouton de Gruyter.

—— and E. B. Ryan (1982) "Prolegomena for developing a social psychological theory of language attitudes." *Attitudes toward Language Variation: Social and applied contexts*. E. B. Ryan and H. Giles, eds. London: Edward Arnold: 208–223.

——, C. Harrison, C. Creber, *et al.* (1983) "Developmental and contextual aspects of children's language attitudes." *Language and Communication* 3(2): 141–146.

—— and J. Coupland, eds (1991) *Contexts of Accommodation: Developments in applied sociolinguistics.* Cambridge: Cambridge University Press.

Gitlin, T. (1980) *The Whole World is Watching: Mass media in the making and unmaking of the New Left.* Berkeley: University of California Press.

Goldenberg, E. (1993) "Notes from the Dean." *LSAmagazine* 2: 3.

Goldstein, E. (1995) "Analysis: accent in Spielberg's *Schindler's List.*" Unpublished ms.

Gomez, G. R. and D. D. Laitin (1992) "Language, ideology, and the press in Catalonia." *American Anthropologist* 94: 9–30.

Gonzales, N. (1993) "Security guards win accent bias ruling." *Philippine News.* April 21–28: 1.

Goodnough, A. (1994) "English for immigrants." *New York Times.* April 10: Section 4A, p. ED8.

Gordon, J. C. B. (1981) *Verbal Deficit: A critique.* London: Croom Helm.

Gould, P. and R. White (1974) *Mental Maps.* Baltimore, MD: Penguin.

Graff, H. (1987a) *The Labyrinths of Literacy: Reflections on literacy past and present.* New York: Falmer Press.

—— (1987b) *The Legacies of Literacy: Continuities and contradictions in Western culture and society.* Bloomington: University of Indiana Press.

Gramsci, A. (1985) *Selections from Cultural Writings.* London: Lawrence and Wishart.

Grant, J. (1993) *Encyclopedia of Walt Disney's Animated Characters.* New York: Hyperion.

Green, F. (1929) *The Film Finds its Tongue.* New York: Knickerbocker Press.

Green, G. and M. Di Paolo (1990) "Jurors' beliefs about the interpretation of speaking style." *American Speech* 65: 304–322.

Greene, B. (1979) "Jive cuts it only on street, not in world." *Chicago Tribune.* December 3. Chicago, IL: section 2: 1.

Greene, R. (1993) "The White man's burden: why turnabout isn't fair play when it comes to racial stereotyping." *LA Village View.* March 12–18: 17.

Greenbaum, S., ed. (1985) *The English Language Today.* Oxford: Pergamon Press.

Greenhouse, L. (1991) "High court upholds exclusion of bilingual jurors." *New York Times.* May 29. New York: A20.

Grimes, M. F., ed. (1992) *Ethnologue: Languages of the world.* World Wide Web http://www-ala.doc.ic.ac.uk/~rap/Ethnologue/.

Grobsmith, E. S. (1980) "Aspects of Lakota bilingualism." *Languages in Conflict.* P. Schach, ed. Lincoln: University of Nebraska Press: 119–128.

Gupta, R. K. (1988) "EEOC orders reinstatement with full relief for an IRS revenue agent trainee denied promotion because of Korean accent." June 8. EEOC press release.

—— (1989) "EEOC finds discrimination on the basis of federal employee's Asian Indian accent." April 5. EEOC press release.

—— (1991) "EEOC opposes speak-English-only rule at work." September 24. EEOC press release.

—— (1992a) "EEOC files class action suit against employment agency for color and accent discrimination." April 27. EEOC press release.

—— (1992b) "EEOC sues Madison Hotel Corporation for accent discrimination." May 22. EEOC press release.

Hacker, A. (1993) " 'Diversity' and its dangers." *New York Review.* October 7: 21.

Haidar, J. and L. Rodríguez (1995) "Power and ideology in different discursive practices." *Language and Peace,* C. Schäffner and A. L. Wenden, eds. Aldershot, England: Dartmouth: 119–136.

Hall, C. W. (1993) "English-first group assails Arlington." *Washington Post.* November 20: C4.

Hall, S. (1977) "Culture, the media and the 'ideological effect'." *Mass Communication and Society.* J. Curran, M. Gurevitch and J. Woolacott, eds. London: Edward Arnold: 315–348.

Halliday, M. A. K. (1989) *Spoken and Written Language.* Oxford: Oxford University Press.

Hamblin, K. (1995) "Speaking well has its merit." *Ann Arbor News.* April 7. Ann Arbor, MI: Opinion Page.

Hamel, R. and T. Schreiner (1989) "Speak English, troops." *American Demographics* 11: 66.

Hanke, K. (1989) *Charlie Chan at the Movies.* Jefferson, NC: McFarland.

Harshaw, T. (1994) "One grammar doesn't fit all." *New York Times.* February 27: Book Review 8.

Harwood, R. (1993) "Language: both ways at once." *Washington Post.* December 11: A23.

Hasselmo, N. (1980) "The linguistic norm and the language shift in Swedish America." *Languages in Conflict.* P. Schach, ed. Lincoln: University of Nebraska Press: 48–57.

Haugen, E. (1980) "Frontier Norwegian in South Dakota." *Languages in Conflict.* P. Schach, ed. Lincoln: University of Nebraska Press: 20–28.

Heath, S.B. (1981) "Introduction." *Language in the USA.* C. A. Ferguson and S. B. Heath, eds, with the assistance of D. Hwang. Cambridge: Cambridge University Press.

—— (1983) *Ways with Words: Language, life, and work in communities and classrooms.* Cambridge and New York: Cambridge University Press.

—— and C. A. Ferguson (1992) "American English: quest for a model." *The Other Tongue: English across cultures.* B. B. Kachru and C. A. Ferguson, eds. Urbana: University of Illinois Press: 220–32.

Heller, M., ed. (1988) "The political economy of code choice." *Codeswitching: Anthropological and sociolinguistic perspectives.* Berlin: Mouton de Gruyter.

Heller, S. (1994) "Dissecting Disney." *Chronicle of Higher Education.* February 16: Scholarship section.

Henry, S. (1993) "Native Americans attempt to save tribal languages for the next generation." *Christian Science Monitor.* June 29: 1.

Herman, E. S. and N. Chomsky (1988) *Manufacturing Consent: The political economy of the mass media.* New York: Pantheon Books.

Herman, L. and M. S. Herman (1943) *Foreign Dialects: A manual for actors, directors and writers.* New York: Theatre Arts Books.

—— (1947) *American Dialects: A manual for actors, directors and writers.* New York: Theatre Arts Books.

Hernandez, R. (1993) "When an accent becomes an issue: immigrants turn to speech classes to reduce sting of bias." *New York Times.* March 2. New York: B1.

Hill, J. H. (1992) " 'Today there is no respect': nostalgia, 'respect' and oppositional discourse in Mexicano (Nahuatl) language ideology." *Pragmatics* 2(3): 263–281.

Hilliard III, A. G. (1983) "Psychological language factors for African-American children." *Education Digest* (October): 52–54.

Hodge, R. and G. Kress (1993) *Language as Ideology.* New York: Routledge.

Holmes, J. (1983) "On speaking Texan." *Publisher's Weekly.* May 20: 154.

Honey, J. (1989) *Does Accent Matter?* Boston, MA: Faber & Faber.

Honeycutt, K. (1993) "Getting down on 'Falling Down': Warners' L.A. story angers some Koreans, Latinos, defense workers." *Hollywood Reporter.* March 2: 3.

Iiyama, P. and H. H. L. Kitano (1982) "Asian Americans and the media." *Television and the Socialization of the Minority Child.* G. L. Berry and C. Mitcell-Kernan, eds. New York: Academic Press: 151–186.

James, C. (1990) "Spike Lee's Jews and the passage from benign cliché into bigotry." *New York Times.* August 16: C1.

Jarrett, V. (1979a) " 'Black English' not spoken here." *Chicago Tribune.* August 17. Chicago: section 5: 4.

—— (1979b) "Who defined 'black English'?" *Chicago Tribune.* August 10. Chicago: section 3: 3.

Jarvis, J. (1993) "The couch critic: the nanny." *TV Guide.* December 18: 8.

Jenkins, S. and D. L. Rubin (1993) "International teaching assistants and minority students: the two sides of cultural diversity in American higher education." *Journal of Graduate Teaching Assistant Development* 1(1) (Spring): 17–24.

John, M., P. Yates, and E. DeLancy (1975) *The New Building Better English.* Evanston, IL: Harper & Row.

Jones, K. (1996) "Weekend co-editor takes introspective look at the best of city." *Michigan Daily.* April 18. Ann Arbor: University of Michigan: 14B.

Jones, R. (1990) "What's wrong with Black English." *Language Awareness.* P. Eschholz, A. Rosa and V. Clark, eds. New York: St. Martin's Press: 93–95.

Jordan, J. (1981) "White English/Black English: the politics of translation (1972)." *Civil Wars.* New York: Touchstone: 59–73.

—— (1985) "Nobody mean more to me than you and the future life of Willie Jordan." *On Call: Political essays.* Boston, MA: South End Press: 123–139.

Joseph, J. (1987) *Eloquence and Power: The rise of language standards and standard languages.* New York: Basil Blackwell.

Kac, M. B. (1988) "Two cheers for prescriptivism." *On Language: Rhetorica, Phonologica, Syntactica: A Festschrift for Robert P. Stockwell.* C. Duncan-Rose, J. Fisiak, and T. Vennemann, eds. London: Routledge: 79–85.

Kalin R. and D. S. Rayko (1978) "Discrimination in evaluative judgments against foreign-accented job candidates." *Psychological Reports* 43: 1203–1209.

Kalin, R., D. S. Rayko, and N. Love (1979) "The perception and evaluation of job candidates with four different ethnic accents." *Social Psychology and Language.* H. Giles, W. P. Robins, and P. Smith, eds. London: Pergamon Press: 197–202.

Kang, K. C. (1994) "No language barrier." *Los Angeles Times.* April 23. Los Angeles, CA: B3.

Kanter, C. E. and R. West (1941) *Phonetics.* New York: London: Harper & Brothers.

Kapoor, S. (1993) "Accent on pain and prejudice." *Vancouver Sun.* March 13. Vancouver: A2.

Karlins, M., T. L. Coffman, and G. Walters (1969) "On the fading of social stereotypes: studies in three generations of college students." *Journal of Personality and Social Psychology* 13(1): 1–16.

Karshner, R. and D. A. Stern (1990) *Dialect Monologues.* Toluca Lake, CA: Dramaline Publications.

Katz, D. and K. Braly (1933) "Racial stereotypes of one hundred college students." *Journal of Abnormal and Social Psychology* 28: 280–290.

Kaufman, J. B. (1988) "Three little pigs – big little picture." *American Cinematographer* (November): 38–44.

Kerr, B. (1994) "Voice of success silences dialect: program helps people shed telltale tones." *Providence Journal-Bulletin.* April. Providence, RI.

Kirby, J. T. (1978) *Media-Made Dixie: The South in the American imagination.* Baton Rouge and London: Louisiana State University Press.

Kliman, B. W. (1978) "The biscuit eater: racial stereotypes 1939–1972." *Phylon* (March): 87–96.

Knack, R. (1991) "Ethnic boundaries in linguistic variation." *New Ways of Analyzing Sound Change*. P. Eckert, ed. San Diego, CA: Academic Press: 251–272.

Koch, E. I. (1989) "Don't ax the mayor" (letter to the editor). *Harper's Magazine* (March) 278: 21–22.

Kochman, T. (1981) *Black and White Styles in Conflict*. Chicago, IL: University of Chicago Press.

Kress, G. R. (1985) *Linguistic Processes in Sociocultural Practice*. Oxford and New York: Oxford University Press.

Kroch, A. and C. Small (1978) "Grammatical ideology and its effect on speech." *Linguistic Variation: Models and methods*. D. Sankoff, ed. New York: Academic Press: 45–56.

Kroskrity, P. (1992) "Arizona Tewa Kiva speech as a manifestation of linguistic ideology." *Pragmatics* 2(3): 297–310.

——, B. Schieffelin, and K. Woolard, eds (1992) *Pragmatics*. Special issue on language ideologies.

Labov, W. (1966) *The Social Stratification of English in New York City*. Washington DC: Center for Applied Linguistics.

—— (1969) "The logic of non-standard English." *Georgetown Monographs on Language and Linguistics* 22: 1–22, 26–31.

—— (1973) "Linguistic consequences of being a lame." *Language in Society* 2(1): 81–116.

—— (1982a) "Building on empirical foundations." *Perspectives on Historical Linguistics*. W. P. Lehmann and Y. Malkiel, eds. Amsterdam: John Benjamins: 17–92.

—— (1982b) "Objectivity and commitment in linguistic science: the case of the Black English trial in Ann Arbor." *Language in Society* 11(2): 165–201.

—— (1991) "The three dialects of English." *New Ways of Analyzing Sound Change*. P. Eckert, ed. New York: Academic Press: 1–44.

—— and W. A. Harris (1986) "De facto segregation of black and white vernaculars." *Diversity and Diachrony*. D. Sankoff, ed. Amsterdam and Philadelphia, PA: John Benjamins.

Ladefoged, P. (1982) *A Course in Phonetics*. 2nd edition. San Diego, CA: Harcourt Brace Jovanevitch.

Laferriere, M. (1979) "Ethnicity in phonological variation and change." *Language* 55: 603–617.

Lambert, W. E. (1967) "The social psychology of bilingualism." *Journal of Social Issues* 23: 91–109.

——, R. Hodgson, R. C. Gardner, *et al.* (1960) "Evaluational reactions to spoken languages." *Journal of Abnormal and Social Psychology* 60: 44–51.

Larmouth, D. W., T. E. Murray, and C. R. Murray (1992) *Legal and Ethical Issues in Surreptitious Recording*. Tuscaloosa and London: University of Alabama Press.

Lavey, K. (1994) "Morning: a calm farewell." *Lansing State Journal*. Lansing, MI: 1F.

Leap, W. L. (1982) "The study of Indian English in the U.S. Southwest: retrospect and prospect." *Bilingualism and Language Contact: Spanish, English and Native American languages*. F. Barkin, E. A. Brandt and J. Ornstein-Galicia, eds. New York and London: Teachers College, Columbia University: 101–120.

—— (1992) "American Indian English." *Teaching American Indian Students*. J. Reyhner, ed. Foreword by Ben Nighthorse Campbell. Normal: University of Oklahoma Press: 143–156.

LeClair, T. (1994) "The language must not sweat." *Conversations with Toni Morrison*. D. Taylor-Guthrie, ed. Jackson: University Press of Mississippi: 119–128.

Lee, F. R. (1994) "Grappling with how to teach young speakers of Black dialect." *New York Times*. January 5. New York: A1–A8.

Lee, Chang-Rae (1995) *Native Speaker*. New York: Riverhead Books.

Leff, L. (1994) "Immigrants weather winter of discontent." *Washington Post*. March 19: B1.

Leitner, G. (1983) "The social background of the language of radio." *Language, Image, Media*. P. Walton, ed. Southampton, England: Camelot Press: 50–74.

Lennenberg, E. H. (1967) *Biological Foundations of Language*. New York: Academic Press.

Levi, J. N. (1994) *Language and Law: A bibliographic guide to social science research in the USA*. American Bar Association.

Levine, K. (1986) *The Social Context of Literacy*. New York: Routledge & Kegan Paul.

Liebman, L. (1993) "Pragmatic Ivey." *New Woman* (February): 14.

Lippi-Green, R. (1989) "Social network integration and language change in progress in a rural alpine community." *Language in Society* 18(2): 213–234.

—— (1994) "Accent, standard language ideology and discriminatory pretext in the courts." *Language in Society* 23(2): 163–198.

Lipton, L. (1992) "After therapy, my Valspeak is still, like, *out there*." *Los Angeles Times*. December 13: E1.

Luebke, F. C. (1980) "Legal restrictions on foreign languages in the Great Plains states, 1917–1923." *Languages in Conflict*. P. Schach, ed. Lincoln: University of Nebraska Press: 1–19.

McArthur, T., ed. (1992) *The Oxford Companion to the English Language*. Oxford and New York: Oxford University Press.

Macaulay, R. K. S. (1988)"The rise and fall of the vernacular." *On Language: Rhetorica, Phonologica, Syntactica: A Festschrift for Robert P. Stockwell*. C. Duncan-Rose, J. Fisiak and T. Venneemann, eds. New York: Routledge: 106–115.

Maccoby, E. E. and W. C. Wilson (1957) "Identification and observational learning from films." *Journal of Abnormal and Social Psychology* 55: 76–87.

McCormick, E. (1993) "Filipino guards sue over 'accent discrimination'." *San Francisco Examiner*. April 15: A-7.

Machlin, E. (1966) *Speech for the Stage*. New York: Theatre Arts Books.

McKay, S. L. and S.-l. C. Wong, eds. (1988) *Language Diversity: Problem or Resource? A social and educational perspective on language minorities in the United States*. Boston, MA: Heinle & Heinle Publishers.

McKenzie, J. N. (1992) "Bad English spoken here." *Wall Street Journal*. April 27. New York: A14(W) p. A20(E), col. 3.

Mahar, W. J. (1985) "Black English in early blackface minstrelsy." *American Quarterly* 37(2): 260–285.

Maltin, L. (1973) *The Disney Films*. New York: Crown.

—— (1987) *Of Mice and Magic: A history of American animated cartoons*. 2nd revised edition. New York: Plume Books.

Matsuda, M. J. (1991) "Voice of America: Accent, antidiscrimination law, and a jurisprudence for the last reconstruction." *Yale Law Journal* 100: 1329–1407.

Maynard, R. (1993) "Improving English skills." *Nation's Business* (May): 68–69.

Mediamark Research (1993) *Television Audiences Report*. New York.

Mencken, H. L. (1956) *The American Language*. New York: Alfred A. Knopf.

Mertz, E. (1992) "Linguistic ideology and praxis in U.S. law school classrooms." *Pragmatics* 2(3): 325–334.

Michigan, State Department of Education (1993) *A Manual to Assist School Districts in Their Work with Students of Limited English Proficiency: Bilingual education program*. Office of enrichment and community services.

—— (1994) *Civil Rights for Language Minority Students.*
Milroy, J. (1989) "On the concept of prestige in sociolinguistic argumentation." *York Papers in Linguistics* 13: 215–226.
—— (1992) *Linguistic Variation and Change.* Oxford: Basil Blackwell.
—— and L. Milroy (1991) *Authority in Language: Investigating language prescription and standardisation.* London and New York: Routledge.
Miron, M. S. (1990) "Psycholinguistics in the courtroom." *Annals of the New York Academy of Sciences* 606: 55–64.
Morgan, M. (1986) "Television and the erosion of regional diversity." *Journal of Broadcasting and Electronic Media* 30(2): 123–139.
Morgan, M. and S. DeBerry (1995) "Lexical grammaticalization and phonological variation in urban African American hip hop." New Ways of Analyzing Variation (NWAVE), Philadelphia. October.
Morris, J. S. (1982) "Television portrayal and the socialization of the American Indian child." *Television and the Socialization of the Minority Child.* G. L. Berry and C. Mitchell-Kernan, eds. New York: Academic: 187–202.
Mufwene, S., ed. (1993) *Africanisms in Afro-American Language Varieties.* Athens: University of Georgia Press.
Murchison, W. (1996) "Our charming speech is gone with the wind." *Dallas Morning News.* March 13. Dallas.
Murray, T. E. (1986) *The Language of Saint Louis, Missouri: Variations in the gateway city.* New York: Peter Lang.
National Council of Teachers of English (1974) "Students' right to their own language." College Composition and Communication series. Urbana, IL: NCTE.
—— (1996) *Standards for the English Language Arts.* Urbana, IL: NCTE.
Nenneman, R. A. (1992) "Language is the guardian of the culture." *Christian Science Monitor.* July 8: 22.
New Mexico, State Department of Education (1979) *Guidelines for Approval of State Programs: Bilingual education.* Santa Fe.
—— (1987a) *Competencies for Teachers of Bilingual Education.*
—— (1987b) *Competencies for Teachers of English as a Second Language.*
Newmeyer, F. J. (1983) *Grammatical Theory, Its Limits and Its Possibilities.* Chicago, IL: University of Chicago Press.
O'Brien, J., ed. (1973) *Interviews with Black Writers.* New York: Liveright.
Ogg, H. and R. K. Immel (1937) *Speech Improvement: A manual for a fundamentals course.* New York: F. S. Crofts.
Orth, J. L. (1982) "University undergraduate evaluational reactions to the speech of foreign teaching assistants." Ph.D. thesis. Austin: University of Texas.
Pais, A. (1990) "Arabs angry from 'The Sheik' to 'Santa Barbara'." *Variety.* December 31.
Pearl, D. (1991) "Hush mah mouth! Some in South try to lose the drawl." *Wall Street Journal.* December 13. New York: A1.
Peet, C. (1929) "The cartoon comedy." *The New Republic* August 14: 341–342.
Peñalosa, Fernando (1981) *Introduction to the Sociology of Language.* Rowley, MA: Newbury House.
Penfield, J. and J. L. Ornstein-Galicia (1985) *Chicano English: An ethnic contact dialect.* Amsterdam and Philadelphia, PA: John Benjamins.
Pettit, A. (1980) *Images of the Mexican-American in Fiction and Film.* College Station: Texas A&M University Press.
Philips, S. U. (1992) "A Marx-influenced approach to ideology and language: comments." *Pragmatics* 2(3): 376–377.
Phillipson, R. (1992) *Linguistic Imperialism.* Oxford: Oxford University Press.
Piatt, B. (1990) *Only English? Law and language policy in the United States.* Albuquerque: University of New Mexico Press.

—— (1993) *Language on the Job: Balancing business needs and employee rights.* Albuquerque: University of New Mexico Press.

Pinker, S. (1994) "Grammar puss." *New Republic.* January 31: 19–26.

—— (1995) *The Language Instinct: How the mind creates language.* New York: HarperPerennial.

Pitts, A. (1986) "Flip-flop prestige in American tune, duke, news." *American Speech* 61: 130–138.

Plato (1970) *Timaeus, and Other Dialogues.* London: Sphere.

Pooley, R. C. (1974) *The Teaching of English Usage.* Urbana, IL: National Council of Teachers of English.

Potter, W. J. and W. Ware (1987) "Traits of perpetrators and receivers of antisocial and prosocial acts on TV." *Journalism Quarterly* 64: 382–391.

Powell, G. J. (1982) "The impact of television on the self-concept development of minority group children." *Television and the Socialization of the Minority Child.* G. L. Berry and C. Mitchell-Kernan, eds. New York: Academic Press: 105–134.

Precker, M. (1993a) "This Aladdin is rated PC." *Dallas Morning News.* October 2. Dallas: 5c.

—— (1993b) "Animated debate." *Dallas Morning News.* July 12. Dallas: 1c.

Pressley, S. A. (1993) "Students return to language roots in Oklahoma." *Washington Post.* November 7: A3.

Preston, D. (1986a) "The fifty some-odd categories of language variation." *International Journal of the Sociology of Language* 57: 9–47.

—— (1986b) "Five visions of America." *Language in Society* 15(2): 221–240.

—— (1986c) "Two heartland perceptions of language variety." *"Heartland" English: Variation and transition in the American Midwest.* T. C. Frazer, ed. Tuscaloosa and London: University of Alabama Press: 23–47.

—— (1989a) *Perceptual Dialectology: Nonlinguists' views of areal linguistics.* Dordrecht and Providence RI: Foris Publications.

—— (1989b) "Standard English spoken here: the geographical loci of linguistic norms." *Status and Function of Languages and Language Varieties.* U. Ammon, ed. Berlin: Walter de Gruyter: 324–354.

—— (1993) "Folk dialectology." *American Dialect Research.* Amsterdam: Benjamins: 333–337.

Purdum, T. S. (1993) "Buttoning every vote." *New York Times.* October 3. New York: section 9, p. 1.

Quinn, J. (1985) "Linguistic segregation." *Nation.* November 9: 479–482.

Quisenberry, J. D. (1993/94) "Linguistic and cultural differences teachers should know." *Childhood Education* 70: 96-K.

Ragno, N., M. Toth, and B. Gray (1987) *Silver Burdett English.* Morristown, NJ: Silver Burdett.

Raspberry, W. (1979a) " 'Black English' sensitivity." *Chicago Tribune.* July 17. Chicago: section 3: 3.

—— (1979b) " 'Black English' study has merits." *Chicago Tribune.* August 28. Chicago: section 3: 3.

—— (1990) "What it means to be Black." *Language Awareness.* P. Eschholz, A. Rosa and V. Clark, eds. New York: St. Martin's Press: 269–272.

Reed, J. S. (1982) *One South: An ethnic approach to regional culture.* Baton Rouge and London: Louisiana State University Press.

—— (1983) *Southerners: The social psychology of sectionalism.* Chapel Hill: University of North Carolina Press.

Reeves, R. (1992) "Make Americans of them." *Sun.* December 8. Tulsa, OK: 21B.

Reinhold, R. (1993) "Horror for Hollywood: film hits a nerve with its grim view of hometown." *New York Times.* March 29. Los Angeles: A1.

Reyes, M. (1991) "Bilingual student writers: a question of fair evaluation." *English Journal* 80(8): 16–23.

Reyhner, Jon (1992) "Policies toward American Indian languages: a historical sketch." *Language Loyalties: A source book on the official English controversy.* J. Crawford, ed. Chicago, IL: University of Chicago Press: 41–46.

Riches, P. and M. Foddy (1989) "Ethnic accent as a status cue." *Social Psychology Quarterly* 52(3): 197–206.

Rickford, J. (1985) "Standard and non-standard language attitudes in a creole continuum." *Language of Inequality.* N. Wolfram and J. Manes, eds. Berlin: Mouton de Gruyter: 145–160.

—— (1992) "Grammatical variation and divergence in vernacular Black English." *Internal and External Factors in Syntactic Change.* M. Gerritsen and D. Stein, eds. Berlin: Mouton de Gruyter: 175–200.

—— (forthcoming) "Regional and social variation." *Sociolinguistics and Language Teaching.* S. McKay and N. Hornberger, eds. Cambridge: Cambridge University Press.

—— and A. E. Rickford. (1995) "Dialect readers revisited." *Linguistics and Education* 7: 107–128.

—— and E. C. Traugott (1985) "Symbol of powerlessness and degeneracy, or symbol of solidarity and truth? Paradoxical attitudes toward pidgins and creoles." *The English Language Today.* S. Greenbaum, ed. Oxford: Pergamon Press: 252–261.

Rickford, J., A. Ball, R. Blake, *et al.* (1991) "Rappin on the copula coffin: theoretical and methodological issues in the analysis of copula variation in African-American Vernacular English." *Language Variation and Change* 3: 103–132.

Riddle, L. (1993) "Sounds like the South is alive and well-spoken." *Los Angeles Times.* February 18: A5.

Robb, D. (1991) "Civil rights commish eyes media images." *Variety.* April 15: 1.

Robbins, J. F. (1989) " 'Broadcast English' for nonstandard dialect speakers." *Education Digest*: 52–53.

Roberts, C., E. Davies, and T. Jupp (1992) *Language and Discrimination. A study of communication in multi-ethnic workplaces.* London and New York: Longman.

Robertson, J. F. (1911) "Pronunciation." *Proceedings of the Indiana Association of Teachers of English.* Bloomington: Indiana University.

Romaine, S. (1980) "Stylistic variation and evaluative reactions to speech: problems in the investigation of linguistic attitudes in Scotland." *Language and Speech* 23(3): 213–232.

Rosenthal, M. (1974) "The magic boxes: preschool children's attitudes toward Black and Standard English." *Florida Foreign Language Reporter* 12: 55–62, 92–93.

Rowan, C. (1979) "Black English is silly." *Chicago Sun-Times.* July 10. Chicago, IL: 36.

Royko, M. (1992) "Pithy questions the presidential debate panel won't ask." *Chicago Tribune.* October 11.

Rubin, D. L. (1992) "Nonlanguage factors affecting undergraduates' judgements of nonnative English-speaking teaching assistants." *Research in Higher Education* 33(4): 511–531.

——, and K. A. Smith. (1990) "Effects of accent, ethnicity, and lecture topic on undergraduates' perceptions of non-native English speaking teaching assistants." *International Journal of Intercultural Relations* 14: 337–353.

Ryan, E. B., E. Bouchard, M. Carranza, *et al.* (1977) "Reactions toward varying degrees of accentedness in the speech of Spanish-English bilinguals." *Language and Speech* 20: 267–273.

Safire, W. (1992) "Who trusts whom?" *New York Times Sunday Magazine.* October 4: On Language.

San Jose Mercury News (1988) "For Santa Clara County." October 18: 6B.

Santa Ana, O. (1996) "Awash under a brown tide: metaphor and the ideology of immigration in American newspaper discourse." Working paper. UCLA.

Sargent, J. A. (1963) "Self-regulation: the motion picture production code, 1903–1961," Ph.D. thesis. Ann Arbor: University of Michigan.

Sato, C. (1989) "A nonstandard approach to standard English." *TESOL Quarterly* 23(2): 259–282.

—— (1991) "Sociolinguistic variation and language attitudes in Hawai'i." *English Around the World: Sociolinguistic perspectives*. J. Cheshire, ed. Cambridge: Cambridge University Press.

Schäffner, C. and A. L. Wenden, eds (1995) *Language and Peace*. Aldershot, England: Dartmouth.

Schanberg, S. (1993) "His job is accent-uating the positive." *New York Newsday* interview with Sam Chwat. June 29.

Schickel, R. (1968) *The Disney Version: The life, times, art and commerce of Walt Disney*. New York: Simon & Schuster.

Schiffrin, D. (1987) *Discourse Markers*. Cambridge: Cambridge University Press.

Schwartz, A. E. (1993) "Dialing for dialects." *Washington Post*. November 8: A21.

Schwartz, J. (1992) "Hispanic affluence has a Cuban accent." *American Demographics* 14: 18.

Shaheen, J. G. (1984) *The TV Arab*. Bowling Green, OH: Bowling Green State University Popular Press.

Shell, M. (1993) "Babel in America; or, the politics of language diversity in the United States." *Critical Inquiry* 20: 103–127.

Shulevitz, J. (1992) "Tongues on wry lend special flavor to movies." *New York Times*. February 9: section 2, p. H13.

Shulman, S. (1993) "Nurturing native tongues." *Technology Review* 96 (May/June): 16.

Shuy, R. (1993) *Language Crimes: The use and abuse of language evidence in the courtroom*. Cambridge: Basil Blackwell.

Sicherman, B. and C. H. Green, eds (1980) *Notable American Women: The modern period. A biographical dictionary*. Cambridge, MA: Belknap Press of Harvard University Press.

Silverstein, M. (1992) "The uses and utility of ideology: some reflections." *Pragmatics* 2(3): 311–324.

Simmen, E., ed. (1971) *The Chicano: From caricature to self-portrait*. New York: Mentor Books.

Sims, C. P. (1992) "Native language assessment of Pueblo Indian teachers in bilingual education." Internal memo, New Mexico Department of Education. Santa Fe.

Sklarewitz, N. (1992) "American firms lash out at foreign tongues." *Business and Society Review* (83) Fall: 24–28.

Skutnabb-Kangas, T. and R. Phillipson, eds (1994) *Linguistic Human Rights: Overcoming linguistic discrimination*. Berlin and New York: Mouton de Gruyter.

Slansky, P. and S. Radlauer (1992) *Dan Quayle: Airhead Apparent*. Berkeley, CA: Behind the News Press.

Sledd, J. (1972) "Bi-dialectism: the linguistics of white supremacy." *Contemporary English: Change and variation*. D. L. Shores, ed. Philadelphia, PA: J. B. Lippincott: 319–330.

—— (1973) "Doublespeak: dialectology in the service of big brother." *Black Language Reader*. R. H. Bentley and S. D. Crawford, eds. Glenview, IL: Scott, Foresman: 191–214.

Smith, E. R. (1992) *Falling Down*. Script revision dated March 17, 1992. Film (1993) directed by J. Schumacher. Arnold Kopelson Productions in association with Warner Bros. Inc.

Smitherman, G. (1977) *Talkin' and Testifyin': The language of Black America.* Detroit, MI: Wayne State University Press.

—— (1995) "Testifyin, sermonizin, and signifyin: Anita Hill, Clarence Thomas, and the African American Verbal Tradition." *African American Women Speak Out on Anita Hill-Clarence Thomas.* G. Smitherman, ed. Detroit, MI: Wayne State University Press: 224–242.

Sonntag, S. K. and J. Pool (1987) "Linguistic denial and linguistic self-denial: American ideologies of language." *Language Problems and Language Planning* 11(1): 46–65.

Sontag, D. (1993) "Oy gevalt! New Yawkese an endangered dialect?" *New York Times.* February 14. New York: 1a.

Spangenberg-Urbschat K. and R. Pritchard, eds (1994) *Kids Come in All Languages: Reading instruction for ESL students.* Urbana, IL: National Council of Teachers of English.

Speicher, B. L. and S. M. McMahon (1992) "Some African-American perspectives on Black English vernacular." *Language in Society* 21(3): 383–407.

Spencer, L. (1995) *Family Blessings.* New York: Jove.

Spicher, L. L. (1992) "Language attitude towards speakers with a Mexican accent: ramifications in the business community of San Diego, California," Ph.D. thesis. Austin: University of Texas.

Spring, J. (1992) *Images of American Life: A history of ideological management in schools, movies, radio and television.* Albany: State University of New York Press.

Stalker, J. C. (1990) "Official English and the English profession." *Not Only English.* H. A. Daniels, ed. Urbana, IL: National Council of Teachers of English: 61–68.

Standing Bear, Luther (1928) *My People, the Sioux.* Edited by E. A. Brininstool. Boston, MA: Houghton Mifflin.

Stannard, D. E. (1992) *American Holocaust: Columbus and the conquest of the New World.* New York: Oxford University Press.

Starks, J. A. (1983) "The Black English controversy and its implications for addressing the educational needs of black children: the cultural linguistic approach." *Black English. Educational Equity and the Law.* J. J. Chambers, ed. Ann Arbor, MI: Karoma: 97–132.

Steele, S. (1991) *The Content of Our Character: A new vision of race in America.* New York: HarperPerennial.

Sterritt, D. (1993) "A dysfunctional movie." *Christian Science Monitor.* March 1: 13.

Stewart, P. and R. F. Fawcett (1994) " 'An' to 'a' in American speech: language change in progress." *English Today* 37, 10(1): 18–24.

Strauss, B. (1990) "'DuckTales: the movie.' Xenophobic waddle to silliness." *Los Angeles Daily News.* August 3. Los Angeles, CA.

Strickland, D. (1983) *Language for Daily Use.* Level 3. New York: Harcourt Brace Jovanovich.

Strobel, L. (1979) "Courts rule spurs Black English row." *Chicago Tribune.* August 8. Chicago, IL: section 1: 1.

Sykes, C. J. (1995) *Dumbing down Our Kids.* New York: St. Martin's Press.

Tapscott, R. (1994) "Schaefer ponders making English Md.'s language." *Washington Post.* May 9. Washington: D4.

Taylor, C. (1994) *Multiculturalism: Examining the politics of recognition.* Princeton, NJ: Princeton University Press.

Thakerar, J. N., H. Giles, and J. Cheshire (1982) "Psychological and linguistic parameters of speech accomodation theory." *Advances in the Social Psychology of Language.* C. Fraser and K. R. Scherer, eds. Cambridge: Cambridge University Press: 205–255.

Thompson, J. B. (1984) *Studies in the Theory of Ideology*. Cambridge: Polity Press, in association with Basil Blackwell.

Tierney, John (1995) "Can we talk?" *New York Times Magazine*. January 22. New York: 16.

Tryfiates, P. G. (1990) "English should be our official language." *USA Today*. February 12.

Tucker, G. R. and W. E. Lambert (1969) "White and negro listeners' reactions to various American-English dialects." *Social Forces* 47: 463–468.

Twomey, S. (1994) "Unneeded in any language." *Washington Post*. March 24: B1.

Tytler, D. (1989) "Prince condemns 'wasteland' of modern English." *The Times* (London). December 20. London: 1, 3.

United States Census Bureau (1990) *Social and Economic Characteristics: Metropolitan areas.*

—— (1994) *1990 Census of Population and Housing*. Revised edition. Washington DC.

United States Equal Employment Opportunity Commission (EEOC) (1988) *Guidelines on Discrimination Because of National Origin*. Washington DC.

United States General Accounting Office (1987) *Employer Sanctions*. Washington DC.

United States Immigration and Naturalization Service (1992) *Statistical Yearbook*. Washington DC.

University of Michigan (1993) Letters *LSAmagazine* (Spring). Ann Arbor, MI: 39–40.

University of the State of New York (1993) *Preparation Guide: New York State teacher certification examinations.*

Valdés, G. (1988) "The language situation of Mexican Americans." *Language Diversity: Problem or Resource? A social and educational perspective on language minorities in the United States*. S.L. McKay and S.-l. C. Wong, eds. Boston, MA: Heinle & Heinle: 111–139.

Veltman, C. (1983) "Anglicization in the United States: language environment and language practice of American adolescents." *International Journal of the Sociology of Language* 44: 99–114.

Verhovek, S. (1995) "Mother scolded by judge for speaking in Spanish." *New York Times*. August 30. New York (late edition): A12.

Verploegen, H. (1988) "Pidgin in classroom stirs spirited debate by seniors." *Honolulu Star-Bulletin*. June 1. Honolulu, HI: A1, A8.

Viereck, W. (1988) "Notes on Black and Red American English." *On Language: Rhetorica, Phonologica, Syntactica: A Festschrift for Robert P. Stockwell*. C. Duncan-Rose, J. Fisiak, and T. Vennemann, eds. London: Routledge: 145–157.

Vincenti, C. N. (1991) "The New Mexico Indian Tribal Court Handbook." Indian Law Section of the State Bar of New Mexico.

Viviano, F. (1990) "Poll contradicts stereotypes." *San Francisco Chronicle*. March 28. San Francisco, CA.

Waggoner, D. (1988) "Language minorities in the United States in the 1980s: the evidence from the 1980 census." *Language Diversity: Problem or Resource? A social and educational perspective on language minorities in the United States*. S. L. McKay, and S.-l. C. Wong, eds. Boston, MA: Heinle & Heinle: 69–108.

Wainess, F. E. (1994) "The presidential search." *Michigan Daily*. March 30. Ann Arbor: University of Michigan: 4.

Walker, A. (1983) *The Color Purple*. New York: Washington Square Press.

Walsh, C.E. (1991) *Pedagogy and the Struggle for Voice: Issues of language, power, and schooling for Puerto Ricans*. New York: Bergin and Garvey.

Walters, K. (1996) "Contesting representations of African American language." *SALSA III*. R. Ide, R. Park, and Y. Sunaoski, eds. Proceedings of the Third

Annual Symposium about Language and Society, Austin: University of Texas: TLF 36, 137–151.

Warner, P. K. (1990) "Fantastic outsiders: villains and deviants in animated cartoons." *Marginal Conventions: Popular culture, mass media and social deviance.* C. R. Sanders, ed. Bowling Green, OH: Bowling Green State University Popular Press: 117–130.

Warren, J. (1993) "English vs English." *Chicago Tribune.* January 17. Chicago, IL: Tempo, p. 2, Zone C, Sunday Watch.

Wax, M. (1973) "Cultural deprivation as an educational ideology." *Black Language Reader.* R. H. Bentley and S. D. Crawford, eds. Glenview, IL: Scott, Foresman: 215–220.

Weinreich, U. (1953) *Languages in Contact: Findings and problems.* New York: Linguistic Circle of Friends.

Weiss, W. (1992) "Perception and production in accent training." Revue de phonétique appliquée 102: 69–82.

Williams, L. (1980) "Type and stereotype: Chicano images in film." *Frontiers* 5(2): 14–17.

Williams, S. H. (1987) "A comparison of cultural values in animated cartoons produced for the theatre and television," Ph.D. thesis. Madison: University of Wisconsin.

Wilson, S. Y. (1993) "Acute accents." *Lingua Franca* (December): 6–7.

Windsor, P. (1993) "Clague teacher's remarks show bias, black parents charge." *Ann Arbor News.* April 22. Ann Arbor, MI: C1–C3.

Winsboro, B. L. and I. D. Solomon (1990) "Standard English vs. 'the American dream'." *Education Digest* (December): 51–52.

Wolfram, W. A. (1969) *A Sociolinguistic Description of Detroit Negro Speech.* Washington DC: Center for Applied Linguistics.

—— and D. Christian (1976) *Appalachian Speech.* Arlington, VA: Center for Applied Speech.

Woolard, K. A. (1992) "Language ideology: issues and approaches." *Pragmatics* 2(3): 235–250.

—— and B. B. Schieffelin (1994) "Language ideology." *Annual Reviews of Anthropology* 23: 55–82.

World Almanac and Book of Facts (1995) New York: St. Martins Press.

Yamamoto, J. and E. Hargrove (1982) "Teachers' attitudes toward recorded speech samples of elementary school children in Hawaii." *Working Papers in Linguistics* 14(2): 109–133.

Yang, C. (1993) "In any language, it's unfair." *Business Week.* June 21: 110–111.

Zelinsky, W. (1980) "North America's vernacular regions." *Annals of the Association of American Geographers* 70(1): 1–16.

Zentella, A. C. (1988) "The language situation of Puerto Ricans." *Language Diversity: Problem or Resource? A social and educational perspective on language minorities in the United States.* S. L. McKay and S.-l. C. Wong. Boston, MA: Heinle & Heinle: 140–165.

—— (1996) "The 'Chiquitafication' of U.S. Latinos and their languages, or why we need an anthropolitical linguistics." *SALSA III.* R. Ide, R. Park, and Y. Sunaoski, eds. Proceedings of the Third Annual Symposium about Language and Society. Austin: University of Texas: TLF 36, 1–18.

Index

FiFth Floor
humanities
1st OFFice on
right